The Linleys of Bath

The Linleys of Bath

by

Clementina Black

with a new introduction by the
Countess of Rosse and a Pedigree of the Linley family
compiled by Sir Anthony Wagner,
Garter King of Arms

Frederick Muller Ltd.

First published, 1911
Revised Edition, 1926
This edition published in 1971
by Frederick Muller Ltd., Fleet Street, London, E.C.4.

Reproduced and printed by
Redwood Press Limited, Trowbridge and London.

SBN 584 10927 X

INTRODUCTION TO 1971 EDITION
by the Countess of Rosse

IT was with great joy that I heard that a new edition of Miss Clementina Black's book was to be brought out. "Who were the Linleys", she asks in her first chapter, "that their sons and daughters should resemble the magically gifted princes and princesses of a fairy tale?"

The branch of the Linley family which moved to Bath from their home on the Yorkshire-Derbyshire border became famous equally for their looks and for their talents. Their gifts were chiefly musical, but by no means exclusively so. They were perfectionists in all that they did; and it was largely through their leadership and example that Bath became in their day a centre of culture as well as of fashion. Elizabeth will always remain one of England's most romantic heroines. She was perhaps the most talented of all, and of such exquisite loveliness that Horace Walpole, even in her later years, placed her "above all living beauties". Her virtue and sweetness of disposition were equally striking in an age when those qualities were but little prized.

Less is recorded of the qualities of their cousins of the same generation who continued to live in the North. But some of the identical characteristics for which the Bath Linleys became celebrated were transmitted to the Sambourne family by two successive marriages in the early nineteenth century.

I write in the drawing-room of 18 Stafford Terrace, a unique survival in Kensington of an almost forgotten past;

a house that has remained unchanged for a century, ever since the day when my great-grandmother Frances Linley came to live here with my grandparents after their marriage, bringing with her some of her own family possessions. Endowed with beauty and talents herself, it was in this house that she encouraged and inspired her son, Linley Sambourne, who learned from her his masterly command of draughtsmanship. Here he designed almost all his famous cartoons, which in typically Linley fashion combine political finesse with superb artistry.

Drawings by my mother in her youth give evidence of the continuation of the talent in her; and both her romantic loveliness and her angelic temperament derived directly from the Linleys. Alas, she did not persist in her drawing, but surely my brother Oliver's imaginative creations in stage design and painting, and subsequently in architecture and landscape too, are altogether in the wide-ranging tradition of Linley interest in the whole gamut of the Arts.

Is it not already possible to detect the same vitally creative urge at work in some of the next generation?

Anne Rosse
June 1971

The Linleys of Bath

by

Clementina Black

With an Introduction by

George Saintsbury

1 9 2 6

London: Martin Secker

INTRODUCTION

It has been held by them of old time that if what is said three times is not always true what can produce three reasons for itself is fairly right.   This Introduction can at least do as much.   Its author lives at present between the Linleys' principal house in Bath and that quaint " Margaret " Chapel in the next street from which they derived some revenue.   (It has had profaner experiences since.)   In his youth he used not infrequently to " sit under " at St. Mary Abbot's, Kensington, the late Archdeacon Sinclair, from whose information Miss Black derived some pleasing stories at the end of her book.   And, in the third place, the first thing that he ever read about Sheridan while still ignorant of him as writer or as politician—indeed at the same time when he went to Old Kensington Church—was Charles Lamb's sentences in " My First Play," Elia being, by the blessing of Providence, very nearly " his first book."   It is true that " the beautiful Maria Linley " of whom Charles speaks, though she was beautiful, was not " Maria " at all, but Elizabeth Ann, and that the elopement, though it took place from Bath, did not take place " from a boarding-school at Bath."   But no person in the lowest degree worthy to enjoy Elia as a literary feeding-bottle could think these trifling errors of any importance at all.

There is, however, no harm in accuracy, though with some kinds of inaccuracy it would be unreasonable to quarrel; and as this excellent book has gone out of print and its author is not alive to represent it, the best thing possible is that it should be presented by somebody else.   Although of course family histories are not unknown they are not (unless devoted to " storied lines " through centuries) common; and this particular family seems to have possessed (one cannot in all respects say " enjoyed ") a certain unicity. It was large; it was unusually beautiful; it was very clever in one great art; it connected itself once brilliantly and not on the whole unhappily, at other times not uninterestingly; and it was an extreme example of that strange curse which used to be called Consumption but which seems recently to have had its terrors abated, some say by calling it tuberculosis and trying new cures on it, others, of the unbelieving kind, by that again strange revolution of things which makes a disease fatal at one time and nearly harmless at another.

These are, whether cheerful or sad, good elements for bookmaking, but it by no means follows that anybody could make a good book out of them. The thing however is done, and done well in the present instance. Nobody has ever succeeded in pointing out, and it may be doubted whether any wise body would ever try to point out, what it is that distinguishes a book from a mere collection of sentences, paragraphs and chapters. But everybody who deserves to read a good book should be able to feel that distinction more or less distinctly. This is a book; the author shepherds and guides her facts, and does not merely shovel them out till the sack is empty. She conducts us through the history of the Linley family to (as nearly the first person who made in English one good book out of many shreds and patches has it) " the dolorous death and departing out of this world of them all." But it is neither a catalogue nor a mere collection of biographic articles; and the fortunate fact that the latest personage to be much spoken of—the Reverend Ozias —was a very quaint individual in the proper, not the vulgar, usage of that word saves the end from being too " dolorous."

Perhaps one secret of Miss Black's success is her avoidance of a pitfall into which the bookmaker of the lower type would pretty certainly have fallen. The Linley girls were beautiful and clever; one of the Linley boys at least was, if not exactly humorous, "humoursome"; the father was a respectable musician. But it may be doubted whether they would have been held in memory if Elizabeth Ann Linley had not married —under perfectly "proper" but rather quaint circumstances— Richard Brinsley Sheridan. Now the average bookmaker, recognising this fact, would pretty certainly have kept the said Richard Brinsley a little too constantly "in the picture," to make sure of the subject seeming important enough. Miss Black has done nothing of the sort. There is quite enough of Sheridan but not in the least too much, and both his merits and his faults, typical Irishman that he was in both ways, are treated fairly but not dwelt on excessively. In fact a carping critic might say that the author has neglected what may be called the fringes of her subject almost too ascetically. A little more could have been said with advantage about Tickell, Mary Linley's husband, and that queer, brilliant if somewhat unscrupulously partisan Rolliad group of which he was a member.

But there is on the whole nothing but praise due to her for sticking to her main business and for devoting most of her time and space to what are certainly the most interesting parts of that business, the interchanges of letters between the two elder sisters, Elizabeth and Mary, and between the youngest, Jane, and her curious lover Charles Ward. He began by being in some mysterious way a "projector" or as we call it now "promoter" of schemes about copper mining which never came off, and ended by being secretary at Drury Lane, a position the conditions of which seem, as far as one can make out, to have consisted in sometimes receiving emoluments from Sheridan, always doing much business for him, and occasionally backing his bills and getting into trouble in his stead.

In these letters all the three sisters show that strong and almost dramatic character which makes eighteenth-century women letter-writers so frequently interesting. There is more of tragedy in Elizabeth, though she is by no means a Julia of The Rivals (*by the way, there is an amusing note in one of the letters something like "if we had a Julia." How many companies have had a real Julia?*) *Her constantly failing health—to which it is only fair to say that Sheridan, whatever his faults, was never indifferent—and the worries of his flightiness of course brought this out. Mary Tickell on the other hand was more of a "Little Comedy," as Goldsmith called someone slightly her senior but who longer outlived her. Mrs. Tickell might sometimes have deserved the worse name of a "Little Spitfire" in reference especially to her mother. But Mrs. Linley's conduct to the still younger sister Jane (a "Maria" came between who is rather a puzzle not merely in the doubling on "Mary") certainly does show her as more than a rather provoking person. On the whole, however, the letters give a sufficiently lively picture of* fin de Siècle *society in this late* 18th *century and (though they are a little older) fit on in a curious comparison-contrast way to Miss Austen's prosopopœia. The two elders, moreover, for a more or less considerable time before their too early deaths, had lived their lives as they had themselves planned them for better for worse. They had, unlike Browning's pair, who made a mess of it, "sighed deep, laughed free," probably not "starved" but certainly "feasted," and if Elizabeth may have "despaired" now and then, had for times and seasons "been happy." Poor Jane's fortune in later years was for a long time rather "despairing," and though it cleared for a little, the family curse gave her short time to enjoy her chances which, though the information is imperfect, would not seem to have been ever of the rosiest. It was hard lines, for she had a few hundreds a year of her own, probably equal to three times as many to-day; she was evidently, though what they would have called " a girl of feeling," quite a sensible girl; and though her lover may have had a bee or two in his bonnet there appears to have been nothing against him either as a good fellow or as a gentleman. But she was quite in her mother's power; while her lover was, for a considerable time, careering about England with vague designs upon properties, the necessary rights over which he generally found (and surely might have found beforehand) to have been already acquired by other people. Jane is not exactly effusive; her affection does not demonstrate itself with such perhaps at first sight a little ludicrous but really pathetic intensity as Elizabeth's for her volatile husband. Nor does she indulge in such partly comic wrath as Mary shows when the conviviality of her husband and his friends keeps her (though she has not " sat up " with or for them) awake half the night. It may not have struck everybody what a nuisance this must have been as a frequent result of the otherwise cheerful hospitality of the ancestors. But there is a sort of steady glow about Jane which is very attractive. And perhaps it was better after all that though things did come right for her the rightness did not last too long. For her Charles, as has been already indicated, would seem to have been rather a poor creature if not at all a bad lot.*

There is, moreover, plenty of interest besides that of these correspondences. Although Sheridan does not figure too much he is bound to figure a good deal, especially in the most eccentric circumstances of the actual elopement and marriage or marriages (for they went through two ceremonies) of himself and his wife, and the equally eccentric but much more unpleasant ones of the double duel with the rascal Captain or Lieutenant Mathews. In all this actual facts accommodated themselves to the theatrical status of the parties concerned in a fashion and to an extent which is quite surprising. It would be an unwise and improper forestalling of the reader's delight in the text to impart to him here the details either of the duels or of the marriages; it must be sufficient to say that Mr. Vincent Crummles might have planned, and that Mr. Vincent Crummles's company might have carried out, all the four schemes and scenes : except that one would not wish even the spiteful coward Lenville to have been left in such physical state of suffering as poor " Dick " Sheridan had, most undeservingly, to undergo after the second encounter. There are many minor events of interest, not a few of them enlivened by epistolary chronicling; there may be said to be practically none of those waste places which so frequently disfigure memoirs and biographies, and the whole book is one which deserves to be kept ready to be read.

GEORGE SAINTSBURY.

CONTENTS

LIST OF ILLUSTRATIONS

xi

LIST OF ILLUSTRATIONS

FOREWORD

IF it had not been for the access to original letters, or to transcripts of original letters, that has been allowed me, this volume must have been meagre indeed. The letters written after marriage by Mrs Sheridan and Mrs Tickell are in the possession of the Sheridan family, and large portions of them were transcribed by Mr Walter Sichel when he was preparing his biography of Sheridan. These transcripts he has, with the permission of Mrs Algernon Sheridan, lent me, and many extracts from them appear. The record of her mother's early life made by Alicia Sheridan (Mrs Joseph Le Fanu) is quoted pretty fully in Fraser Rae's " Sheridan," and I have generally taken her statements from his pages, but sometimes from those of Mr Sichel. The letters of Jane Linley and of Charles William Ward have remained in the hands of his family, and these, together with the other letters employed in the last chapter, have been entrusted to me by Mrs Ward of Iver, who has also permitted the reproduction of the portrait of Jane Linley. For the discovery of the date and place of Mr and Mrs Linley's marriage I am indebted to the Rev C. W. Shickle, of Bath, who lent me his copies of church registers belonging to the parishes of that city and its neighbourhood, and who also helped me to find the books of water and church rates by means of which the residence of Thomas Linley in Orchard Street has been established beyond all question. Some valuable notes about early Linleys were lent me by

Miss L. M. Middleton; and my attention was called to the
presence of three Lyndeleys at Agincourt by Mr E. L.
Trustram, himself a relative of the family. Mr H. Linley
Howlden, of Freshford, near Bath, pointed out to me that
the name previously read as "Waton" must be "Norton,"
and gave me some interesting information about the Linleys
of Norton, who were, almost certainly, the ancestors of
Thomas Linley as well as of himself. Mr Joseph Tickell,
of Whittlesford, and Mrs Tickell, of Hampstead, have
kindly lent me pedigrees of the Tickell family which have
confirmed the fact—sufficiently proved by her will and by
original letters—that Elizabeth Ann, the daughter of Mary
and Richard Tickell, was not the mother of John Arthur
Roebuck.[1] To the clergy of Norton, of Malton, of Badminton, of Didmarton, of Tisbury and of Broseley I owe
not only information about entries in the registers of their
various parishes, but also several helpful and valuable suggestions. To all these kind helpers, and to various others who
have assisted me in more ways than it is possible to enumerate
here, I beg to offer my sincere thanks.

Finally I may add that a good many details of interest to
a biographer remain still unelucidated. Among these are
the precise parentage of William Linley, born, according to
his own account, at Norton, Derbyshire, in 1704; the
maiden name and family of his wife, Maria, born probably
in October 1701; the parentage and family of Mrs Thomas
Linley (Mary Johnson), born in 1729; and the whereabouts
of several Linley portraits known to have existed but not
at present traceable. Among these are three—one of
Mrs Ward (Jane Linley), in crayon, by Lawrence; one of
Mrs Linley, by Oliver; and one of Ozias Linley, by the

---

[1] The Christian name of Mrs Roebuck is given in Armitage's
"Chantry Land" as Zipporah.

xiv

same painter—which were once in the possession of the Governors of Dulwich College, and are in their official catalogue until 1892, but not in later editions. No person at present connected with the gallery has been able to give me any information concerning any of these three portraits, and it seems sadly probable that they have disappeared for ever. Of Mrs Linley and of Jane there are other portraits, but of Ozias in manhood there is, as far as I know, no other, and it is a great disappointment to me that none can be included in this volume.

C. B.

CHAPTER 1. THOMAS LINLEY, MUSICIAN

CERTAIN mysteries of inheritance and of family resemblance seem likely long to elude the researches and the explanations of the scientific inquirer. Instances occur in which all or nearly all the children of a particular pair of parents will present marked characteristics not conspicuous in the family of either parent, nor perhaps strongly persistent in their own descendants. Generally, indeed, there will be discernible traces of the prevailing qualities in at least one parent and in at least one descendant, but it is to a single generation that the great development—the sudden burst of blossom—belongs.

With a family group exhibiting this phenomenon the present volume deals. The father, whose own father was a respectable and prosperous craftsman, not at this distance of time remarkable, except as a writer of verses that were not good, was a musician of some distinction; the mother, of whose antecedents nothing has been discovered, was not intellectual, nor refined, nor amiable; both were above the average in the matter of good looks, and both more than a little difficult in the matter of temper. Who would have dared to prophesy, when young Thomas Linley, the harpsichordist and singer, married, at nineteen, the somewhat older Mary Johnson, that the children born to them would be lavishly endowed with talent, beauty, individuality and distinction? Not only did all of them—all, that is to say,

B

who lived to grow up—inherit in a high degree the musical gifts of their father, but at least four were quite unusually handsome, and at least three had some literary talent, while four were notably witty. In the next generation are found a granddaughter who was a paler Linley, a grandson in whom the Sheridan preponderated over the Linley, and in every one of that grandson's children a recurrence of outstanding beauty, accompanied in several instances by charm, brillance and talent of various kinds. Who were the Linleys that their sons and daughters should resemble the magically gifted princes and princesses of a fairy tale ?

Of the remote ancestry of the family whence these wondrous young creatures sprang it is not possible to speak with certainty; a fine field in which to exercise the sport of ancestor hunting lies open to any modern owners of the pretty surname of Linley. That name is probably a territorial one, and may be derived from Linley, near Broseley, in Shropshire. This ancient manor, and modern parish, was held early in the twelfth century by Richard de Linley, described in an ancient charter as " Richard son of Baldwin de Lintlega." In other documents down to the year 1200 occur the names of Richard, Ralph, Philip and Sibyl de Linley. In 1200 the direct male line must have become extinct, for the inheritance passes to the husbands of two co-heiresses.[1] Of course there may have been collateral branches through which the family name was carried on, and from one or more of which the Linleys of Bath as well as the Linleys of to-day are descended. There are no Linleys to be found at present in Linley by Broseley, nor at Linley in Wiltshire.

In varying forms—Lynley, Linlie, Lindley, Lingley, Lingly, or Linley—the name emerges now and again in

[1] Eyton, " Antiquities of Shropshire," vol. ii., pp. 39–42.

2

various English records from the twelfth century to our own.

Not until about two centuries ago can anything like a settled clan be pointed out. By that time a family group of Linleys was established at Norton, in Derbyshire, near to Sheffield, and from this group came William Linley, who was the father of Thomas Linley, who in his turn was the father of the beautiful Elizabeth Ann Linley, the first wife of Richard Brinsley Sheridan. William Linley recorded upon the leaf of a family Bible, still preserved, that he was born in 1704 in a parish in Derby, near Sheffield, in Yorkshire. The name of the parish was read as Waton, and under that name it could not be discovered. That the true reading was Norton was suggested to me by Mr Linley Howlden, who himself belongs to the Norton family, about which he has been kind enough to give me a few particulars. One Samuel Linley, was the owner of an early Sheffield trade mark for scythes: the "old O"; and any person still possessing an excellent scythe blade with that mark upon it may look back gratefully to the old craftsman who first tempered and stamped such blades. Another early Linley was a wholesale vendor, and probably a manufacturer, of "Broseley clays," which are, I am informed, churchwarden pipes of superior size and quality. The circumstance suggests that, as late as about 1770, there were still Linleys not quite detached from the place in which I suppose their name to have originated. The old home of the Norton Linleys is Bole Hill, a stone house of considerable antiquity, which has evidently received additions at various times. A photograph which is in my possession of this interesting homestead was taken in the year 1901 by the late Linley Sambourne, who was a descendant of the Linleys and was born in the house. It is noteworthy that the Christian

3

names most prevalent among the early Linleys of Norton were Samuel, Thomas, William and Elizabeth Ann, all of which appear among the children of Thomas Linley of Bath.

The reprehensibly lax manner in which our ancestors too often kept their parish registers renders it a matter of little surprise that no entry appears at Norton of William Linley's baptism, but the omission leaves us in ignorance of his parentage and connections, and we know of him, up to the time of his son's baptism, only what the page of his family Bible tells. Upon it he gives with great particularity the birthday of his wife—19th of October 1701—and her Christian name—Maria—but omits to mention either her surname or the date of their marriage. His son Thomas is recorded as having been born at Badminton on the 17th of January 1733, and on the 20th of that month his baptism is entered in the church register of that place. At Badminton also were born Isabella, who was baptised on the 9th of October 1737, and William, baptised on the 29th of July 1744. The register in each case records the name of the parents as "Lingley." Whether this spelling was the father's own or was due to the writer of the entries cannot now be ascertained, and it may be a mere coincidence that in the registers of St James's, Clerkenwell, four entries occur between 1690 and 1696, in all of which the name is spelled "Lingly," whereas in others of 1698 and 1712—the latter of which seems to be the marriage of a child baptised in 1690 —the form "Linley" is used. These facts would appear to indicate that the registrant rather than the possessor of the name was responsible for the variation.

William Linley, or Lingley, is reported to have been a carpenter, and in the early accounts of his son's career is generally said to have belonged to Wells. That there was some connection with that place, and that some of the family felt the bond very warmly, is certain, but at present the links have not been fitted in. Later in life, probably soon after the birth of his second son, William Linley moved to Bath, where he appears as a builder and where he became a prosperous person, who, after living for twenty years in a good house of his own, died in it at the age of eighty-eight, his wife, who was three years his senior, surviving him but a couple of months. A tablet to their memory may be seen in Walcot Church, Bath.

Concerning the boyhood and youth of Thomas Linley we have little knowledge, but many stories. That which describes him of having studied in Italy under Paradies, or Paradisi, can be true only on the supposition of his having gone at an extremely early age to that country, and as he could not himself, at that period, have earned enough money to pay for the journey, it would become necessary also to suppose that he was sent at the expense of some one else. It may be remembered that he sent his own son to Italy when the boy was but twelve years old. That a marked talent revealed itself very early, and that he was taught by Chilcot, the organist of Bath Abbey, are accepted facts. If it is true—as I am inclined to believe—that he attracted the attention of Chilcot when the latter was playing at the Duke of Beaufort's at Badminton, the connection must have begun before the settlement of the lad's parents at Bath. Mr Emanuel Green, that most industrious of investigators, says that Linley began life as Chilcot's errand-boy[1]; but the "Notes and Notices of Thomas Linley printed during his Life" upon which he bases the statement are by no means very trustworthy, and neither he nor any later writer seems

[1] Emanuel Green, F.R.S.L., " Thomas Linley, Richard Brinsley Sheridan and Thomas Mathews, their Connection with Bath," p. 4.

5

to have asked himself why an organist should want an errand-boy. The services of a boy, Chilcot, like any other eighteenth-century organist, and many a country organist to-day, would indeed require, not for running errands but for blowing the organ. I venture to believe, without any scrap of documentary evidence to support me, that the young Thomas Linley blew the bellows of the organ in Bath Abbey, and, unlike most performers of that necessary function, found full compensation for its monotony in listening to his master's music. That he somehow imbibed or developed a genuine and unselfish devotion to music which became and remained the passion of his life is unquestionable, and that somebody taught him extremely well is almost equally certain. It may reasonably be assumed that he was apprenticed to Chilcot in the same manner as various pupils both male and female were afterwards apprenticed to himself.

The next fact in his history is one for which documentary evidence can be cited. On the 11th of May 1752 he was married, at Batheaston, to Mary Johnson. Unfortunately the register of that parish is extremely laconic, and communicates no particulars beyond the two names and the date. Even this scanty information, however, is partly new, since neither the date nor the place of the marriage was known to the descendants of it until the kindness of the Rev. C. Shickle enabled me to discover these particulars, in the spring of 1910, from the copies made by him of church registers in and around Bath. The Sheridan family was unacquainted even with the family name of Mrs Thomas Linley, but this appears in the Tickell pedigree, where, also, her date of birth is given as 1729. As she herself wrote in June 1819 to one of her grandchildren: " I am now entered into my ninety-first year," that entry is pretty evidently correct.

6

Mr William Linley—an old gentleman whose accuracy was sometimes but approximate—calls his daughter-in-law Maria, and notes the date of her marriage as the 22nd of August 1752, four months later than its actual celebration. The discrepancy is so considerable as to suggest that the young people may, to use a phrase of their day, have "stolen a wedding," and that the bridegroom delayed confession to his family.

Of Mrs Linley's antecedents nothing is known. Her not uncommon surname appears occasionally in the registers of Batheaston and of neighbouring places, but there is no clear indication of any settled family to which she can be assigned. Michael Kelly says that she belonged to Wells, a statement which he received in all probability from herself or from one of her family, but no register of her birth is to be found either at Wells Abbey or at St Cuthbert's. Kelly, who was often at her house, describes her as a " kind, friendly woman and in her youth reckoned beautiful," a cautious phrase from which it seems fair to infer that the writer, who saw her for the first time in March 1787, when she would be fifty-eight years old, did not perceive any traces of beauty remaining.

Her young husband, who at the time of their marriage had not passed the half year between nineteen and twenty, was unquestionably endowed with good looks, and Gainsborough's portrait, painted some eighteen or twenty years later, shows that from him the most beautiful of his daughters inherited her finely cut brows and mouth. From him, too, his children one and all derived their musical talent, and, possibly, that fatal delicacy of constitution which carried off one after another of his five daughters before they reached the age of forty. In person he was tall, in colouring dark, and in manner reserved and somewhat stern. Yet we hear frequently of his shedding tears; he laughed boisterously, though not perhaps often, and had fits of talkativeness in which he told interesting anecdotes. It is a pity that these have not descended to us, since his reminiscences must have been peopled by a large number of conspicuous contemporaries. Parke, speaking from personal observation, declares him to have been "so devoid of envy that he was not only ready to admit the talents of every rival in his art but to contend for the merits of his contemporaries." One instance indeed exists of a quarrel, in which no less a man than William Herschel complained loudly of having been unfairly used by Linley; and signs are not entirely absent that at a later time the Drury Lane company considered the Linley family to preponderate unduly. With most contemporary musicians, however, he certainly was on friendly terms, and throughout his life many of England's best singers were those who had learned their art with him. Of his unremitting zeal and industry as a teacher many stories are extant. Kelly, for instance, reports how Mr Linley heard him sing, over and over again, the song with which he was to make his first appearance at the concerts of ancient music, and says that his success on the occasion was due to the "masterly instruction" thus given him.

Linley, indeed, was probably the best master of singing whom England has ever possessed. Whether he was altogether and invariably amiable in that capacity may be doubted. An assertion that his pupil, Miss Phillips, afterwards Mrs Crouch, trembled at the sight of him is thus dealt with by her niece and biographer: "This she has certainly said: 'There was never a greater contrast in human forms than is evinced in my first and last music master. Mr Wafer is of fairy race, light-complexioned and of meek appearance. Mr Linley, in comparison, is dark, stern and gigantic; I

8

tremble sometimes when I look at him, for I actually believe that my poor, dear, little, old master might go into the sleeve of Mr Linley's greatcoat.' "

Of the early married life of Thomas and Mary Linley we have no connected record; but entries in church registers and advertisements in Bath newspapers provide a chain of stepping-stones and enable us to fix some few events with complete precision. Several of these items have been gathered together by Mr Green, in papers read to the Bath Natural History and Antiquarian Field Club, in 1902 and 1903, and reprinted in pamphlet form in the latter year. Most of these references, but not all, I have, following in Mr Green's track, looked up; and I shrewdly suspect him of having wilfully left at least one error for the careless to trip over.

In the course of eighteen years the baptisms of twelve children were registered in Bath, as follows:—

1753, 12th March, at the Abbey, George Frederick.

1754, 25th September, at St Michael's, Elizabeth Ann.

1756, 11th June, at St James's, Thomas.

1758, 10th February, at St James's, Mary.

1759, 15th May, at St James's, Thurston.

1760, 23rd June, at St James's, Samuel.

1761, 8th September, at St James's, William Cary (brought to church to be received, after having been privately baptised).

1763, 10th October, at St James's, Maria.

1765, 22nd August, at the Abbey, Ozias Thurston[1] ("son of Thomas and Mary Linley, of St James's ").

---

[1] "Thurston" in the register; but "Thurstan" in the entry of his matriculation at Oxford; and "Thurstan" on the tombstone of his nephew, Charles Thurstan Ward.

1768, 17th February, at the Abbey, Jane Nash and Charlotte, twins ("daughters of Thomas and Mary Linley, of St James's parish, Bath." Brought to church to be received after having been privately baptised).

1771, 27th February, at St James's, William.

The birthday of Elizabeth was the 5th of September, that of Thomas (according to a manuscript account of him in the British Museum), the 5th of May; Mary's, the 4th of January, and Jane's, the 18th of the same month.

The eldest child is said to have been named in honour of Handel—a very probable conjecture, considering the admiration of Thomas Linley for that master, but one of which I have not found first-hand confirmation. That this boy did not live to grow up is certain; that he died very early is probable; but no register of his burial has yet come to light. He may have died away from home. The burial of Thurston is recorded, in May 1763, at St James's, with the note that he was "a child," and in the previous year (October 1762) the burial of William Linley is registered. Whether this was the little William Cary who had been privately baptised some thirteen months before, or whether it was that child's uncle, the William who was baptised at Badminton in 1744, remains uncertain. In any case, William Cary must have been dead before 1771, when the grand-paternal name was bestowed upon a second infant. No later mention of William of Badminton can be positively identified, although an advertisement as late in date as 1772 may possibly refer to him.

The name of Linley is to be found not only among baptisms and burials in Bath, but also among marriages, both at St James's and at the Abbey. On New Year's Day 1754 a certain Margaret Linley was married at St James's to Robert Smith, a widower, of Lyncombe and Widcombe.

That this Margaret should have been entirely unrelated to the family with which we are concerned is highly improbable. A daughter of William Linley's she can scarcely have been or he would not have omitted her from the record of his family Bible; whether she was his niece, his cousin, or even perhaps his sister, we must remain ignorant.

At the Abbey, on the 7th of October 1764, Isabella Linley, spinster, was married to Richard Philpot, bachelor, and both were described as " of this parish." The witnesses were James Davis and Mary Linley. This bride was unquestionably the daughter of William Linley, baptised at Badminton in 1737, and therefore now twenty-seven years old. Her husband was, we may feel pretty sure, the Richard Philpot whose advertisements appear in *The Bath Chronicle* (as Philpott, Phillpot and Philpot) in the years 1767 and 1768, and in which he describes himself as a carpenter. His may have been a case of the industrious apprentice who married his master's daughter.

Among the private houses and old furniture shops of Bath still linger, no doubt, unidentified, some of the tables, chairs, clock cases, " Buffetts with Glass Doors " and bedsteads with fluted or carved pillars that were fashioned in the workshop of Richard Philpot, and at the manufacture of which those pretty boys, Tom and Sam Linley, must, if they at all resembled ordinary boys, have sometimes looked on with interest. " Aunt Bel " is frequently mentioned in the letters of her nieces, and it is clear that cordial relations existed between her and her brother's children. I have come upon no positive evidence that she had children, it may have been her daughter who lived at Wells and but was held in high esteem and affection by Jane Linley, and in the Bath Directory for 1800 the name of John Philpot, musician, appears at 12 Kingsmead Terrace. The conjunction of name and calling suggests that Linley blood ran in the veins of this John.

The baptism of a child at the Abbey would lead to the supposition that in 1753 Thomas Linley was living in the Abbey parish, and similar evidence in 1754 applies to the parish of St Michael. But children were often baptised at churches other than that of their parish, and the earliest printed notice of their father's dwelling-place is a concert advertisement of the year 1759, in which tickets are announced as on sale " at Mr Linley's in the Abbey Green."

Abbey Green, which must not be confounded with the Abbey Churchyard, lies on the other side of York Street, and is nowadays a forlorn and poverty-stricken little square, from the central space of which all greenness has been trodden. The houses, however, have been good, and a hundred years ago must have been far from despicable. In one of them the lovely Elizabeth Linley may perhaps have been born. It seems unlikely that, at his first establishment, Thomas Linley could have afforded the whole of a house so large as these, unless, indeed, he let part of it. The taking of lodgers was a method of adding to the family income that commended itself greatly to Mrs Linley, who insisted, to the annoyance of her youngest son and daughter, in pursuing it long after it had ceased to be necessary. That a household dependent upon the earnings of a young and comparatively unknown musician must at first have been a modest one is evident, even without the confirmation of a positive statement made by Alicia Sheridan. Speaking of her first meeting with her sister-in-law (in 1770, when the Linleys were already comparatively prosperous) she says that her father " had some years previous to that period rendered some service to Mr Linley at that time in very narrow circumstances." As the earlier visit of the elder Sheridan to Bath took place in 1764 it is a fair inference that, as late as twelve years after their marriage, the Linleys were still struggling. At a later date they became not merely prosperous, but wealthy, and in the spring of 1772 were living in one of the fine new houses in the Crescent, now called Royal Crescent, and familiar under that name to the whole reading world as the scene of Mr Winkle's nocturnal adventure with a sedan-chair.

During the intervening years, or some of them, they have long been believed to have lived at 5 Pierrepont Street, and many accounts of Mrs Sheridan declare her to have been born there. In 1903, however, Mr Green laid before the Bath Field Club cogent reason for thinking that Thomas Linley never lived in Pierrepont Street at all. He had discovered an advertisement of the sale of concert tickets " at Mr Linley's in Orchard Street " in 1767.

Orchard Street, the name of which will not be found in current maps of Bath, was the turning now known in its northern half as Pierrepont Place, and its southern as Manvers Place.

Some reader may reflect, as I did, that concert tickets might conceivably be sold at the grandfather's and that, possibly, not Thomas, but William Linley was the tenant in Orchard Street. This doubt, however, is set at rest by an old church-rate book in the vestry at St James's Church, wherein, under the heading of Orchard Street, " Mr Thomas Linley's House " is inscribed with admirable legibility opposite to an entry of ten shillings for the year 1771. The rent is set down as £45.

Why the Linleys should have moved from Orchard Street to the Crescent is easy enough to understand; by the middle of 1771, when the family was in receipt of a large income, the eleven-roomed house in which they had dwelt for four years, and probably longer, had grown too narrow for the accommodation of father, mother, five daughters, four sons, and at least one maid-servant.

Among the advantages of the house in Orchard Street quiet cannot have been included, since the New Theatre, built in 1750, stood on the same side of the way and not many doors distant. The performances, however, began at half-past six, as did also the Bath concerts, so that the Linley babies were not kept awake by the departure of audiences to hours quite so undue as those to which modern infants would be exposed. Moreover there are indications that the children were to a considerable extent brought up away from home. Elizabeth and Mary were at a boarding-school near Wells, and Jane tells her lover that she lived till she was thirteen in a country town with a grandmother and great-aunt. Ozias and William continued to live in Bath after their parents had removed to London, one under the care of Mr and Mrs William Linley, the other under that of Mr and Mrs John Symmons. Tom was absent in Italy for two years, if not indeed for three. Thus the " neat convenient house," in Orchard Street, so described in an advertisement in 1771, may have been not so crowded after all.

It was in any case a busy hive enough. The father, always an industrious man, gradually accumulated pupils, few of whom, in all probability, showed so much talent as the tiny creatures in his own home; he sang and played at concerts; he may, perhaps, since he performed on the organ as well as on the harpsichord, have officiated at one of Bath's many churches. Mrs Linley, we may be very sure, was not idle. Labour-saving contrivances were few in her day; gas and electricity, the sewing machine and the vacuum cleaner were unthought of. Doubtless she and one servant, with help from her daughters as they grew up, kept the house in order, purchased and carried home provisions from the neighbouring market, then well stocked and flourishing, that lingers still in a decayed and discouraged state behind the Empire Hotel; cooked, washed dishes, and performed those endless tasks of sewing which kept eighteenth-century needles so busy. She, in all likelihood, made, and, after they had been washed at home, " got up " the many frilled shirts of her husband and her boys, mended their long stockings, and while her children were young probably manufactured with her own hand every garment, inner and outer, into which their little persons were tied and buttoned. That she fulfilled efficiently the housewife's Sisyphean task of "keeping down the bills" cannot be doubted. At every period of her life, and long after her husband had become a wealthy man, she economised, to use a gentle term, in coals and candles, and even, although not with quite so ardent a zeal, in clothes. The children began to work when they were little more than babies. Ozias Humphry, the painter, who lodged with the Linleys, and from whom the sixth of their sons is supposed to have derived his unusual Christian name, describes the little Elizabeth at eight years old as knowing all the songs in *Thomas and Sally*, *The Beggar's Opera*, *The Chaplet*, and *Love in a Village*. " These," J. T. Smith tells us, in " Nollekens and his Times," " she would sing so sweetly that many a day at the young Painter's solicitation, she chanted them, seated at the foot of his easel looking up at him, unconscious of her heavenly features, with such looks and features as prevailed upon the motley visitors of Bath when she gracefully held up her little basket with her father's benefit tickets at the door as they passed in and out of the Pump Room." It was from her father that she had learned thus early to sing, and it speaks well for his care and knowledge that her voice in womanhood was absolutely unimpaired by its exercise in childhood. Thomas also showed a precocious and remarkable talent, and was " by the tuition of his parent perfectly grounded in both theory and practice " before he was seven years old. At that age the proud father put him under the instruction of Dr Boyce, with whom he remained for five years.

Up to 1767 or thereabouts the expenses of the household must have been heavy and the father the only breadwinner. By the end of the year 1765 there were six children, the eldest of whom was but a little over eleven years old, while the age of the youngest was still reckoned in months. One of the girls was certainly at boarding-school, and the second probably already with her. Tom was with Dr Boyce, to whom, either in the form of premium or of fees, some payment must have been made. The boy was by this time a skilled violinist. Samuel, born in 1761, would hardly yet have begun taking lessons from any master but his father, though he may by this time have known his notes and the respective values of crochets and quavers. After the first dozen years of family life, however, the children, instead of impoverishing their parents, began to enrich them, and before another half-dozen years were over the earnings of Elizabeth alone were sufficient to have supported the whole household in affluence, while Tom and Mary, although not commanding payments so large as hers, were successful and prosperous public performers.

The conduct of the father who thus early trained these exquisitely endowed and highly strung little creatures to such a degree of technical proficiency, and who pocketed as a matter of course the proceeds of their labours, has to modern eyes an ugly look; but in measuring it by our own standards, we do a grave injustice to Thomas Linley.

We must remember that in his lifetime, and for many years after his death, it had not yet occurred to anybody that the young and growing human being was likely to be injured by overwork of hand or brain. Nor did any father in his day dream that the earnings of his child ought equitably to be the child's property rather than the parent's. Even the earnings of a grown woman were not her own, but her husband's, until well within the memory of many persons still living; and at the present day there are many working-class parents who appropriate as a matter of course the earnings of unmarried daughters. For his three eldest children, in particular, the affection of Linley was intense, and when the last of them died, his life broke too and a mere wreck of himself was left to linger out three melancholy years. In these children his passion for that art which was his very element seemed almost to take bodily form; he must have loved them, not only because they were his own, but because they were music's own. Moreover, of Elizabeth, less than twenty-two years his junior, he might have said, as Goethe's mother said of her wonderful boy: "We were young together." He was not yet thirty-five when, in May 1767, he led Elizabeth, something over twelve years old, and Thomas, something under eleven, upon the concert platform at Bath, the girl to sing, the boy to play the violin. Young though they were, this was probably not their first appearance. A note in the Egerton MSS. in the British Museum, which seems to have been copied from some newspaper paragraph, says: "Mrs Sheridan, daughter of Mr Linley . . . first appeared at Covent Garden in Fairy Favour." What character she played I have not been able to discover, but that taken by her brother may be learned from Mr Green's paper. He tells us of a reference in *The Bath Journal* to a paragraph in *Lloyd's Evening Post*,

for 19th of February 1767 (which paragraph however
Mr Green has sought in vain), wherein Master Linley is
to have played a violin solo at a concert by command of their
Majesties. The information is added, whether from the
Evening Post or from the *Journal* itself, that "this is the
little gentleman that played the part of Puck in the Fairy
Favour whose abilities as a child are beyond description."
In the absence of a playbill, the date at which *Fairy Favour*
was performed cannot be settled, but we may, I think, take
it for granted that the two children did act in it at some
time probably in the winter of 1766–1767. That Tom
may well have made the tricksiest and most engaging of
Pucks may easily be believed by anyone who studies the
picture which Gainsborough made of him and his elder
sister in May 1768. Roguish, yet wistful, the boy's eyes
look out beneath his thick curly hair; the dimple of a smile
hovers at the corner of the sensitive yet determined mouth.
Even when at twenty or so he had grown into the pale,
trim, somewhat self-satisfied young gentleman of his later
portrait, with the curls all brushed down into powdered
smoothness, his cravat up to his chin and a smart cocked hat
under the arm of his smart red coat, the look of Puck still
lingered in the long eyes, and the hint of a smile still hung
about the lips, close pressed now and firm almost to hardness.
Scarcely a spoken or a written word of Tom Linley's remains,
only certain elaborate and beautiful musical scores with their
free, flowing quill-drawn lines, and that childish answer—
and even that is sometimes attributed to Samuel: "We
are all geniuses here, sir." But on the testimony of
Gainsborough I at least am ready to believe that Thomas,
like Elizabeth, like Mary, like Ozias, and like Jane, had a
pretty wit.

With their invariable trick of attracting the interest of

interesting people the Linley family early possessed themselves of Gainsborough's affections. How, indeed, could he fail to be enchanted with them, he who adored beauty and music almost equally? He painted the father, he painted Tom, and Sam; he painted Elizabeth and Tom together; Elizabeth and Mary together; Elizabeth alone, twice if not three times; Mary alone; Mary's husband and Elizabeth's husband; and Elizabeth's son. He also on two occasions modelled and coloured a head of Elizabeth in clay. What would we not give for either of those models? But alas, each in turn was broken by some too zealous maid in the course of officious dusting. Finally, when he and they alike had moved to London and were all prosperous together, Gainsborough adopted a little boy of three years old for the avowed reason that he looked so like the Linleys. To him, more than to any of the many artists who painted her, we owe it that we know so well what that most exquisite of creatures, Elizabeth Linley, looked like. Of that further charm that lay in her voice only dull printed words can now tell us, but they tell us enough to make us understand how perfectly it matched her face, and how truly both were the expression of a very rare and lovely nature.

No account seems to be extant of the concert at which, as far as we know, Elizabeth and Tom appeared for the first time in Bath; but in *The Bath Chronicle* of 14th of May—that *Bath Chronicle* in which so much of her romantic story was to be recorded, and the reading of which must so often have caused her angry tears—the proud father printed " his most grateful acknowledgment to the Company for the great Honour and Encouragement his Children received at their Concert; to merit their future Favour, it shall be his constant Study by every Effort in his Power to promote their Improvement."

In November, when the Bath season began again, he gave another concert, at which a musical version of *Lycidas* and "Wharton's *Ode to Fancy*" were performed, Elizabeth and her father singing, while Tom played a solo between the acts. This is one of the concerts for which tickets are advertised to be sold at Mr Linley's in Orchard Street. *The Bath Journal* in its next issue recorded that "the whole audience expressed their approbation by loud and unusual applause."

It is, indeed, clear that both children made their mark at once; and we may conclude that the songstress of twelve years old returned no more to the boarding-school at Wells. Her portrait when she was thirteen years old looks at the first glance like that of a girl of eighteen, the elaborate edifice of her hair and the womanly costume helping to deceive the eye; her face, however, has the rounded contour and the immaturity of her real age; compared with later portraits by the same hand the countenance is almost empty, and there is actually more of definite character in that of her young brother.[1] But from this painting we can judge that the Miss Linley of the concert room ceased very early to look like a juvenile prodigy, and also that her characteristic air of pathetic dignity was not acquired as a result of experience and suffering, but was inborn. Before she was sixteen she was a well-known and greatly admired public singer and was also one of the acknowledged beauties, if not indeed *the* beauty of Bath.

Mary's first appearance was almost certainly made in 1770 at Covent Garden. A newspaper cutting in the British Museum (Egerton MSS.) dated 9th July 1770, runs as

[1] Some writers have erroneously supposed this portrait to represent Mary, but this is impossible. It was painted in the summer of 1768 when Mary was but ten and a half years old.

follows: "The young lady who so admirably performed the part of Sally in the new piece called *Man and Wife* is about eleven years of age, and is daughter to Mr Linley, an ingenious Composer at Bath, whose eldest daughter lately made a great figure in the world as a musical performer." Mary's voice must have been of the same type as her sister's, since she was able, in the absence of Elizabeth, to supply her place, but it was admittedly not so fine. Both were sopranos, and, even allowing for the lower concert pitch of their period, must have commanded unusually high notes. In looks Mary resembled her sister sufficiently to be sometimes mistaken for her, and was probably—as her own letter seems to imply— not flattered by the Dulwich portrait. Her nose, however, was not, as was her sister's "of that most elegant of shapes, Grecian"; she and Jane, as she merrily writes, when an epidemic of silhouettes had overtaken her household, "don't happen to think so well of your *Profiles*." In general intelligence Mary was fully her sister's equal, and in wit her superior. The two were devoted to each other—how, indeed, could either find elsewhere equal talent, charm and comprehension? Tom, persevering—or sometimes, it would appear, not persevering very much—with his fiddle, went to Italy probably in the autumn of 1768, and remained there until 1770 at least. He was already composing, and indeed is said to have written six violin solos before he left England.

For their father those must have been happy years. Not only was the public confirming his fondest hopes of Elizabeth, Thomas and Mary; Samuel, two years younger than Mary a lad of extraordinary beauty, who closely resembled his eldest sister, would by this time be showing that he too had the family endowments, and even the little Maria had perhaps already given promise of the wonderful voice that was to be

21

hers. The most brilliant expectations can hardly have seemed to him exaggerated.

Moreover, the commercial aspect of their success must have removed from him that dread of leaving his flock unprovided for, which makes uneasy the mind of so many a professional man. The present was made prosperous, the future secure; Thomas Linley might rest from the anxieties to which his temper was prone; Mary Linley might, with a good conscience, have ceased from the sparing and paring that had become habitual, and that, unfortunately, remained so to the end. Early in 1771 the last and longest-lived of their children, William, was born, and the first stage of the family's history reached its conclusion.

CHAPTER 2. THE MAID OF BATH

Mr Thomas Sheridan, a worthy, pompous, cantankerous and eminently respectable man, believed elocution to form a very important part of education, and made it his business not only to teach it to such pupils as presented themselves, but also to impress upon all his compatriots the desirability of getting themselves trained as orators. To this end he wrote various works, and gave from time to time courses of lectures, to which he gave the name of " Attic Entertainments." They consisted mainly of recitations and were interspersed with songs or music. In the early part of 1769, when the Linleys were in London fulfilling musical engagements, Elizabeth was the singer at one of these courses; and when towards the end of the next year Mr Sheridan brought his family to live in Bath, he again secured her help. The songs which she then sang have been recorded and are of the ballad type, Scotch, Irish and English. The perfect voice production for which she was praised by musical contemporaries must have been particularly appropriate to the occasion.

Mrs Sheridan, an amiable and cultivated woman, who had written a novel and some plays of considerable merit, had been dead for some years, and had left two sons and two daughters: Charles Francis, born in 1750, Richard Brinsley, born in 1751, Alicia, called in the family " Lissy," born in 1753, and Anne Elizabeth Hume Crawfurd (Betsy), born in 1758. It is a complicating circumstance that the husbands whom these sisters eventually married were brothers: Joseph and Henry Le Fanu, and the application to both of them of the name " Mrs Le Fanu " has led to some confusion of identity. It is well to remember that the account of what happened in Bath when she was young was written by Mrs Joseph Le Fanu, Alicia, who at the time of these occurrences was seventeen or eighteen years old, not thirteen, as Mr Green, who supposes the writer to be Mrs Henry Le Fanu, Elizabeth, says. While she here and there makes a slip upon points not within her personal knowledge, her record must be considered as by far the best-informed and most trustworthy that remains. To prefer the statements of contemporary newspapers is to prefer third-hand to first-hand evidence. Except the hero and heroine, no person in the world was so well aware of the facts; moreover, upon many points her narrative is corroborated by the independent testimony of witnesses who were never acquainted with it.

From her statement, quoted pretty fully by Mr Fraser Rae and Mr Sichel, we learn that her father had some years previously rendered some service to Mr Linley, " who took an early opportunity of inviting Mr Sheridan's family and some of their friends to a small musical party at his house. This was the first introduction of Mr R. B. Sheridan to Miss Linley." This meeting, as we now know, must have taken place in Orchard Street. " She was then principal singer at the Bath Concert, though not more than sixteen years of age. The young people were all much pleased with each other, but the elder Mr Sheridan, who had never introduced his daughters before to any person in public life, desired his elder daughter, then about Miss Linley's age, not to cultivate too great an intimacy, though he permitted the acquaintance to go on. Charles Sheridan became strongly attached to Miss Linley; his brother was apparently entirely engaged in the amusements of the place."

In fact, Thomas Sheridan, actor and lecturer, thought his own social standing considerably more exalted than that of Thomas Linley, the musician. In his " Plan of Education," published in 1769, Mr Sheridan had remarked that music " often draws persons to mix with such company as they would otherwise avoid." No doubt his attitude towards the Linleys was in some degree influenced by the recollection, which seems to have been always in the background of his mind, that he himself belonged to a good old family, honourably adorned with Bishops and Doctors of Divinity, whereas the father of Thomas Linley (although now growing rich and about to settle down in his own excellent home in Belmont) was from the point of view of descent a mere nobody.

If he could but have heard of the old Linleys of Broseley and known that there was a Linley Hall still existing there, he might possibly have looked with other eyes upon the marriage of his younger son—and, indeed, that son himself would greatly have preferred that his wife should have possessed some ancientry of lineage. But the Linleys, I am very certain, knew nothing about those early glories of their name; and nothing would have been more alien to their whole disposition than to claim any distinction that was not theirs. They were, as they had very good reason to be, proud of themselves as they were, and in their private communications with one another they did not conceal the well-founded conviction that to be a Linley was to be made of finer stuff than their neighbours.

Though Dick Sheridan might appear engrossed in the mere amusements of Bath, his mind was really much occupied by literary efforts and projects, and a large proportion of such verses of his writing as remain belong to this period of his life. It must have been an added charm in Eliza Linley[1] that she too wrote verses and could turn a pretty rhymed reply to a poetical compliment. Several of the Linleys, indeed, had a literary talent, well marked in their letters, and William Linley, their grandfather, wrote verses—but his, it appears, were bad. Eliza's always show a good ear and a perfect sincerity of feeling; concision, indeed, that highest of technical merits and surest warrant of survival, they lack, but even at their most diffuse they breathe something of her individual charm. There was a sort of fragrance about this delightful woman, something gentle and tender and touching, yet passionate and spirited. Character as well as talent belonged to her, and an innate refinement. In the love letters of her girlhood she is, it is true, once or twice " gushing," a few phrases run over into sentimentality; but of what love letter written by a girl in her teens was the wording ever perfectly simple and free from amplification? If for a few brief weeks Elizabeth Linley did pose to herself as a persecuted heroine of romance, she did but share the secret belief of every young girl in love with a forbidden suitor—and it must be admitted that she had unusual justification. Never again does a touch of affectation show itself; and the more nearly we come to know her, the more surely do we perceive how solid were her fundamental qualities, how sensible she was, how active minded, how capable, how devoted. The germs of all these qualities must have existed even at sixteen, and they were to come to maturity in spite of some of the most demoralising experiences to which life can expose a young woman: she was to attract

---

[1] Her parents called her " Betsy " but her young contemporaries preferred what was then the romantic form " Eliza." Elizabeth Bennet, it may be remembered, was " Lizzy " to her family, but " Eliza " to her friend Charlotte and to the fashionable sisters of Mr Bingley.

the love, good or bad, of nearly every man she met, and was
to become the victim of such outspoken discussion as even
the least restrained of modern journalists would hardly
permit himself in England to-day. Her best support,
probably, lay in her professional work. The subordination
of self to something larger—and any art is so much larger—
gives a certain standing place beyond petty personal cares;
Elizabeth, though she loathed—or perhaps it would be truer
to say, came to loathe—appearing in public, loved music,
and music, we may be certain, stood her friend in return.

The list of men known to have been in love with her
before her marriage runs well into two figures. It included
Sheridan's brother as well as his old Harrow schoolfellow,
Nathaniel Halhed, now at Oxford, who was collaborating
with him in a book of professedly translated verses. These
and others, however, were impecunious young men, and for
suitors of that description the eighteenth-century parent had,
if I may be pardoned the Americanism, no use. In the eyes
of Mrs Linley, as in those of most of her contemporaries, it
was the first of maternal duties to get a daughter wealthily
married. In fact the Linleys, husband and wife, who had
themselves made an imprudent match and found it turn out
successfully, were extremely anxious to preserve their
daughter from taking any such risk. Eliza, it must
further be remembered, was articled to her father until she
should come of age, and her earnings, which legally were
his, made a handsome addition to the family income. It
must have been at about the end of the year 1770 that a
suitor presented himself who was entirely to the taste of the
elders but by no means to that of the young lady. This
was Mr Walter Long, who was rich and elderly, and
inhabited a good house in Gay Street. Miss Linley was
sixteen; Mr Long was much her senior. The antithesis

of sixteen and sixty was obvious. All the contemporary satirists and scandalmongers labelled Mr Long as sixty; Mrs Le Fanu, writing many years later, and probably without personal knowledge, followed them; and subsequent writers have followed her. But the fact that his name appears in the Bath Directory for 1800 arouses a suspicion that he may not improbably have been considerably younger. No doubt he pursued the correct course and made his proposal to the lady's father, who no doubt accepted it on his daughter's behalf. At Mr Long's desire she ceased to appear in public. Settlements were made, handsome jewels presented to her; the date of the marriage was apparently fixed. Driven to desperation, Elizabeth seems to have found it easier to appeal to Mr Long, than to her parents. She wrote to him, "declaring," says Alicia Sheridan, "her reluctance to the proposed match on the ground of her attachment to another, and requesting he would withdraw his suit in order to shield her from her father's displeasure." It is believed that Mr Long's family, on their side, urged him to give up his project; and perhaps second thoughts had whispered to him—a kind and reasonable man—that happiness, either for himself or for his wife, did not lie in the direction of marriage with a girl who was some thirty years at least his junior and who belonged to an entirely different world. He withdrew his proposal and respected Elizabeth's secret.

Mr Linley, incensed at the slight apparently cast upon his daughter, threatened to sue for the price of her services during her temporary retirement, and she naturally was greatly alarmed lest Mr Long should justify himself by handing her father her letter. But he never did so. He accepted quietly the *rôle* that she had assigned to him, suffered in silence the jeers and slanders of contemporary gossip, and

28

pacified the irate parent by settling on Elizabeth three thousand pounds and leaving in her hands the jewels, estimated at another thousand. He retained to the end of her life a friendship for her, and both she and her husband regarded him with well-deserved esteem. One can but feel, in spite of the glaring disparity in age, that worse fates might have befallen Elizabeth Linley than that of becoming Mrs Long.

An article that appeared in *The London Magazine*, September 1772, and that in some points is curiously well informed, says that she disliked being dragged from "the kind eye of the public who had so often caressed and applauded her," a statement quite incompatible with her steady distaste for singing in public. When, however, the tale proceeds: "she told her father so, and added with a truly English spirit that if she married at all she would marry to be *free*," we seem to hear the voice of the real Elizabeth. Gentle though she was, she had a temper that could flame out upon occasion, and, in spite of her awe of her father, may well, in a moment of sudden provocation, have turned upon him with some such words.

The marriage, then, with Mr Long was safely averted; but the circumstances were not permitted to fall naturally and slowly into oblivion. That odious person, Samuel Foote, perceived in the story material for one of his scandalously personal plays, gave to his piece the name of *The Maid of Bath*—by which Miss Linley seems to have been already known—and produced it at the Haymarket in the summer of 1771. Apart from its bold introduction, under the most transparent masks, of living and recognisable people, the play is neither better nor worse than scores of others. The whole essence of it is its unabashed personality. "Solomon Flint," who represents Mr Long, is a mere compound of senile

29

miserliness, cowardice and meanness; "Major Rackett," at once recognised as Ensign Thomas Mathews, whose Christian name he shares, is little better than a professional seducer; while the two elder women, Mrs Linnet, mother of the heroine, and a certain Lady Catherine, are entirely mercenary. Among these sordid personages, and against a background of local caricatures, moves Miss Kitty Linnet, simple, modest, refined and sensible. Even Foote did not attempt to make Elizabeth Linley a figure of parody. There is no mention of her father. Perhaps Thomas Linley, with his imposing stature, his stern concert conductor's eye and his reserved demeanour struck Foote as a man with whom it might be better not to meddle; but more probably (since such considerations would have been equally effectual in restraining him from ridiculing Mr Linley's wife) the very reserve, silence and quiet dignity of the musician offered to satire none of those salient points in which Mrs Linley, it must be confessed, abounded. Between her and her proto-type the likeness is cruelly exact, more exact, indeed, than, one would suppose, the author could easily have been aware. So precise are several little details that when I found Mrs Linnet accused of being " proud and pragmatic as the Pope 'cause her great-aunt by the father's side was a clargyman's daughter," I at once inclined to believe that Mrs Linley— a regular churchgoer—came in fact of a clerical stock. It is certainly the case that there was a clergyman attached to Wells Cathedral (his name appears frequently in the register as having officiated at marriages) whose name was E. Johnson, and who may easily have been her relative.

To Mrs Linley the rupture of her daughter's engagement with the owner of ten thousand a year—the figure is Foote's —must have been a disappointment of the severest kind; and often, we may be sure, did her active tongue reprobate the treachery of Mr Long, or turn to rate Betsy for her stupidity in not managing to retain such a prize. In her own way she was devoted to her children, and she was perfectly convinced that their real happiness must be determined entirely by their wealth. She would have been fully as ready as Mrs Linnet in the play to scout the notion that any disparity of years or tastes could counterbalance the benefits of a good income. Thirty years later, when her last surviving daughter, possessing three hundred a year of her own, determined to marry a poor man to whom she had been engaged for over two years, Mrs Linley spared no effort to divide them, and showed few scruples as to the methods which she employed. Not from her did her daughters acquire their rectitude.

It is, however, in regard to the character of Mathews that *The Maid of Bath* is of most importance to the present history. Major Rackett appears, newly arrived at that famous Bath Inn, " The Bear," where he at once encounters his old acquaintance, Sir Christopher Cripple. From Sir Christopher's conversation we learn that the Major, during his last visit to that city, created a great scandal by carrying off one Miss Prim, apprentice to a milliner " in the Grove." He inquires after " my little flame, *la petite Rosignole*," and is told that she is about to marry the aged Solomon Flint. The two men hereupon set themselves, with the assistance of various subordinates, to scare Flint out of his design, and, partly owing to their machinations, partly owing to the discreditable behaviour of Flint himself, the match is broken off. Sir Christopher, who has all along suspected Rackett of being in love with Miss Linnet, forces him into a proposal of marriage. " Sir," says she to Sir Christopher, " there is first an account to be settled between this gentleman and an old acquaintance of mine." " Who? " asks Sir Christopher.

And she replies: "The Major can guess—the unhappy Miss Prim." So she refuses his offer and declares her intention of continuing in her present condition.

This portrait of Mathews corresponds very closely with another written many years later in a production called *Bath Characters*. "Rattle," who unquestionably stands for Mathews, says: "Fallen is my pride among women. There was a time, indeed, when I made a figure with the sex, and could select from my list of conquests a fair specimen of every degree of rank from the duchess to the spouse of the squire." A lady-killer, then, was Captain Mathews—the superior grade was generally given to him by his fellow-townsmen—according to the general opinion of Bath; and Alicia Sheridan's account of his conduct, which is also confirmed by contemporary letters, accords precisely with the pictures of him given in print by the two authors.

It is of some importance to recognise this concurrence of testimony, because Mr Green has in some of his investigations endeavoured to whitewash Mathews at the expense of Sheridan, and to discredit the narrative of Sheridan's sister, about whose own identity he is in error. To represent Mathews as a safe and trustworthy friend for a beautiful young girl of a rank inferior to his own becomes possible only by ignoring alike *The Maid of Bath*, *Bath Characters*, Alicia's statement, and Elizabeth's own subsequent letters. Elizabeth Linley, even at seventeen, had far too much experience of lovers to suppose herself persecuted by a man's attentions unless she really were so. We must never forget that it was she, not Sheridan, who was Alicia's informant.

Nor does any resentment seem to have been felt by Mathews or his friends at the character of "Major Rackett," whereas those of Mr Long were indignant at that of

"Solomon Flint," and there were paragraphs and letters in the *Chronicle* suggesting the probability of an action against Foote. Possibly the military gentleman did not dislike to be thought dangerous.

Thomas Mathews belonged to a good family, settled in Wales, but perhaps originally Irish. He had held a commission in the Militia, and although he never seems to have called himself "Captain," other people did so to the end of his life. He married, probably in 1770, a Welsh lady, became a permanent resident in Bath, and lived to write an authoritative and often reprinted handbook of whist. Mr and Mrs Mathews lived, and eventually died, at 19 Portland Place, Bath, at which address his name may be found in the early Bath Directories as "Mathews, Mr Thomas," in 1800, and as "Matthews, Captain," in 1809. I looked with some interest at the house when I happened to pass it. It is the last house towards the west, on the south side, its exterior is grey, gloomy and uninviting, and it has an air, such as some old Brighton houses have, of shrugging itself together from the wind.

Whether Elizabeth Linley was ever in this house (some accounts describe her as meeting Sheridan there) appears to me very doubtful. It is more likely that Mathews would continue, after his marriage as before, to visit at the musician's house, but that Mrs Mathews would scarcely consider the family as socially qualified to be invited as her guests. Both Mrs Le Fanu and *The London Magazine* tell us that Mathews had known the Linleys since Elizabeth was a child; and the former, whose information came direct from Elizabeth herself, expressly states that, as she grew older, he made love to her, and that she was afraid to tell her father of her distress lest he should risk his life by challenging her persecutor—one instance among many of the manner in which the custom of duelling, supposed to protect women from insult, really exposed them to it.

"He threatened sometimes to destroy himself," says Mrs Le Fanu, "at others to injure her character to the utmost of his power if she persisted in refusing to listen to his addresses." Whether Mathews was the man whom Elizabeth had in her mind when she wrote to Mr Long that her affections were fixed upon another person cannot be declared with certainty. We do know from her own written word that she did not at that time love Sheridan; and undoubtedly gossip connecting her name with that of Mathews was rife in Bath. It is quite possible, however, that the man by whom she was attracted at the age of sixteen or seventeen was one whose name has never reached us at all. A girl so much wooed is apt to bestow her affections where they have not been sought; and it is likely that Sheridan, who refrained so long from declaring his feelings, gained an advantage thereby.

Such was the exceedingly explosive state of affairs among the group of young people in Bath at the close of that agitating year, 1771. To increase the perils, Mr Sheridan withdrew his severe surveillance and went to fulfil his theatrical engagements in Dublin, never suspecting, poor autocratic parent, into what extremely distasteful complications he was to be plunged during his absence.

The Irish visit of Mr Sheridan no doubt facilitated intimacy between his children and the Linleys. Charles Sheridan, however, prudent and cautious even at two and twenty, after taking counsel with himself had decided that his attachment to Miss Linley would certainly bring him more trouble than happiness, or, in his own phraseology, that he was "indulging a passion which could only make him acquainted with the pains of love and never taste its sweets." He sent her, by his younger sister, a formal letter of farewell, and went to lodge at a farmhouse some miles away, in order to avoid the too attractive company of the sweet young singer. Later in the year he described himself to his uncle as cured of "his very ridiculous attachment." Yet after the lapse of seven and twenty years he told Jane Linley that the resemblance between her eyes and her sister's made him "tremble again."

In the absence of their two elders, therefore, Richard, Alicia and Elizabeth Sheridan were keeping house together, and it must have been about this time that Alicia became the recipient of confidences from her friend on the one hand and from her brother on the other. Dick confessed that he too was in love with Miss Linley—a confession never yet made to herself. Throughout these eventful months, indeed, he showed a power of self-control very remarkable in a youth of his age. Presently Elizabeth in her turn confided to Alicia her distresses. Cruel, indeed, had been the poor girl's position for many months past. What must she have endured, proud, sensitive and modest as she was, in knowing that her own story was being acted almost under her own name on the public stage; in being aware, every time she stepped forward to sing, that every person in her audience had canvassed, or was canvassing the most intimate details of her personal history. To these sufferings were added the disturbing conduct of Mathews and her terrors lest her father, discovering that conduct, should, in the phrase of the day, "call him to account."

The attitude of Elizabeth's parents seems, as far as we know enough to judge it, culpably negligent. That Linley observed nothing for himself we may well believe. Fathers, until experience is forced upon them, are proverbially blind to the love affairs of their children; and his head was full of many other preoccupations. But *The Maid of Bath* had been acted; and he cannot have remained ignorant of its main lines. " Major Rackett " ought to have aroused the attention—to say no more—of even the least observant of parents. His daughter, as her fears of a possible duel prove, believed him entirely unsuspicious. We cannot, of course, tell how specious and plausible a person Mathews may have been, nor how he may have posed to the elders as a safe old friend and protector. After all, they were only beginning their experience as the parents of daughters whose position, standing as they did neither wholly within nor wholly without the fashionable society of the place, was more than a little anomalous. Perhaps Linley's pride refused to suppose that his daughter could be in danger under his roof; perhaps he may have dreaded to make an enemy who might do harm to the professional popularity of the family; perhaps to him, after twenty years of married life and of unromantic hard work, the flutterings and murmurings that circled round his girl may have seemed but excessively trivial details of the general social game. That he realised in the smallest degree his daughter's distress of mind, or dreamed that she might be nearing the edge of a precipice, is quite incredible.

But that Mrs Linley should not have seen enough to make intervention her duty is more difficult to believe. She was not absorbed by the claims of an art; she was not possessed, as her husband must often have been, by the insistent haunting of a half-shaped melody, nor by the executant's brooding over this and that possible improvement. Nor was she a woman insensible to the importance of good repute. Though she was capable of many small meannesses, though she was domineering and violent tempered, though she was neither delicate nor refined, there is every reason to suppose

that she had a genuine sense of duty, especially towards her own family, and that she had the virtues as well as the vices of that eighteenth-century middle class to which she belonged. On such a point as the acceptance by an unmarried girl of the love of a married man her verdict would pretty certainly have been entirely that of Mrs Grundy. Yet so far as we know she did not interfere.

That Elizabeth did not confide in her was but natural; mother and daughter though they were, there was a total lack of affinity between them; in fact, in contemplating the character of the daughters belonging to this family—of whom we have more intimate records than of the sons—the question constantly presents itself: Where, in these women, is a trace discernible of their mother? And yet the mother's was a well-defined and developed individuality, likely, one would have supposed, to leave its mark very clearly upon her offspring. There may have been—there must have been—in that narrow, bustling, energetic, harsh, yet warm nature qualities that passed themselves on and existed also in those open, generous, artistic, impulsive and exquisite creatures whom she bore, nursed, cradled and out-lived. We can only say that the traces are hidden, and that, so far as we can see, sons and daughters alike were Linleys and not Johnsons.

In *The Gentleman's Magazine* for October 1825 was published a letter which purported to be written by Elizabeth Linley, and to give an account of her experiences at this period. It was declared to have been addressed to her " confidential friend Miss Saunders "; but the document is not in her hand-writing, nor can the date of " May 2nd, 1770 " possibly be a genuine one for a letter that describes events known to have occurred in the year 1772. But the paper communicated to *The Gentleman's Magazine* might

37

have been a transcript of a genuine letter, and the error of date a mere copyist's mistake for "May 2nd, 1772." If so, it is reasonable to ask: Where is the original, and why has it never been produced? Does it give the address of Miss Saunders—whose name is otherwise unknown? Is the place indicated by the initial D. written at full length? The earlier biographers of Sheridan, Moore and Fraser Rae, both unhesitatingly declared the letter to be a forgery, but Mr Sichel, whose extensive acquaintance with the correspondence of the Linley and Sheridan families give sparticular weight to his opinion, says: "Though it cannot be an original, a minute analysis convinces me that it is a transcript —however garbled—from a genuine letter." He proceeds to cite several points in it that are confirmed by information existing in family papers unpublished at the time of its appearance.

Having reread the letter with care, I find myself coming to very much the same conclusion. There are passages in it that recall the phrases and the turn of thought of Elizabeth —passages of which, as one reads, one murmurs involuntarily: "This must be hers"; but there are other passages of which, with equal conviction, one murmurs: "This she never wrote."

Apart from any discrepancies or concurrences in detail, there is a sort of verbosity and a flavour of self-conscious silliness about the letter as it stands, entirely out of accord with the character of any of the Linley sisters. To pose and to languish did not belong to their first-hand temperaments; and the real seriousness of this letter lies not in the probability that it may lead readers astray as to the succession, or indeed the occurrence, of certain subsidiary events, but in the danger that it may give them a wholly inaccurate impression of Elizabeth Linley.

In justice then to her memory, this doubtful letter should be carefully eliminated from the data upon which any estimate of her character is founded; and it will be wise not to consider as valid any statement contained in it for which there is not independent evidence.

To return to the group of young people in Bath. Alicia, who in January 1772 had reached the mature age of nineteen, found herself thus standing as a trusted confidante between her brother, who had completed his twentieth year in the previous September, and her friend, who in the same month had entered her eighteenth. Alicia, like Richard, seems never to have been a favourite child of her father, who preferred his elder son and his younger daughter. Thus the motherless elder girl had no doubt early learned to think and act for herself. The story of Miss Linley's woes was before long shared with Elizabeth Sheridan, and the sisters considered that their brother was " designed by nature to act the part of a knight of the olden time." At their request his aid was invited; he knew Mathews, and seems to have done something in the way of expostulating with him. In the case of almost any other youth one might hesitate to believe that any influence could be brought to bear upon a man eight or nine years his senior by a lad of twenty who, moreover, might be reasonably suspected of being a rival admirer. But the persuasive powers of Sheridan were remarkable, and it seems possible that he did induce the military gentleman to leave Miss Linley in peace, at any rate for a while. The tongues of Bath were by this time coupling their names pretty freely; the gossip may have reached the ears of Mrs Mathews, and she may have intervened. Or Sheridan may have hinted that the eyes of Mr Linley were beginning to open, although this does not appear to have been really the case. Whatever form his

39

interposition may have taken, it is fairly clear that Elizabeth
thought herself served by it, and that she thereafter unfolded
to him and his sisters a plan which appears as her own in
Alicia's narrative, but as his in the mysterious letter. Her
dislike to the publicity of her profession had become, as we
may well believe, increasingly acute since she had found
herself the subject of general discussion, and had now grown
into an eager desire for escape. She thought she might hide
herself in a French convent until the age of twenty-one
should at the same time free her from the obligations of her
apprenticeship and enable her, out of the money settled upon
her by Mr Long, to compensate her father for the loss of
her services in the meantime. To Alicia it seemed " meri-
torious to assist a young person situated as Miss Linley was
in getting her out of the difficulties that surrounded her,"
and she offered " letters of introduction to some ladies she
had known in France where she had resided some years,
and Sheridan offered to be her conductor to St Quentin
where these friends lived. . . . At length they fixed on an
evening " (it was Wednesday, 18th of March) " when
Mr Linley, his eldest son and Miss M. Linley were engaged
at the Concert (Miss Linley being excused on the plea of
illness) to set out on their journey. Sheridan brought a
sedan-chair to Mr Linley's house in the Crescent in which
he had Miss Linley conveyed to a post chaise that was waiting for them on the London Road. A woman was in the
chaise who had been hired by Sheridan to accompany them
on this extraordinary elopement."

For Mr Linley the young man had left a letter in which
he gave apparently an account of the conduct of Mathews,
and that account Mr Linley seems to have accepted.
Perhaps it was accompanied by a letter from his daughter,
perhaps Alicia Sheridan repeated to him her story.

A letter written to Sheridan and signed with the initials,
" W.B.," which are supposed to stand for the name of
William Brereton, who was a friend of the Linley and
Sheridan families, gives first-hand information about the
position in Bath, and incidentally suggests that the writer
had been aware beforehand of the intended expedition. I
cannot help suspecting that money had been borrowed of
him for the journey. He commends Sheridan's action and
rejoices that Miss Linley

has a prospect of enjoying a calm peace of mind . . . the
morning after you left Bath Mathews came to me and has
repeated his visit several times. It is impossible to give an
account of his conversation, it consisted of many dreadful
oaths and curses upon himself and his past life, but in my
opinion they were little to the purpose. I am afraid his
present situation and feelings are not to be envied. But, bad
as he is, the town has so little charity for him that they make
(him) worse perhaps than he deserves. I carried two messages for him to Mr Linley, but he would not hearken to a
word about him. He said he had been deceived once and
he never would trust him more, since that he has heard so
many reports to his prejudice that their meeting may be of
bad consequence, and I shall endeavour by all means to prevent it. In my last conversation with Mr Mathews, I
ventured to affirm that he had nothing now to do but to
settle his affairs and leave Bath with a resolution never to
return again. This scheme (if anything he says can be depended upon) he solemnly promised should be immediately
put in execution. After which, I know Mr Linley's plan
is to get his daughter to return to Bath, in order to put an
end to the many wicked suggestions, which the malice of
his enemies have propagated, and Betsy may expect soon to
be persuaded to take this step by letter, or, perhaps, by Mr
Linley in person.

The date of this communication is 22nd of March, four days after the departure of the fugitives. From it we get a glimpse of Linley's attitude, who is seen to distrust Mathews so entirely as even to defer the urgent matter of bringing back his daughter until Mathews should be safely out of the way. Naturally the "town" is talking of the affair, and its opinion is adverse to the "Captain."

At the other household, in Kingsmead Street, the Sheridan sisters were left alone, and Mr Bowers, their landlord, thinking, as every man of his time did, that young ladies should never be unprovided with a male protector, went to seek out their brother Charles, who, having had no idea of any attachment between Dick and Miss Linley, was "violently agitated at the intelligence, conceiving himself to have been deceived by both parties. He hastened to Bath, and on his arrival found Mr Mathews at the house, endeavouring to get news of the fugitives. Charles Sheridan unguardedly dropped some expressions of displeasure at his brother's conduct, which the man treasured up. He was outrageous at having been induced by R.B.S. to give up his pursuit of Miss L——, and though he had been married many years, made no scruple of avowing his passion and his hopes of success, but for the intervention of her young friend."

These, it should once more be noted, are the words of Alicia, about what happened in her own presence. Mr Green is quite wrong in attributing them, as he appears to do, to Mr Fraser Rae.

Nor did Mathews confine his expressions of anger to third parties; he wrote, as we learn from a later letter of Charles Sheridan to his uncle, "the most impertinent letters" to Sheridan himself "upon a supposition that my brother had married Miss Linley and would never return to Bath." Finally he inserted in *The Bath Chronicle*, 9th of April 1772, the following advertisement :—

BATH, *Wednesday April 8th, 1772.*
Mr Richard S******* having attempted in a Letter left behind for that Purpose to account for his scandalous Method of running away from this Place by Insinuations, derogating from *my* Character and that of a Young Lady *innocent* as far as relates to *me* or *my Knowledge*; since when he has neither taken any Notice of Letters or even informed his own Family of the Place where he has hid himself.—I can no longer think he deserves the Treatment of a Gentleman and therefore shall trouble myself no further about him, than in this public Method to post him as a *L**** and a treacherous *S*********

And as I am convinced there have been many malevolent Incendiaries concerned in the Propagation of this infamous Lie, if any of them unprotected by *Age, Infirmities, or Profession*, will dare to acknowledge the Part they have acted, and affirm *to* what they have said *of* me, they may depend on receiving the proper Reward of their Villainy in the most public Manner. The World will be candid enough to judge properly (I make no Doubt) of any *private* Abuse on this subject for the Future; as nobody can defend himself from an accusation he is ignorant of.   THOMAS MATHEWS.

The tone of this effusion speaks for itself. Alicia, very indignant, we may be sure, "called him to severe account for this step, when he had the insolence and baseness to assert that her brother Charles was privy to what he had done. On speaking to him on the subject he was greatly shocked, for, however displeased with his brother he was incapable of countenancing such conduct, and nothing but Mr Mathews' quitting Bath at the time, prevented his taking up the matter in a very serious manner."

43

Thus Mathews did retire from Bath, and the date of his retirement must have been not much subsequent to that of his advertisement. Some days later Mr Linley set out from Bath to fetch his daughter. Whether he had only just learned her whereabouts, or whether he had waited, as Brereton's letter implied that he intended to do, until he was sure of Mathews' absence, is doubtful. Since those "most impertinent" missives from Mathews eventually reached Sheridan's hands, it must be presumed that letters from Linley would do the same. Be this as it may, nearly a month from her departure had elapsed before he followed his daughter. We do not hear that he ever expressed any doubt of Sheridan's honourable behaviour towards her; whereas he refused to hear from Brereton a word in favour of Mathews. Probably either Sheridan or Elizabeth had been able to enclose for his perusal some letter in Mathews' own writing.

The objections of Linley to Sheridan as a son-in-law were of a financial, not of a personal, nature; for the young man himself he seems to have entertained a genuine liking that ripened later into warm and almost fatherly affection.

About the 20th of April, then, the gossip of Bath was left for the moment without new events to feed upon. The romantic couple were still absent, Mr Linley had lately departed, and Mathews had left the town some ten days previously. The curtain was down upon the first act, and the onlookers turned their attention otherwhere until it should rise upon the second.

CHAPTER 3. THE FLIGHT TO FRANCE

OF that strange night journey to London on 18th of March 1772 no account remains; nor has the third traveller been identified. A discreet person she must have been, and honourable, since she never brought her wares to the market in which she could so easily have made money of them. What would not some scandalous papers of that day— nay, and some respectable biographers of this—have given for her history of Elizabeth Linley's brief visit to France?

Early on the 19th the chaise reached London, and Sheridan introduced Miss Linley to a friend and relation then in town as an heiress who had consented to be united to him in France! It may have been at this time and under this pretext that he borrowed money of Mr Ewart, the friend and relation in question, and also of his son, since we learn from a subsequent letter of Charles Sheridan that " Ewart was greatly vexed at the manner of your drawing for the last £20," and that " old Ewart is already surprised at Mr Linley's long delay, and indeed I think the latter much to blame in this respect." Clearly the loan from " old Ewart " had been for some purpose of which Mr Linley thought himself bound to assume the responsibility. The younger Ewart, who presently in his turn eloped, with a genuine heiress, was in all likelihood deeper in the confidence of the fugitives. In the course of the day Sheridan met another friend, whom Alicia describes as " the son of a respectable

brandy merchant in the city," and who suggested a free
passage to Dunkirk in a vessel of his father's that was about
to sail. This alteration of plan, as making a pursuit more
difficult, was immediately adopted, and the old gentleman,
not being entirely let into the secret, accompanied the young
couple on board his ship, recommending them to the care
of the Captain as if they had been his own children and
giving them letters of introduction to " his correspondent
at Dunkirk." As Goldsmith touched nothing which he did
not adorn, so those favourites of nature, the Linleys, seem
to go nowhere without setting up some interesting association. If Tom goes abroad to study he falls in with Mozart,
who conceives a friendship for him and by-and-by tells the
friendly gossip, Michael Kelly, that " Linley was a true
genius; and he felt that, had he lived, he would have been
one of the greatest ornaments of the musical world." And
so the benevolent owner of the trading vessel in which
Elizabeth and her escort were to be conveyed, and whose
name was Field, was the godfather of no less a man than
Charles Lamb, the parents of whom were actually sitting at
cards in Mr Field's parlour when Sheridan and Miss Linley
entered. Lamb, in recalling the incident, calls the latter
" Maria," a mistake that may be accounted for by the fact
that since he himself was not born until 1775, Maria would
be the only one of the sisters whose singing in public he
could possibly recollect. To him the story had a personal
importance, for Mr Field's kindness was " requited years
afterwards by Sheridan with a free pass to Drury Lane, and
this became the means of admitting the boy-essayist to his
first play," a link delightful to remember.

The crossing, occurring, as it did, at the March equinox,
and in a vessel not equipped for passengers, was a bad one
and Miss Linley was alarmingly ill. Many years later

46

Sheridan, at a time when he was again apprehensive of her
death, wrote of the restless waters, over which " I bore
poor E., who is now so near me fading in sickness, from all
her natural attachments and affections, and then loved her
so that, had she died as I once thought she would in the
Passage, I should assuredly have plunged with her body to
the Grave."

Mr Field's correspondent at Dunkirk gave them intro-
ductions to friends at Lille, and to Lille they went, by way
of Calais. "After quitting Dunkirk," says his sister,
" Mr Sheridan was more explicit with Miss Linley as to
his views in accompanying her to France. He told her he
could not be content to leave her in a Convent, unless she
consented to a previous marriage, which had all along been
the object of his hopes, and she must be aware that, after
the step she had taken, she could not appear in England but
as his wife. Miss Linley, who really preferred him greatly
to any person, was not difficult to persuade, and at a village
not far from Calais the marriage ceremony was performed
by a priest who was known to be often employed on such
occasions." The ceremony, which was no more than a
ceremony, and which certainly had no legal force, the
contracting parties being both minors and both Protestants,
was apparently intended to remain secret unless scandal
should render its publication necessary. Sheridan's object
probably was, as Mr Sichel says, " to bind her in some way
to himself, to preclude her from being again sacrificed." It
gave him, he may have thought, some claim to act in future
as her defender.

One vivid incident of their travels, narrated by Sheridan
to Rogers, stands out. The wanderers went to a theatre,
where two French officers stared at Miss Linley, to the
indignation of Sheridan, who stared back at them, con-

temptuous but perforce silent, as they also were, he knowing no French, and they no English.

Arrived at Lille, Elizabeth succeeded, though not apparently without difficulty, in getting rooms in a convent, and he, his sister says, " remained a few days at Lille to be satisfied that she was settled to her satisfaction." She became ill, however, and an Englishman, " Dr Dolman of York," was called in. He " wished to have her more immediately under his care than he could in the Convent, and he and Mrs Dolman most kindly invited them to their house." Happy Dr and Mrs Dolman, who thus entertained an angel unawares! Often, no doubt, did they relate to friends at York how the beautiful Mrs Sheridan stayed with them at Lille, and how the great Mr Sheridan spent evenings with them. A little note from the kind Doctor to " Monsieur Sherridan, Gentilhomme Anglois, à l'Hotel de Bourbon sur la Grande Place " remains, and indicates both that by the time it was written (15th of April) Miss Linley also was residing at the hotel, and that he supposed the pair to be married. Certain powders are to be given twice daily, " in a glass of white wine." " Don't wait supper for me because my time is not my own. Compliments and wishes of health to your lady."

On the same day Sheridan wrote for the first time since his departure to his brother. He mentions that " we have never received one line from Bath "; he supposes that " there are letters somewhere," and is endeavouring to obtain them. Miss Linley is now " fixing in a Convent—a much more difficult point than you would have imagined." He speaks of her recent illness, says he shall soon be back in England, and hopes his brother " could never have been uneasy lest anything should tempt me to depart, even in thought, from the honour and consistency which engaged me at first."

He had written, "above a week ago," to Mathews, "which I think was necessary and right. I hope he has acted the one proper part that was left him; and to speak from my feelings I cannot but say I shall be very happy to find no further disagreeable consequences pursuing him."

The next event was Mr Linley's arrival at Lille; but of precisely what passed between him and the fugitives we remain tantalisingly ignorant. Alicia, commendably refraining from a report of what she did not herself know, merely says that "after some private conversation with Mr Sheridan, he appeared quite reconciled to his daughter but insisted upon her returning to England with him to fulfil several engagements that he had entered into on her behalf," an insistence which, since the engagements dated probably from before her departure, can hardly be considered unreasonable. "The whole party," continues the narrative, "set out together next day." Mr Green, to whose theory of Sheridan's blameworthiness such a display of amity on Mr Linley's part would be disturbing, inclines to doubt this friendly return in one party; but the letter in which Charles Sheridan speaks of "Dick's safe return from France with Mr and Miss Linley" is surely decisive.

Either from Mr Linley or from letters received about the same time, Sheridan had now heard of Mathews' advertisement, and thereupon, he tells us, declared that he would never sleep in England until he had called him to account. True to this promise, he sat up all night at Canterbury, and on arriving in London at nine o'clock on the night of Wednesday, 29th of April, learned from his friend, Ewart, that Mathews was in London and resolved to call upon him immediately. He reached Mathews' lodgings, "at Mr Cocklin's in Crutched Friars," about half-an-hour after midnight and was denied admittance. "The key of Mr

E

Cocklin's door was lost "—as flimsy a pretext surely as was
ever offered to an importunate young man in a passion. " By
two o'clock he got in," having presumably stood outside and
disturbed the repose of Crutched Friars for over an hour.
Mathews had at last come down and promised from behind
the door that the visitor should be admitted, " and had retired
to rest again." At this point the sequence of Sheridan's
narrative becomes a little confused, since Mathews must
surely have put on some clothes before rather than after
letting in the besieger. Sheridan's words, however, are:
" He dressed, complained of the cold, endeavoured to get
some heat into him, called Mr Sheridan his dear friend and
forced him to sit down." The narrative here diverges with
some scorn to recall the previous threats of Mathews, his
warning to Ewart that Sheridan had better not come in his
way without a sword, the letter in which he had assured his
adversary that he was " to be met with at any hour and
begged him not to stand on ceremony." Yet here he was,
after having vainly attempted to keep the young man out,
receiving him with none but friendly words. He had never
meant to quarrel. Charles Sheridan and " another gentleman
at Bath " were the real sinners. The conversation was
prolonged until seven in the morning Mathews, when he
found that the insulting advertisement had never been seen
by Sheridan, explained it away, " assuring him," says Alicia,
" that it was nothing more than an enquiry about him
published with the sanction of his family." They arranged
to meet again, on friendly terms, the next day, and it was
probably then that Matthews drew up the communication
to the newspaper of which Charles Sheridan wrote to his
uncle. " Mathews' behaviour," he says, " was so very con-
descending "—a word of which the significance was not at
that period quite the same as it is now—" that Dick let him

off for a very small concession to be made in the Bath paper." This would be on Thursday, and as the Bath papers appeared on Wednesday and Thursday respectively, there was no use in hurrying down. Sheridan did not arrive in that city until late in the afternoon of Saturday, 2nd of May, and he probably travelled with Mr Linley and Miss Linley. The words of his sister are: " Mr Linley, his daughter and R. B. Sheridan proceeded to Bath."

The 2nd of May, it may be recollected, was the date of Miss Linley's supposed letter to Miss Saunders. If she and her father came home on the evening or late afternoon of that day, she not having seen her mother, brothers or sisters since the 18th of March, is it conceivable that she could have had time to write this exceedingly long letter? On the other hand, if she had waited to finish it until Sunday, 3rd of May, there would have been a new and alarming incident to communicate of which the letter contains no hint—although the mind of the supposed writer was full of it.

Sheridan, before rejoining his family in Kingsmead Street, visited the office of *The Bath Chronicle*, and perused Mathews' advertisement. With easily imaginable surprise and indignation he beheld himself stigmatised as a liar and a treacherous scoundrel, and read the insinuation against Elizabeth. " He then thought," says Charles Sheridan, very moderately, " the apology then made by Mathews was no concession at all for so signal an insult." Going home, the younger brother instantly demanded of the elder an explanation of his share in it. The explanation was easily given; but Charles, in his turn, reproached Dick for the elopement. " However," proceeds their sister's story, " the family spent the evening amicably together, and after the young ladies had retired for the night, the two Brothers set out Post for London to have

an explanation with Mr Mathews." Charles, coinciding
with his junior's views, or, to use his own expression, " this
being also the opinion of everybody else," thought it incumbent upon him " to accompany him to prevent mischief if
possibly consistent with his honour."

The girls coming down to their Sunday breakfast, found
themselves once more destitute of fraternal " protection,"
and some obliging inhabitant of the house, whether a servant
or some member of the excellent Mr Bowers' family does
not appear, having heard high words between the young
gentlemen, started the consoling notion that they had gone
off to fight each other. " Though they did not credit this
report, yet they feared some danger to their Brothers and
Miss Sheridan proposed Miss Linley as the person most
likely to be informed of her brother's intentions, but that
young lady did not know of their having left Bath and was
completely overcome with distress at being considered the
cause of so much misery. Repeated fainting fits obliged her
father to call in medical aid and Miss Sheridan was nearly
in the same situation. A very remarkable person happened
to be present at this scene; the late Dr Priestley, who lodged
at Mr Linley's at the time. At length when they were a
little recovered Mr Linley put Miss Sheridan into a chair
and taking her sister by the hand conducted them to the
melancholy home." A very distressing Sunday, to be sure,
for all the pacific persons concerned, and one scarcely likely
to leave Elizabeth with much either of time or of inclination
for going on calmly with that long-winded exculpation to
Miss Saunders.

The brothers, reaching London on that same Sunday,
abstained from going to the house of their uncle, Mr
Chamberlaine, an omission afterwards excused by Charles
on the ground that " the purport of our coming must have

been very disagreeable to you." Charles "waited on M.
that evening and after two hours' altercation could get him
to make no further concessions." Nothing therefore
remained but a duel. The prudent Charles foresaw all the
disagreeable consequences attendant on coming to extremi-
ties, "did all I could to prevent it, but a young man's
stamping on himself the character of coward was worse than
anything that could happen." Mr Brereton was now in
town, and they seem to have stayed with him; young Ewart
was engaged to act as Richard's second; Captain Knight, an
uncle of Mathews, attended him in that capacity. Mathews,
who as the party challenged had the right to choose the
weapons, and who, according to Henry Angelo, "had
learnt fencing in France and was considered very skilful in
the science," decided for swords. Sheridan had taken lessons
some years earlier from that famous master, young Angelo's
father, who was a friend of the elder Sheridan; but, although
the quickness and readiness of his temper were qualities
conducive to good fencing, it is not probable that he was the
equal of Mathews. Yet in this first duel it was Sheridan
who had the advantage, and at their second meeting Mathews
was for pistols.

The meeting, which was fixed for six o'clock on Monday
evening in Hyde Park, seems to have been very little to
Mathews' taste. "He objected frequently to the ground,"
says Sheridan. "They adjourned to the Hercules Pillars"
(a tavern). "They returned to Hyde-Park. Mr M.
objected to the observation of an officer. They returned to
Hercules Pillars. They adjourned to the Bedford Coffee-
house by agreement," it being, no doubt, by this time dark.
"Mr M. was gone to the Castel Tavern" at the corner
of Henrietta Street and Bedford Street. "Mr S. followed
with Mr E." In a room at the Castle Tavern they

eventually fought, Ewart holding up the candles that had now
become necessary. A precise account—or rather an account
as precise as a man engaged in such a struggle can possibly
give of it afterwards—was written by Sheridan about two
months later in the form of a letter to Captain Knight:
" I struck Mr Mathews' point so much out of the line that
I stepped up and caught hold of his wrist or the hilt of his
sword, while the point of mine was at his breast. You ran
in and caught hold of my arm, exclaiming, ' *Don't kill him !* '
I struggled to disengage my arm and said his sword was in
my power. Mr Mathews called out twice or thrice: ' *I
beg my life.*' We were parted. You immediately said:
' *There, he has begged his life and there is an end of it* ';
and on Mr Ewart's saying that, when his sword was in my
power, as I attempted no more, you should not have inter-
fered. You replied that you ' were wrong ' but that you
had ' *done it hastily and to prevent mischief,*' or words to that
effect. Mr Mathews then hinted that I was rather ' *obliged
to your interposition* ' for the advantage. You declared that
before you did so ' both the swords were in Mr Sheridan's
power.' Mr Mathews still seemed resolved to give it
another turn and observed that ' *he had never quitted his
sword.*' Provoked at this, I then swore (with too much heat
perhaps) that he should either give up his sword and I would
break it, or go to his guard again. He refused but on my
persisting either gave it into my hand or flung it on the
table or the ground. . . . I broke it and flung the hilt to
the other end of the room. He exclaimed at this. I took
a mourning sword from Mr Ewart, and presenting him with
mine, gave my honour that what had passed should never
be mentioned by me, and he might now right himself again.
He replied that he ' *would never draw a sword against the
man who had given him his life* '; but upon his still exclaim-

ing against the indignity of breaking his sword . . . Mr
Ewart offered him the pistols, and some altercation passed
between them. Mr Mathews said that ' *he could never show
his face if it were known that his sword were broke—that such
a thing had never been done—that it cancelled all obligations,*'
etc., etc. You seemed to think that it was wrong, and we
both proposed that if he never misrepresented the affair it
should not be mentioned by us. This was settled. I then
asked Mr Mathews whether (as he had expressed himself
sensible of, and shocked at the indignity he had done me in
his advertisement) it did not occur to him that he owed me
another satisfaction; and that as it was in his power to do
it without discredit, I supposed he would not hesitate. This
he absolutely refused, unless conditionally; I insisted on it,
and said I would not leave the room till it was settled. After
much altercation and with much ill grace, he gave the
apology which afterwards appeared."

The matter being thus settled in Sheridan's favour, he
and his brother, neither of whom had in the interim sent
any communication to the anxious girls in Bath, returned
to that city on Tuesday night, and entered it, " much
fatigued, never having been in bed from the time they left
Bath." Richard triumphantly handed to Alicia the apology
wrung from the reluctant Mathews; it was immediately
sent to *The Bath Chronicle*, and may still be read there in
the number dated 7th of May 1772. Thus it runs:

Being convinced that the Expressions I made use of to
Mr Sheridan's Disadvantage were the Effects of Passion and
Misrepresentation, I retract what I have said to that Gentle-
man's Disadvantage and particularly beg his Pardon for my
Advertisement in *The Bath Chronicle*.

THOMAS MATHEWS.

55

Less than this could hardly pass as an apology for denouncing a man publicly as a liar and a scoundrel.

Miss Linley and Sheridan were now both back at Bath; Mathews had withdrawn his accusations, and, in the words of one of Charles Sheridan's letters to his uncle: "Thus is the affair concluded highly to the honour of Dick who is applauded by every one and whose conduct I hope you will approve of." This letter, received by Mr Chamberlaine, as he has methodically noted upon it (would that all recipients of letters in the Linley and Sheridan correspondence had but done the same), on the 13th of May, was followed by another dated from Bath on the 18th of that month. Charles cannot be sufficiently grateful to his uncle's last very kind letter with its generously warm approval of what had been done in the trip to London. He and Richard had feared that "from the difficulties my brother had unnecessarily brought himself to" his subsequent conduct "might have been deemed the effect of youthful heat and indiscretion." The necessity of the last step was evident, but as to that former one which led up to it Charles cannot speak with so much conviction, "however, I am certain his motives were good, and by the event he has acquired great credit and honour." Moreover the elder brother is surprised, not unreasonably, "that in this age, when the world does not abound in Josephs, most people are (notwithstanding the general tendency in mankind to judge unfavourably) inclined to think he acted with the strictest honour in his late expedition with Miss Linley, when the circumstances might allow of their being very dubious on this head without incurring the imputation of being very censorious." Mr Sheridan, in Ireland, too, whose views of these adventures had at first partaken of strong disapprobation, was now "well enough reconciled" to the part taken by his younger son after Charles had "convinced him that his motives were wholly honourable and that Dick could scarcely have acted otherwise consistent with humanity."

For the moment, youth and imprudence were very much in the ascendant. At no time of her life does any fellow-creature seem to have been capable of thinking or speaking unfavourably of Elizabeth Linley. Even Foote, the un-scrupulous caricaturist, presents her as pure and dignified. The public of Bath, seeing her sweet, pathetic face and hearing her sweet, pathetic voice, could believe no ill of her, and her freedom from blameworthiness involved that of her champion. Instead therefore of tasting public disgrace they found themselves the popular hero and heroine. But Mr Sheridan came home to Bath, and it is not to be supposed that recent events had at all weakened his aversion to any violent intimacy between his own flock and Mr Linley's. Nor were the parents of the young lady in any way disposed to let her champion become her husband. Not even Alicia seems to have been aware at this time of that secret ceremony performed somewhere near Calais, although the present brought home to her by her brother, and still preserved, a "French watch with the lovers' hair interwoven" must have signified an acknowledged affection on both sides.

The lovers met, but they did not meet openly even as lovers, much less as man and wife. It does not appear that they quite regarded themselves as being so. They do not write to each other, as Jane Linley and Charles Ward, in affirmation of the unalterable and solemn character of their promise to each other, constantly did, by the titles of "wife" and "husband." That they met secretly has been often asserted and hardly needs assertion; but it is scarcely possible that such meetings can have been frequent. Mrs Linley had become a very Argus; no longer was Elizabeth allowed to walk out unaccompanied by either father or mother; no longer, we may be sure, could she and Alicia Sheridan hold long confidential conversations or together devise romantic schemes. Everything was now under strict parental supervision, very orderly, very tranquil—on the surface, and entirely undisturbed. Mathews had retired into Wales, and everybody except Sheridan had a bad word for him. That magnanimous youth, he assures us, "gave Mr Mathews credit," as he had promised to do, until Mathews' own misstatements obliged him and his friend to tell the truth.

Letters and verses passed between the lovers. The first of the collection tells him that she will be at Mrs "Lyn's," "this evening," bids him not tell "Lissy" (Alicia), "as I promised her I would not tell you," and concludes with the cryptic remark: "Only think of Captain Hodges! I am frightened out of my wits."

A long, undated letter, marked "Eleven o'clock," may perhaps have been written on the same evening, after returning from Mrs Lynn's:

Though I parted from you so lately, and though I expect to see you again so soon, yet I cannot keep my fingers from the pen but I must be plaguing you with my scrawl. Oh, my dearest love, I am never happy but when I am with you. I cannot speak or think of anything else. When shall we have another happy half-hour? I declare I have not felt real joy since I came from France before this evening.[1] Perhaps now while I am writing and amusing myself by expressing the tender sentiments which I feel for you, you

---

[1] It is not easy to believe that the girl who wrote this can also have written of the day on which she set out for France as "that fatal Wednesday"—an expression that appears in the doubtful letter.

are flirting with Miss W., or some other handsome girl, or making speeches to [illegible] scold. I do not believe any such thing, but give me leave to doubt that I may with greater pleasure be convinced to the contrary. No, my life and Soul, I love you to such a degree, that I should never bear to see you (even in joak) show any particular attention to another. Judge then by my writing if I doubt your constancy. When shall I hear from you? Let me have that satisfaction at least, although it is impossible to see you so often. If you do speak to that woman I think we might contrive to send our letters there, directed under feigned names. I could easily frame some excuse for getting them. Till then I shall expect you will write your letters and give them yourself—for I do insist on hearing from you, for I am sure it is nothing but laziness that prevents you.

I really think Charles suspected something this evening. He looked amazingly knowing this evening when I came down. Duce take his curious head. I wish he would mind his own business and not interrupt us in our stolen pleasures. Is it not amazing, my dear Love, that we should always have so great an inclination for what is not in our possession? . . .

Let me see, what have I more to say?—nothing but the same dull story over and over again—that I love you to distraction, and that I would prefer you and beggary before any other man and a throne. I will call you Horatio—that was the name you gave yourself in that sweet poem—write to me then, my dear Horatio, and tell me that you are equally sincere and constant. . . .

My hand shakes so at this moment I can scarce hold the pen. My father came into my room this moment, and I had just time to stuff the letter behind the glass. 'Twas well he did not take much notice of me, for I was . . . Good-bye. God bless——I will . . .

Another letter, equally undated, bears the heading, " Twelve o'clock."

You unconscionable creature to make me sit up [to] this time of the night to scribble nonsense to you, when you will not let me hear one word from you for this week to come. Oh, my dear, you are the Tyrant indeed. Yet do not fancy I would do this if it was not equally agreeable to myself, Indeed, my dearest love, I am never happy except when I am with you or writing to you. Why did you run away so soon to-night? Tho' I could not enjoy your conversation freely, yet it was a consolation to me that you was so near me. I gave up my cards the moment you left me, as I could not play with any patience. My father and I had a long conversation this morning. He wanted me to go to a private concert at Dr Davenport's, but I availed myself of his promise and excused myself, as I am resolved not to go so much to those kind of meetings. He says he shall have a concert for my brother's benefit in a fortnight, and he shall expect my performance without any objections. You know I could not refuse him; but I am resolved never to go into public but on these occasions.

My mother and me called on Miss Roscoe this evening, when we talked a great deal about you. Miss R. said she was sure you and I should make a match of it. Nay, she said the whole world was of the opinion that we should be married in less than a month. Only think of this, bright Hevn's! God bless you, my dear, dear love. I am so weary I must go to bed. There is but one thing that could keep me awake and that is your company. Once more adieu . . .

Upon my knees, half nacked, once more I am going to tire you with my nonsense. I could not bear to see this little blank without filling it up. Though I do not know with what, as I have almost exhausted the Budget of news which I had collected since our long absence. I do insist that you write to me, you lazy wretch, can't you take so small a trouble? I can receive your letter by the same method. My sister is very impatient that I don't come into bed, but I feel more happiness in this situation, tho' I am half froze than in the warmest bed in England. . . .

But though a young lady, kneeling without her gown, to write letters towards one in the morning might find herself " half froze," the hot weather in which Bath becomes empty was at hand; Mr Linley had as usual made engagements elsewhere for the slack season, and the lovers were about to be divided by actual distance, more imperative than any parental disapproval. On the eve of her journey Eliza again writes at midnight:

Wednesday night, 12 *o'clock.*

The anxiety I felt while in my dear Horatio's company to-night would not let me feel the pains of separation, but now that I am retired, and at full liberty to give way to my own unpleasing ideas, I cannot describe what I feel to be so long divided from you. Oh, my love, how vain are your doubts and suspicions; believe me, if I thought it possible to change my present sentiments of you, I should despise myself. Never shall you have the least reason to suspect my constancy or my love. I am in a very gloomy disposition to-night, but I will not give way to it. I will try to forget every disagreeable circumstance, and only look forward to those happy hours which I hope are still in store for us. With what rapture shall we meet when we can do so without constraint, when I may live in your arms without the fear of parents [   ] or the ill-natured world. I could write to you without ever leaving off, but my sister insists on my coming to bed. It is now near one o'clock, and I am to be up by five to-morrow. God bless you, my ever dear Horatio. Think of me while I am absent and don't let any idea disturb your peace in regard to me, for while I live I can never cease to be your own Eliza.

Next morning, no doubt, the family party of Mr, Mrs, the two Misses Linley and Mr Tom Linley were duly conveyed away in coach or chaise. They went to Chester, to Cambridge, and eventually to Oxford, whence Eliza wrote to her Horatio. That city was not strange to her; she had sung there in the previous year, when she had enchanted Sheridan's friend, Halhed, now in India, and possibly on other occasions. One wonders whether she gave a sigh to the exile who had gone away so heavy-hearted on her account, or whether she had no thoughts to spare from herself and Sheridan. She arrived at Oxford on Monday, 29th of June, which is the date of the following letter:

How shall I account to my dear Horatio for my long silence? Will he permit me to excuse myself by pleading the perpetual hurry I have been in since I parted from him? Indeed, nothing should have hindered my writing but the shocking situation I was in, all day confined to my business and at night my mother took away the candle for fear I should read. It was an absolute impossibility to elude her vigilance. We came here this morning, and I have taken the first opportunity to assure you of my unabated love.

Whilst I was at Chester I went to the Masquerade, but such a scene of confusion and fright I never saw, and sincerely hope I never shall again. Mrs Williams (whose husband was the principal leader in the affair) made it her business to insist on our going with her and she was so pressing my father could not resist her. I own as I had never seen anything of the kind I had some curiosity, but it is perfectly satisfied. I would not go through the fatigue of another for the world. We had two dresses apiece. Mine was a pilgrim and a Spanish lady; Polly's a shepherdess and another pilgrim. The crowd was so great at the door, that, before I could get into the room, the fright overcame me

and I fainted in the midst of them. On the return of my
senses I found somebody going to pull me by the legs as you
would a dead horse; this roused me, and I gave them a
hearty kick.

Luckily a gentleman that I knew came by who took care
of me home, where I was going to pull off my finery and
stay at home, but I was prevented by Mrs Williams who
came to fetch me to my mother and sister who had made
their way through the crowd and was got safe. At last I
got to this famous affair, but never was disappointment equal
to mine, to see such a nonsensical puppet show. I walked
about as tired of the Masquerade as I am of a long sermon.
The impudent looks and speeches of the men were too much
for me. I forgot that I had a mask on and really felt myself
very much affronted at their ill-bred stares. So much for
the Masquerade.

At Cambridge there was nothing but the music which was
very fine. I was extremely ill for two days. I was taken
ill in the church during the Oratorio of Samson. I fainted
and was carried out. This raised no small bustle among the
Cantabs. as they call them. I need not describe them to
you, they are a strange set; though, upon the whole, I
really think they are more rational beings than the
Oxonians. It seems there is to be a very great riot here
on one of the nights. They don't like the music, and
intend calling the Governors to an account. How it will
end God knows.

I have not been out since I came here. I shall be very
happy when I am once more in Bath. I cannot tell how
much I long to see you, to ask you a thousand questions.
Oh, my dear Horatio, I have had many perplexing thoughts
since I have been absent but I will hope for the best. If I
find you well and happy on my return, I shall be content.
It is much if I am not with you as soon as this letter. Till
then receive my tenderest affections, and let me find you
constant as I left you. If my prayers are granted, I shall

once more embrace my Horatio, and convince him how sincerely I am his Eliza.

Little did poor Eliza guess, as she despatched her loving letter, upon what sort of business it would find Horatio engaged, nor how far from happy was to be that return to Bath of which she was so hopefully thinking.

CHAPTER 4. AFFAIRS OF HONOUR

MR THOMAS MATHEWS had retired to his Welsh property, where he found himself looked upon somewhat askance, his behaviour in the duel—which had come to light by way of contradiction to his own account of the matter—not being considered to reach the standard of courage demanded by the public opinion of his day. Alicia Sheridan (who, however, can hardly have had any direct evidence upon the point) says that he was " shunned and despised." One Mr Barnett or Barnard, who was his neighbour, is credited with having suggested to him that the best way of re-establishing himself would be to fight Sheridan a second time. Be that as it may, upon some day in June 1772 Messrs Mathews and Barnett came to Bath and opened negotiations. Mathews drew up his version of the Castle Tavern meeting, and Sheridan was pressed in vain to sign it. " Messages conveyed in the most opprobrious terms " were delivered to him, and upon his final refusal to furnish his signature, Mathews sent him a challenge, and also, either previously or simultaneously, " a letter filled with the most scurrilous abuse." Having already encountered Mathews, Sheridan would, according to the current " code of honour," have been justified in declining to receive such a challenge, and had indeed been resolved against receiving it. But the tactics had been skilful, and those opprobrious messages had done their work; the temper of the baited youth was up, and he accepted the challenge. If Mr Thomas Sheridan, if even

Charles Sheridan, had been at home, calmer counsels might perhaps have prevailed; but Charles, who had been appointed Secretary to the Swedish Legation, was in London, making his preparations, and his father had accompanied him.

The decision appears to have been made no earlier than the evening of Tuesday, 30th of June, and the meeting was fixed for an extremely early hour next morning. The place was to be Kingsdown, about four miles out of Bath, whence departure towards London would be easy for either combatant who might find flight necessary. Meanwhile Sheridan had to provide himself with a second, and his hurried selection of Mr or Captain Paumier was no very good one, that gentleman being young and without experience. Sheridan's preparations, Alicia says, consisted solely in the writing of three letters, " one to his father, one to Miss Linley and one to his sisters." But here she must surely be in error. That letter to Captain Knight, which gave a full account of the former duel, and which has been already quoted, is dated " July 1st," and can hardly have been either written or dictated by a man lying seriously ill immediately after receiving a number of wounds and losing a quantity of blood. At three in the morning he drove out with his second to Kingsdown; their chaise and that of Mathews stood by throughout the conflict, and the evidence of the postilions was afterwards taken before a magistrate in the presence of Mr Sheridan and his elder daughter—a circumstance which gives weight to the accounts which each wrote of the matter.

Mathews being this time the challenger, the choice of weapons lay with Sheridan, who decided upon swords, and refused to yield to Mathews' wish for pistols. Had pistols been employed, English literature might have possessed no *School for Scandal*, and poor Eliza, sleeping unapprehensive

in Oxford, might have awakened to an even greater sorrow
than that which lay before her. As to the precise details of
the duel there are variations of statement, but its main facts
are clear. After some undecisive passes, Sheridan pressed in
upon Mathews, and his sword broke. Mathews tripped him
up; both men fell, and the second sword also was broken.
Mathews, being uppermost, and having apparently the more
effective of the broken weapons, continued to stab his
unarmed adversary, who persistently refused to beg his life,
and whose dexterity in warding off any fatal blow shows
that he must have retained great presence of mind. At last
the brutal scene was ended by the interposition of the seconds,
and Mathews, who, according to Mr Sheridan, had been
cursing horribly, went off, Alicia says, " exclaiming with
an oath: ' I have done for him.' " In all probability
Mathews really believed that he had done what he came out
to do—killed the young man who had stood so much in his
way, and avenged himself, incidentally, upon Elizabeth
Linley. He had provided everything necessary for escaping
to France, and drove off at once with Barnett towards the
coast. He too was wounded, but not seriously. Sheridan
was put into the other chaise, and driven back to the White
Hart Inn. Twenty years later, crossing Kingsdown on the
way to Bristol with his dying wife, he turned aside to revisit
the place, and wrote of it to the Duchess of Devonshire as
" the spot where my life was strangely saved once. It is
marked with a great stone cut by the man who, I remember,
used to make a show of our broken swords, and a sleeve
button of mine, and the setting of her Picture which was
broke on my neck and placed where he found the blood.
At this man's cottage, I remember, I got some water, and
I remember many thoughts that passed in my mind, believing
as I did, that I was dying. What an interval has passed

67

since, and scarce one promise that I then made to my own soul have I attempted to fulfil." The White Hart Inn, to which he was conveyed and which has appeared so often in English fiction, no longer exists, and is replaced by the Pump Room Hotel. Doctors were called who declared the patient's condition to be very serious and removal impossible. " His sisters," says Alicia, " were informed of the business the following morning "—she must mean the morning of the same Wednesday—" and going to him they found his situation from noise and heat so very uncomfortable, they obtained leave from the Medical gentlemen to have him carefully removed to his own house."

As the duel had taken place upon a Wednesday and *The Bath Chronicle* appeared on Thursdays, hundreds of persons were early on Thursday reading the following statement in its columns :—

This morning about 3 o'clock, a second duel was fought with swords, between Captain Mathews and Mr R. Sheridan, on King's Down, near this city, in consequence of their former dispute concerning an amiable young lady, which Mr M. considered as improperly adjusted; Mr S. having, since their first rencontre, declared his sentiments respecting Mr M. in a manner that the former thought required satisfaction. Mr Sheridan received three or four wounds in his breast and sides, and now lies very ill. Mr M. was only slightly wounded and left this city soon after the affair was over.

The words, " this morning," do not indicate, as they have been taken to do, that the duel occurred on Thursday, 2nd of July; they indicate the day on which the *Chronicle* was printed, which, as any reflecting person will easily understand, was one day earlier than that on which it was distributed. The first part of this announcement looks rather like a statement put forth on behalf of Mathews, and I suspect was handed in to Mr Crutwell's printing office before the duel had actually occurred. The second portion —which begins, it may be observed, with a name at full length, instead of the " Mr S." of the earlier sentences—is evidently a report after inquiry. Among the persons whom the news reached were the father and brother of the wounded man. Mr Sheridan returned at once to Bath, in a very bristling state of temper, and Charles wrote a letter so characteristic that I cannot forbear to quote it. It is dated 3rd of July, and the receipt of it can hardly have tended to allay any fever from which the younger brother may have been suffering.

It was with the deepest concern I received the late accounts of you though it was somewhat softened by the assurance of your not being in the least danger. You cannot conceive the uneasiness it occasioned to my father. Both he and I were resolved to believe the best, and to suppose you safe, but then we neither of us could approve of the cause in which you suffer. All your friends have condemned you. You risked everything where you had nothing to gain, to give your antagonist the thing he wished, a chance for recovering his reputation. Your courage was past dispute: he wanted to get rid of the contemptible opinion he was held in, and you were good-natured enough to let him do it at your expense. It is not now a time to scold, but all your friends were of opinion you could with the greatest propriety, have refused to meet him. For my part, I shall suspend my judgment till better informed, only I cannot forgive your choosing swords. I am exceedingly unhappy at the situation I leave you in with respect to money matters, the more as it is totally out of my power to be of any use to you.

And he proceeds to give the comforting intelligence already given of Ewart's being " greatly vexed " at the manner in which Dick had drawn upon him for twenty pounds, and of "old Ewart's" surprise at not having already received payment from Mr Linley.

As for Mr Thomas Sheridan, he was "so grieved and incensed at his son's second duel that he even refused to see him on his arrival"—one wonders whether the invalid felt this refusal as a deprivation or as a reprieve—"and strictly forbade all intercourse between his daughters and the Linley family. The youngest, however, contrived to convey some intelligence to her brother when she perceived how unhappy he was on that subject. In the course of a few days Mr Sheridan was prevailed on to see his son and all displeasure seemed over."

By the 9th of July Mr Sheridan was able to write to his brother-in-law a full account of the duel, for which he had not chosen to ask his son until that morning. He adds:

Never was more concern shown on any occasion than was here to be seen in all classes of people on my son's account, for he bears an excellent character, and is much beloved. And never were more execrations poured upon any head than that of the vile assassin. Never was man so universally detested, and I do verily believe were he to appear in the streets of Bath by day, he would be stoned to death by the populace. If ever he were to show his head here again he will be shunned as one infected by the plague.

Popular indignation, however, like popular applause, soon evaporates, and the man who had after all not killed Sheridan, and not abducted Miss Linley, continued to live unstoned and unshunned in Bath for the better part of half-a-century. He died in 1820, and an oval tablet on the walls of the Abbey records his name, but is discreetly silent as to his virtues. Mrs Mathews, that strange, silent figure in the background of all these violent doings, survived her husband by a couple of years and inherited from him " everything of every kind without the exception of the most trifling article."

Naturally the story was not long in reaching Oxford, but the news and the papers were carefully kept from Elizabeth, " as her father was well aware she could not have appeared in public had she known what had passed." On the last day of her stay in Oxford she sang at a concert where probably she alone, of all the persons present, was ignorant of the event that so closely concerned her. Alicia recalls how Mr Thomas Grenville, a pupil of the elder Sheridan and a friend of the younger, spoke of the compassion aroused by the poor girl's appearance on this occasion:

I perfectly remember his saying that Miss Linley's appearance on that day inspired the greatest interest in the company present. As her ignorance of the duel and its consequences were known to every person, and her beauty, joined to the effect of her truly enchanting powers, could not fail of exciting a degree of sympathy in youthful and susceptible minds when they thought of the heavy calamity that hung over her.

Immediately after the performance, Mr Linley's family left Oxford on their return to Bath. Within a few miles of that place the party were met by a Mr Panton, a clergyman and a friend of the family. This gentleman proposed her quitting her father's chaise and accompanying him the rest of the way. He then in the most cautious manner informed her of what had passed; but all these precautions were not sufficient to prevent her being dreadfully affected by the stroke, and during her agitation she insisted on being permitted to see him, declaring she was his wife and as such entitled to attend on him.

But with Mr Sheridan at home, pronouncing excommunication against the whole Linley household, her wish stood very little chance of fulfilment; and her unwary declaration, far from leading the disapproving elders to feel their opposition useless, rather incited them to stronger measures; in Alicia's words: " Miss Linley's assertion of her marriage had answered no end but suggesting the idea to both Fathers of breaking off the match." Elizabeth was kept away from the dangerous city which contained Kingsmead Street, " sometimes at Bristol, and sometimes at Wells with her relations." But of course they wrote to each other. Mr Paumier conveyed to her some message from the wounded man, and carried back to him the following letter:—

I cannot resist the opportunity of thanking my dearest Horatio for his concern for me. Believe me I have not been in my senses these two days, but the happy account of your recovery has perfectly restored them. Oh! my dearest love when shall I see you? I will not ask you to write as I am sure it must hurt you. I am going to Wells to-morrow. I am obliged to be there before my father returns, and I expect him very soon. I shall not be happy till I hear from you there. Oh! my Horatio, I did not know till now how much I loved you. Believe me had you died, I should certainly [   ] dressed myself as a man and chalenged M. He should have killed me or I would have revenged you and myself. I cannot stay to write more as Mr P. is waiting. I suppose you can trust him. I will not write again till I hear from you at Wells as I do not know how to direct safely. God in heaven bless you my dearest Horatio and restore you once more to health to happiness and the arms of your Eliza.

The happy account of his recovery may have reached her by means of the *Chronicle*, which one week after the duel announced that Mr Sheridan was declared to be out of danger. At first Sheridan cannot have been able to write with his own hand. Verses, however, can be composed without the aid of bandaged fingers; and an invalid tended by two devoted sisters must have had opportunities of dictating. It is supposed to have been at this time that he made a charming variation upon his friend Halhed's line:

Dry be that tear; be hushed that struggling sigh.

From Wells, somewhat later, comes a very anxious letter:

Saturday morning.

To what can I impute your silence? At a time, too, when you must be certain that I am in the most dreadful state of suspense. . . . I was surprised not to find a letter [   ] when it was my particular request. I received a letter from my mother which has if possible increased my uneasiness. After telling me that my father and yours have had many serious conversations, she adds, " I could say more but am not permitted."

I am ordered to stay here a week longer. My father wrote two or three lines at the bottom of my mother's letter, where he tells me how your father has behaved and of your sending him a note, but he says that it is of no use to him as you are under age, and he does not suppose it will be [   ] your power to keep your word. . . . It is strongly reported that we [   ] and that I discovered it in my fright when I first heard of your duel. Then there is a long lecture with hopes that it is not true and that I will convince the world I have more spirit and prudence, etc.

Now what am I to think of all this? Can you imagine, Horatio, that I can be easy under these circumstances? For God's sake write to me. Tell me what has happened and do not hide anything from me. I have been tortured with ten thousand apprehensions ever since your first letter. And now if possible I am more so . . . [   ] from you by the next post I [   ] to think my happiness is no longer [   ] to you. Therefore if you wish me still to believe you faithful do not fail to [   ] your sincere Eliza.

73

The gaps in the above letter (and those in many letters still to come) indicate portions illegible owing to the seal of the original. Mr Fraser Rae generally filled these blanks conjecturally, but I prefer to leave them to the imagination of the reader.

The note that had been sent from Sheridan to Mr Linley was probably some promise to leave Eliza's fortune in her father's hands, in case of marrying her.

Evidently the strain under which they had now been living for some months was beginning to tell upon the nerves of both lovers. Other letters written after they had seen each other again show signs of irritation and impatience on both sides. There were now no more meetings in the house of either family; but the neutral domain of friendly houses was still open. It must have been after some occasion upon which they had met, but probably had not spoken to each other, that she wrote to him:

How can you my dear Horatio torment yourself and me with such unjust suspicions? My behaviour last night proceeded from the anxiety I felt on perceiving you look so remarkably grave. If I was prudent it was my father's conversation that made me so. He declared he would sooner follow me to the grave than see me married to you as you would ruin me and yourself in a short time by your extravagance. I know he watched us last night; 'twas that which made me cautious. If I said anything in my note to offend you, impute it to my desire to have you esteemed by your father.

You cannot have any doubts in regard to R——. Believe me I have wrote to him to put an end to every future hope. I never can think of another. I do not know how to see you. My situation at present is very disagreeable. I am not suffered to go out without my father or mother, and I am so watched I can scarce find a moment to write. We must

74

have patience. In the meantime assure yourself of the sincerity of my intentions for I will ever be my dear Horatio's Eliza.

The position is clear enough. Sheridan, fundamentally kind and affectionate, was nevertheless inconsiderate and neglectful; even when he was deeply in love he could not be trusted to write with decent regularity; and although in matters of real importance he was magnanimous and devoted, he could never control a rather petty jealousy upon trifling occasions. On the evening in question, for example, because she had avoided any special mark of interest in him "Horatio" had evidently sulked, and on going home had at once written her a letter calculated to torment her and himself; and this at a time when their only chance of success lay in absolute unanimity. The two fathers, of one mind in opposition to the marriage of their children, were otherwise at variance, and indeed seem never again to have been on good terms. Mr Sheridan, who thought his son altogether Miss Linley's social superior, may not improbably have expressed that opinion in terms offensive to Mr Linley, who, on his side, seems to have considered, with some reason, that a young man of twenty without property, profession, prospects or thriftiness of disposition, was a very poor match for a girl inhabiting a fine house in the Crescent, earning a large yearly income and possessing three thousand pounds.

The situation presently came to a crisis. Mr Sheridan resolved that, on his own return to Ireland, his whole family should remove from Bath. At the prospect of this impending separation all Elizabeth's vexations melt away. Once more she writes as ardently as ever, and once more at the romantic hour of midnight. Apparently Mrs Linley, true to the traditions of fiction, had removed the heroine's inkstand, and her outpourings had to be written in pencil.

75

Tuesday night, 12 o'clock.

You see to what shifts I am reduced. I have lost my ink, but I hope you will be able to understand me as I could not resist the inclination I had to thank my dear Horatio for his sweet letter—but is it possible you can ever believe I can change or bestow one serious thought on any object or any other person in life? My whole soul is devoted to you, nor would I change my present situation to be wife to any man. Yet though I despise the ties that govern vulgar souls, yet I must look sometimes towards a time when I hope it will be in my dear Horatio's power at least to make me his in every sense of the word. . . . But as it is we must submit till fortune puts in our power to be happy our own way.

How could you tease me about Miss C——? Indeed, my love, if you believe her you would hurt me very much, as I give you my word and honour I never gave her the least reason to think that you was of the least consequence with me more than as a friend. Nor could the hints that Lissy dropt proceed from anything I ever said, as I assure you I never have nor ever will make a confidant of any one; be easy then, my dearest love, on that head, as I am resolved for once to convince you that I can keep a secret. How beautiful at this moment does that bright moon appear! Yes, my Horatio, it was conscious that thy Eliza's thoughts were wholly fixed on thee, nor can any other idea remove thy loved remembrance from my heart. I feel I love you every day more tenderly, I cannot support the idea of a separation, and yet I have sometimes horrid thoughts of your going to Dublin. Oh, my loved Horatio, what will then become of your Eliza? But I will not make myself unhappy with imaginary evils. If you love me, and will always be constant in every situation, I will yet be at peace and in that hope even, it is impossible but I must be happy. " One woe doth tread upon another's heels; so fast they follow." I had before lost my ink, and now my candle is just burnt out. God bless you, my dear, Dear Love; believe me tenderly and sincerely your Eliza.

It was not, in fact, Dublin, but St Quentin upon which Mr Sheridan had fixed as a place of exile for " Horatio," and the brother and sisters were to have been all together. But in the meantime the father discovered, apparently with surprise, and certainly with violent anger, that his son " continued privately to see Miss Linley." Possibly he suspected his daughters of complicity; for he now resolved upon taking them with him to Ireland while the culprit, their brother, was to be established, under the care of the father's " particular friends," Mr and Mrs Parker, at Waltham Abbey. Anger proved on this occasion, as on so many others, a poor counsellor; Mr Sheridan, in leaving his son so near to London, where the Linleys generally had engagements in the spring, was really leaving open a door between him and the beautiful Eliza. He trusted no doubt in the extorted promise of the convalescent not to write to Miss Linley, and in his " oath equivocal," as Alicia calls it, not to marry her. This latter the graceless Dick perhaps reconciled to his conscience by reflecting that the French ceremony was a marriage binding in honour, if not in law, and that therefore, since they were really married already no future rite would be a marriage, but merely a reaffirmation. Perhaps, however, there was a moment in which he himself believed these promises and honestly resolved to conquer his attachment. A few days after his arrival at Waltham he wrote to his father, for whom, despite all parental ungraciousness, he had a genuine affection, in the following terms:—

I left you, Sir, at a time when from appearances you had reason to suppose I had not been dealing ingenuously with

77

you. I certainly had in some degree deserved the suspicion; however some accidental circumstances served greatly to strengthen it. There were circumstances attending that connexion which you so much wished me to break off, which made it almost impossible to deal with proper candour on all sides; and I can only reassure you that what might strongly seem to be a departing from my word, and your injunctions, was, sincerely, and to the best of my judgment, enter'd on with a view to secure to myself the power of adhering effectually to both for the future. The merit or demerit of my having so involved myself, is not now a question; but I can now have no motive in solemnly declaring to you that I have extricated myself, and that on this subject you shall never again have the smallest uneasiness.

The meaning of these generalities seems to be that he felt bound to explain to Elizabeth his father's " injunctions " and to obtain her consent before agreeing to conform to them. Mr Sheridan, we may presume, went away with his daughters to Ireland, satisfied that he had put an end to the troublesome boy's infatuation, and that he was no longer in any danger of having a " public performer " as his daughter-in-law. The young man, shaken by six months of extraordinary agitation, sat down in the dullness of Waltham to read law, and to put out of his heart that lovely creature whom her contemporaries persistently called " the Syren."

Elizabeth Linley stayed on in Bath, ripening both in beauty and in talent, turning more heads, refusing fresh lovers and learning by degrees to believe that the man upon whose constancy she had reckoned was after all forgetting her. For the moment age and prudence were in the ascendant while youth and ardour were left, not only defeated and disheartened but—worst defeat of all—distrustful of themselves.

To be a biographer is notoriously to assume responsibilities the complete fulfilment of which demands a sublimity of virtue beyond mortal attainment. In biography even more conspicuously than in most human undertakings we all sin continually against absolute veracity, against our predecessors, and against our subjects—to say nothing of our readers. Few of us, however, it is to be hoped, sin quite so unpardonably as did Mr Thomas Moore, whose pernicious practice it was to mark, in original documents entrusted to him, the passages " which he wished to be put in type " and to send these originals to the printer. " It is not wonderful in these circumstances," says Mr Fraser Rae, " that a few of the papers went astray." Among those which have thus vanished are four pages of Alicia Sheridan's statement; and their absence leaves in permanent obscurity the steps by which the youth and maiden who, in the autumn of 1772, were separated, estranged and unhappy, came, in the spring of 1773, to be blissfully united as bride and bridegroom.

Estranged at one period they certainly were. Sheridan's letters to his friend Thomas Grenville contain passages that point to his having, while at Waltham, passed through one of those periods of reaction that occur in the course of every strong feeling, and often in the course of feelings comparatively weak. Even the steadiest family affection has its warmer and its colder fits, its intervals in which charms and merits are perceived with singular force, and its other intervals in which, often very unjustly, faults start into surprising relief. The wise, as they grow older, learn to allow for the inevitable weakness in themselves and in others, to curb the caustic comment that presses to the tongue, and wait for the mood to pass; but to youth, with its ardour, its inexperience, and its invariable expectation of an abiding rapture always at the highest pitch, the chill of reaction when it comes seems as permanent and as definitive as the rapture itself, and the unreasonable expectation is followed by as unreasonable a despair. Such a fit of chill seems to have befallen Sheridan at Waltham. At first his heart was entirely fixed upon Eliza. On the last day of August he was writing to his friend that he had passed two days in excessive melancholy, and that a lover absent from his beloved would be less unhappy in a desert than in a paradise. He hopes Grenville has seen " her."

I hope you have talked to her; if you *have*, and should again, I am sure your own feelings will suggest to you what I would say. Tell me she is happy; if she is otherwise tell her to be so. Upon my soul, it were the part of an angel to come down from Heaven, to watch over her, and reconcile her to peace. I wish dying could assure me of the power to come from Heaven to her with that happiness which I fear she will never know here. It is impious to say it, but I believe I should exchange a Robe of Glory for *her* Livery.

In a few days Grenville replied. He had not spoken to Miss Linley, whom he had seen but for a moment and who was now gone to Winchester and Gloucester. His sympathy, though warm, was by no means encouraging; he wished it were in his power " to reconcile your mind to the loss of what you so much regret, or what I fear *is* and *must be* impossible, and make you happy in each other." Sheridan, it appears, had promised his friend some " memoirs " of the whole story; but no trace of such a narrative has been discovered, and perhaps no line was ever written.

Sheridan's health was probably still weak from the effect of his wounds; his anxiety must have tended to retard complete recovery, and now some of those unromantic ailments that dog a lowered vitality descended upon him in

the shape of a bad cold, toothache, and an abscess (a
" tumour " is his own term) in the jaw. " I am sick and
without society," he wrote; " my love is almost the only
feeling I have alive." Yet in the same letter there are
symptoms of reaction; he is giving up hope—sure sign in a
young man of a change in inclination. He agrees with
Grenville that to hope for happiness from this attachment
" *is* and *must* be impossible." Moreover he had

received a letter from her . . . (contraband!) filled with the
violence of affection, and concluded with prayers, commands
and entreaties that I should write to her. I did not expect
such a desire, as she acquiesced to my determination of not
corresponding. Indeed as we had always other subjects to
employ us when together, she hesitated less in agreeing to a
distant mortification, and I by that had less necessity to
explain properly to her the necessity of it. I cannot now do
it; for to tell her *why* I am right is to plunge into the wrong.
To tell her why I did *resolve* is to break my resolution, yet
to deny her, and not excuse my denial, is a hard mortification.
I am determined *not* to write, not from a conviction of the
necessity of such a determination, but I cannot break a solemn
promise. How strange is my situation! If I consult my
reason, or even one half of my *feelings*, I find conviction that
I should wish to end this unfortunate connexion. What
draws the knot, rejects the influence of reason, and has its
full moiety of the feelings (dearest, tenderest!) with the
passions for its hold. Perhaps then, it is best that there is
an *artificial*, but powerful bond, that keeps me to the other
party.

It would be interesting to know whether Sheridan ever
saw the September number of *The London Magazine* with
its outrageously personal article headed: " Anecdotes of the
Maid of Bath." This contains an unabashed account of
Elizabeth's private concerns, and displays more detailed

knowledge than one would think could have been honestly
come by. The personalities, indeed, are spiced with praise;
after mentioning that her first appearance was made at the
age of twelve, the writer proceeds: "Even in those first
efforts she charmed all who listened; there was in her
voice the extensive power of commanding all sounds and
every sound was harmonised by such softness that it was
impossible to resist her influence; she sung to the heart,
from this time therefore she was present at every concert
and held the station of principal singer." In regard to
Mathews, *The London Magazine* is of some interest; it
expressly declares that "among the earliest in his attendance
on Miss L. was Mr M——ws, a circumstance which was
far from favourable to her fame, for this gentleman was at
the time married. . . . The censorious as usual took the
alarm and became very anxious for her virtue without knowing whether it was in danger." The story of Mr Long is
of course told; and on the whole accurately, although the
writer is a good deal astray when he supposes the reluctance
of the young lady due to dislike at being dragged "from the
kind eye of the public who had so often caressed and applauded
her." The article is particularly explicit as to the circum-
spect conduct of Sheridan during the elopement, and as to
the constant presence of that mysterious chaperon. Finally
it winds up, in a manner that must have been singularly
exasperating to both fathers, thus: "Whether they are
married or not, their respective parents have since that time
been very industrious in keeping them separate."

The extremely calumnious portrait accompanying this
article has been reproduced by Mr Green, and has suffered
in reproduction. Bad as it is, *The London Magazine* portrait
is not quite so bad as that. The original indeed is hard-
featured enough, and lacks all beauty; yet the likeness to

Elizabeth Linley can be traced. Even this travesty shows the peculiarly graceful set of the head, the pathetic lift of the brows, the something tragic and touching that marks every portrait of her in which the eyes are shown. Nay, as we continue to gaze at the harsh and libellous woodcut in the yellowed pages of the old magazine, the curious fascination of the face gradually asserts itself; and we begin to feel that even if the girl did, in her young immaturity, ever look as ill, as lean, as hard as this, it would still remain not strange that men and women alike adored her. But in fact we know that her young immaturity, like her childhood, like her womanhood, was lovely; Gainsborough's portrait, already spoken of, shows us what she was at thirteen; Ozias Humphrys shows what she was shortly after her marriage; it is quite inconceivable that between those stages can have intervened one so extraordinarily different from either. Moreover there is the testimony of Wilkes, who wrote, in a letter to his daughter: " I have passed an evening with Mr Brereton's family and the two Misses Linley. The elder I think superior to all the handsome things I have heard of her." He adds that " she does not seem in the least spoiled by the idle talk of our sex, and is the most modest, pleasing and delicate flower I have seen for a long time; the younger a mere coquette, no sentiment."

The latter judgment, it may be stated, is unfair in the highest degree. Mary Linley was at least as remarkable a woman as her sister, full of feeling and of character, and perfectly capable of summing up the great Mr Wilkes in one glance of her mirthful eyes. Not to a person of this kind would she reveal her real self.

By the end of October, Sheridan, now an exile of two months' standing, could write in a calmer mood and could assure his friend that he now had " better health and more animal spirits than I ever remember to have had "; that he kept regular hours, used a great deal of exercise, and studied hard. Towards the close of the letter comes this passage: " You will observe that I have omitted to say anything *de amore aut de Caeciliâ meâ (utinam quidem mea esset)*! I have kept absolutely to my resolution. But (from a late accident) I will defer saying more till I see you."

" Saint Cecilia " was one of the several pretty nicknames by which Elizabeth Linley was known; under it Sir Joshua Reynolds described the portrait which he painted of her, and by it the susceptible Halhed, now far away in India, had been accustomed to write about her. The resolution to which Sheridan had " kept absolutely " was, I presume, that of not replying to the poor girl's letters; while the " late accident " must refer to some going astray of a letter.

Sheridan's prospects must have seemed to him at this time more uncertain than ever; the plans of his father for him fluctuated continually. Now, Dick was to study for the Bar; now, again, he was, after all, to go to France, with his sisters. By-and-by the young man, who in September had come of age, heard " from a third hand " that Lord Townshend had promised " to do something handsome for me immediately " and anticipated that the something would not be to his own taste. Anything more unsettling and demoralising than the six months spent in this manner it is difficult to conceive; and if the Sheridan of later days was deficient in the habit of regular industry, if he worked by fits and starts, if throughout life he failed in those prime duties of a man of business, the answering of letters and the keeping of appointments, surely much of the blame must rest with the father who, after suffering him to hang about unoccupied, at Bath, ever since he left Harrow, had now, in addition, cut him off from his family and friends and left

84

him, as unoccupied as ever, to eat out his heart in isolation. That, in his disappointed and solitary state, he escaped falling into any very serious mischief was owing probably to that fastidious delicacy which made him throughout life detest coarseness of speech or behaviour. Moreover, when the Linleys came—as they usually did in the spring—to perform in London, was it to be expected that the lad's smouldering passion would not revive, and that he would be able to resist the temptation of seeing Elizabeth again?

A letter of Mr Linley's, quoted by Mr Percy Fitzgerald, serves, although it must have been written at some earlier date, to show very clearly his professional aims and hopes. It is in reply to one from Colman, the manager of Covent Garden Theatre:

I think, as she has acquired a reputation, I ought to have the advantage of her first performing in London myself. . . .

Were I properly settled in London, I think I could conduct the business of oratorios regularly; therefore I do not relish giving the prime of my daughter's performance to support the schemes of others. Still as you are so earnest, I would take two hundred guineas and a clear benefit, with the choice of oratorios. In regard to her engaging as an actress, I shall never do that, unless it were to ensure to myself and family a solid settlement by being admitted to purchase a share in the Patent on reasonable terms, or something adequate to this; either of which I see no possibility of obtaining; and I shall never lay myself at the mercy of my children, especially when their power of being of service to me depends so entirely on chance.

This letter shows how ridiculous it is to talk, as Mr Green does, of the elopement as " half-ruining her father," or as " This sad act " which " broke up the prosperous Bath home and largely tended through disappointment and a constant lasting regret to break up the life, if not the heart of the father." To remove to London and to secure a share in the Patent of one of the two theatres had long been Linley's hope and desire, and within four years from the night of the elopement, Sheridan offered him the chance of fulfilment. From the point of view of Thomas Linley's ambitions, the day was a lucky one on which he gave his daughter in marriage to Richard Sheridan.

In December some kind friend in Bath informed Sheridan that Sir Thomas Clarges was "either going to be married to or to run away with Miss L." The good Grenville was able to reassure him. "I have seen Sir T. Clarges," he writes, "who is at Oxon. I have talked with him upon the subject. He wonders at the report, denies it totally, and goes abroad in a week's time." Sir Thomas's wonder can hardly have been very profound, since the fact was that that music-loving young gentleman had actually offered himself to Miss Linley and been refused, and that his friends were sending him abroad to get over his disappointment.

In the first week of the new year (1773) Sheridan writes :

Eliza is within an hour's ride of me, and must have been for some time, yet, upon my honour, I have and do industri-ously avoid knowing the particular place that is blest with her inhabiting. I was obliged to go to London the other day, and I protest to you, no country girl passing alone through a Church-yard at midnight, ever dreaded more the appearance of a ghost than I did to encounter this (for once I'll say) *terrestrial* being. But I cannot say anything on this subject on paper.[1]

[1] Fraser Rae, " Sheridan," vol. i., p. 251. Sheridan seems to have been mistaken as to Miss Linley's whereabouts. *The Bath Chronicle* advertises " Miss M. Linley's concert " for the 6th of January at the New Assembly Rooms. " Vocal parts by the two Miss Linleys."

Eliza herself was no longer the entirely trusting and patient adorer of "Horatio." Tales, not wholly without foundation, had been reaching her of his making love to ladies in Waltham. It was no doubt a dull spot, in which romantic young gentlemen of leisure were not common, and the unoccupied ladies of the neighbourhood seem to have done what they could to spoil the new-comer. Gossip arose; his name became involved in the differences of a certain indiscreet "Mrs L." with her husband. Mrs L. carried her grievances to Miss Linley, and was confirmed by Miss C——y; or perhaps Miss C——y brought the story, and the denials of Mrs L. were unconvincing. Several letters of Elizabeth's have been printed by Mr Fraser Rae, which must belong to this period, although indications of date and place are lacking. Though she was gentle, she was never tame, and what her sister Mary calls "the spirit of the Linleys" now flamed out.

I have been so deceived by you and by everyone that it has almost deprived me of my reason, but I have paid too, too dear for my experience ever to put in your power or anyone's to impose on me again. I did not expect you would attempt to vindicate your conduct. You cannot to me. Think! oh! reflect one moment on what I have suffered, and then judge if I can again consent to risk my life and happiness. For God's sake, S——n, do not endeavour to plunge me again into misery. Consider the situation I am in. Consider how much your persisting to refuse my letters will distress me. Reason, honour, everything forbids it. This is not a sudden resolution, but the consequence of cool, deliberate reflection. You are sensible it is not from caprice, but when I tell you I have lately had some conversation with Mrs L. and Miss C——y, you will not suppose I will be again deceived. Farewell! If you value my peace of mind return my letters.

Those words about his attempt " to vindicate his conduct " point to his having broken through his resolution
and written to her. He must have done so again, in reply
to her, for a second letter from her followed:

Thursday night, 12 *o'clock.* I did not think to have opened
another letter of yours but was deceived by your telling the
maid they were my *papers.* I am too well convinced you
have art and eloquence sufficient to impose on one less
credulous than me. For *that* reason, tho' I was sure you
could not so far clear yourself, as to induce me to disbelieve
what I have such undoubted proofs of, I did not chuse to
enter the lists with so subtle an arguer, but you oblige me
(contrary to my intention) to take up the pen. Why, S——n,
will you thus distress me? Why endeavour to disturb *that*
repose which for some time I have tried to court? I conjure
you, by all you hold dear, cease to persecute me. I *never* can
be *yours.* There are now insuperable bars between us. Do
not let the mistaken notion of pity impose on you. *You are
Deceived.* You know not your own heart—it is not in your
nature to be constant, especially to *one* who is so much in
your *Power,* but if you still persist in thinking your happiness
connected with mine, I now assure you it is not in your power
to make me happy. I have gone through such scenes from
my infancy of distress Disappointment and Deceit, it has
taken from me that keen sensibility which has been the cause
of all my misfortunes. My Heart is no longer susceptible of
Love; 'tis dead to every tender feeling. You think I hate
you, Heaven knows I do not, but I cannot *love* you nor any
Man. Your coldness, your neglect, your contempt at a time
when I stood so much in need of every consolation to support
me, prey'd on my mind, and the convincing proofs I have
since received of your Behaviour, completed my *cure.* I saw
you in such a light—I could not but despise you, but tho' I
do not now look upon you in that light, I own to you I do
not love. What was it that first induced me to regard you.

You are sensible that when I left Bath I had not an idea of you but as a friend. It was not your person that gained my affection. No, S——n, it was that delicacy, that tender compassion, that interest which you seemed to take in my welfare, that were the motives that induced me to love you.

When these were lost, when I found you no longer the man my fond imagination painted you, when, instead of respect, I found myself spoken of with *contempt*, laugh'd at, made the Sport of your Idle Hours, and the subject of your Wit with every Milener's Prentice in Bath! When I was convinc'd of *this*, how could I *love*, how could I continue blindly to esteem the *man* who had used me so basely. In regard to your omission in writing to me, I assure you, that is the least crime my heart accuses you of, but I assure you I wrote *twice*, and put the Letters in the Post Office myself, they could not *miscarry*. In the first (which you say was *cold*) I beg'd, I entreated you to write; but receiving no answer, I again renew'd my request, and urg'd it by every sacred tie. In answer to this, P—— showed me what you had writ to him, where you desire to know if I *insisted* on your breaking your promise to your father and where you offer to come to Bath. I own I was hurt. What could I have said more than I had already done? Were not my entreaties and supplications sufficient to prevail (if your own affection was not strong enough to prompt you) but you must ask if I *insisted* on your compliance? You know, S——n, I could not *insist*, I had put it out of my power. I told you, before we Parted that I might *Desire, Request* but should never insist on anything from *you*. Your proposal of coming to Bath I looked upon as mere *Words*, as you was well assur'd your father would not permit it. Besides how ridiculously contradictory did it appear that *you*, who held a promise so *sacred* as to refuse writing, would yet break thro' every tie of honour to see *me*. How could you suppose me so blind as not to see the absurdity of such a proposal? In regard to P——, upon my honour, his behaviour to *you* in regard to

89

me, has been consistent with the strictest friendship, and I sincerely believe he has been basely belied, for I am well convinced he is a worthy man. At present you see everything through the mist of passion, but let reason once more chase the cloud of suspicion from your *mind*, and you will think with me that P—— has not deserved your resentment.

I do not judge from appearances. If I did, I should be weak enough to listen to your *plausible excuses*, but, S——n, I cannot be again deceived, I am altered in every respect. I look back on my past conduct with *Horror*; I cannot be *happy*, but yet I trust I shall not be *miserable*.

.   .   .   .

I am acquainted with your Behaviour to your father and Lissy. I know by what means my Letters were made Publick. In short there is not a circumstance, nor a disrespectful *word* of *yours* that I am not acquainted with, tho' I did not get but little intelligence by Miss C. It is useless therefore your endeavouring to extenuate your behaviour. I cannot look upon you in the light I formerly did. Besides, supposing you was even to convince me you had never been guilty, I never could be yours. The remorse, the Horror which I feel when I reflect on my past conduct, would not permit me to marry the man who would have it so much in his power to upbraid me. After this declaration I hope you will no longer refuse returning me my letters; be assured this is the last you will ever receive from me.

You say you will not give them up till I declare I love another man. Do not distress me so much as to continue in that resolution. Believe me, I am incapable of loving any man. They cannot be of any use to you. Do not think I shall alter my resolution, or that I am to be terrified by your threats. I will not think so basely of your principles as to suppose you meant anything by them. There are insurmountable obstacles to prevent our ever being united, even supposing I could be induced again to believe you.

I did not think to have told you of a great one, but I must or you will not be convinced that I am in earnest. Know then that before I left Bath, after I had refused Sir T. C., and other gentlemen of fortune, on your account, who I found had given up all thought of me, in the anguish of my soul which was torn with all the agonies of remorse and rage, I vowed in the most solemn manner upon my knees, before my parents, that I never would be yours, by my own consent, let what would be the consequence. My father took advantage of my distress, and my upbraidings mixed with persuasions, prevailed on me to promise that I would marry the first man (whose character was unexceptionable) that offered. I repented I had made this promise afterwards, for though I resolved never to be yours I had not the least intention to be another's. I comforted myself with thinking I should not be solicited, but I was deceived.

My father before we left Bath, received proposals for me from a gentleman in London, which he insisted on my accepting. I endeavoured to evade his earnest request, but he urged my promise in such a manner that I could not refuse to see him (at least). He has visited me two or three times since we have been here. He is not a young man, but I believe a worthy one. When I found my father so resolute, I resolved to acquaint the gentleman with every circumstance of my life. I did, and instead of inducing him to give me up, he is now more earnest that ever. I have declared it is not possible for me to love him, but he says he will depend on my generosity—in short there is nothing I have not done to persuade him to leave me, but in vain. He has promised my father not to take my fortune, and you may be assured this circumstance will have great weight with him. You see how I am situated. If this was not the case, I could never be your wife, therefore once more I conjure you to leave me and cease persecuting me.

My father has this minute left me. He knows I am writing to you, and it was with the greatest difficulty I pacified him. He was going immediately to your lodgings. He has given strict orders to Hannah to bring every letter to him. You will make me eternally miserable if you persist after what I have told you. Be assured I will not open any letter of yours, nor will I write again. If you wish me to think my happiness is dear to you, return my letters. If not, I cannot compel you, but I hope your generosity will not permit you to make an improper use of them. For God's sake write no more. I tremble at the consequences.

From the same letter or from one about the same time comes also the following paragraph:

Do not think I have been influenced by Mrs L. or Miss C.; 'tis true I have had some conversation with them both. Mrs L.'s assurance led her to suppose she could make me believe she was entirely innocent in regard to you, and that she never entertained a thought of you but as a friend. I was a good deal surprised at her endeavouring to vindicate her conduct to me, but her behaviour only heightened the contempt I before felt of her; Miss C. I own I pity. Why do you abuse her, what have you to alledge against her? If she was hurried on by the violence of her love for you to the commission of a crime, she has since repented. Surely the remorse, the anguish which she feels, hourly joined to the opinion she is sensible you entertain of her, is punishment sufficient.

The foregoing letters, parts of which are printed in *The English Illustrated Magazine* for April 1887, and parts in Mr Fraser Rae's first volume, come, the latter informs us in his Prefatory Note, from a collection purchased by the late Mr MacHenry, and after his death by Mr Augustin Daly, who allowed Mr Rae to make what extracts he pleased from them. Whence they came has not been ascertained; and Mr Percy Fitzgerald, who had not apparently seen the originals, denied their authenticity. Mr Rae, who had seen the originals, and who was well acquainted with Mrs Sheridan's handwriting, accepted these as genuine examples of it; and at least one, moreover, of the collection bears confirmatory postmarks. Mr Sichel also believes them to be "certainly genuine"; and several points in them are confirmed by Sheridan's letters to Grenville, which were not published till long after the purchase of these documents. In the absence of any testimony as to their origin it is only possible to say that the evidence in their favour, especially the internal evidence, preponderates. They possess in their very wanderings and repetitions a note of reality that appears to me singularly lacking in the supposed letter to "Miss Saunders." It is very much to be regretted that they should ever have passed from the keeping of the writer's family, and not easy to imagine how they can have done so without some infringement of honesty.

As to their contents, it may be said with reasonable certainty that Sheridan was guilty of the lesser offences with which Miss Linley charged him, and innocent of the greater. That he did leave her letter or letters unanswered we know from his own to be true; that he did send through P—— (no doubt Paumier) the message which so deeply and not unnaturally incensed her, can hardly be doubted. But that he ever spoke of her with contempt, laughed at her, made her the sport of his idle hours and the subject of his casual chatter, no person will believe who has studied with any attention the real facts of Sheridan's life. His weakness was never the exposure of secrets; it lay rather in a fondness for needless secrecy; and even supposing—as nobody, how-ever, can suppose who understands his character—that he had not good feeling enough to preserve him from such gross misconduct, he had undoubtedly more than enough

93

good taste. No, the sins against her which Elizabeth rightly
considered unpardonable were sins of which her lover had
not been guilty—as no doubt he succeeded in convincing
both her and her father. Mrs L—— whose full name is
signed to a letter from her still preserved by the Sheridan
family, was probably the maker of the mischief; but it may
be conjectured that some letter from Elizabeth had actually
fallen into the hands of her lover's father, and in so doing
furnished a nucleus of truth for the fiction about her letters
having been " made public."

At the season when she was writing these impassioned
letters, Elizabeth was reaching the summit of her professional successes. Fanny Burney's " Early Diary" of
March or April 1773, says that the town " has rung of no
other name this month." She describes poor Mr Linley,
whom apparently she had never seen, as " a very sour, ill-
bred, severe and selfish man." As for Elizabeth, she is
" believed to be very romantic . . . has met with a great
variety of adventures and has had more lovers and admirers
than any nymph of these times. She has long been attached
to a Mr Sheridan, . . . a young man of [   ] very well
spoken of, whom it is expected she will speedily marry. The
applause and admiration she has met with can only be
compared to what is given Mr Garrick. The whole town
seems distracted about her. Miss Linley alone engrosses all
eyes, ears, and hearts."

Critical notices of her singing are so rare that the remarks
on this point of Miss Burney and of her sister Susan (who
was an accomplished musician) are of interest. " Her voice,"
says the former, " is soft, sweet, clear, and affecting. . . .
She has an exceeding good shake and the best and most
critical judges pronounce her to be infinitely superior to *all*
other English singers." But her " cadences " were not

perfect. Although they showed great fancy and even taste, they were more florid than a " finished singer " would have made them. Susan Burney, comparing Mrs Sheridan and Miss Harrop, considered the manner of the latter " much more Italian." But Miss Harrop now and then permitted things to escape her that were " really vulgar," particularly in recitative; moreover she was guilty of " a howl and bad manner of taking her notes " which Mrs Sheridan was always free from. " *She* was never *vulgar*, though without the soul or refinement of a great Italian singer."

Fanny Burney, whose short sight prevented her from judging at a distance of Miss Linley's beauty, was taken behind the scenes, where she found Mr and Mrs Linley, Mary and Tom, as well as the enchantress herself, and where her observant woman's eye at once noted various details that give to her account a precision lacking in those " angels," " flowers," and " Syrens " of which contemporaries were so lavish.

Had I been for my sins born of the male race, I should have certainly added one more to Miss Linley's train. She is really beautiful; her complexion a clear lovely animated brown, with a blooming colour on her cheeks; her nose that most elegant of shapes Grecian; fine, luxurious, easy-sitting hair, a charming forehead, pretty mouth and most bewitching eyes. With all this her carriage is modest and unassuming and her countenance indicates diffidence and a strong desire of pleasing—a desire in which she can never be disappointed.

The colour of those " most bewitching eyes " Miss Burney does not tell us. Judging from the portraits of Gainsborough, who knew their faces so intimately, Elizabeth, Thomas and Samuel all belonged to that admirable type in which the hair is dark and the eyes grey; Mr Linley, Maria and Mary were brown-eyed. Among the charms of grey eyes is the power of looking sometimes light and sometimes dark; and it must have been in a moment of apparent darkness that Foote met the gaze of Elizabeth Linley, or he could never have made his " Solomon Flint " speak of " her lovely black eyes."

The Bath Chronicle of course followed, with interest, although not always with exactitude, the doings of the Linley family in London. On the 18th of March, in its London letter (dated 13th of March), the world of Bath is informed that their Majesties were on Wednesday and Friday at the Oratorio at Drury Lane to hear Miss Linley, and seemed much pleased. A fortnight later, on the 1st of April, there are two items, a sort of leading article, and a paragraph from town, dated 26th of March. The former begins skilfully with personal gossip, and then declines on theatrical news:

It is now publicly said that, Mr Richard Sheridan is actually married to Miss Linley, and has been for some time. Thus this charming Syren has put it out of her power to listen to the addresses of any man.

The two Linleys carry all before them. The benefits of the first actors have been materially hurt through the attention of the town being rivetted to the Drury Lane Oratorios alone. Covent Garden and the Haymarket theatres are very little frequented on the Wednesday and Friday evenings, and the loss to each party must be as considerable as the gains of Mr Stanley will be immoderate. It is imagined that the receipts of Drury Lane house, each Oratorio night have rather exceeded than fallen short of £500.

The paragraph from London is headed: " True Intelligence Extraordinary," and declares that " To-day the two

celebrated Miss Linleys dined by invitation with the Lord
Bishop of Bristol, at the Deanery House, St Paul's"; and
a facetious hope is expressed that "these young ladies" may
soon be introduced to the choir of St Paul's and promoted
to Minor Canonries.

The number published on the 13th of April—the actual
date of Elizabeth's marriage—has a paragraph of London
news, dated three days earlier, and furnished by some
particularly well-informed correspondent, either Linley himself or some person who received the report directly from
him:

Yesterday se'nnight Mr Linley, his son and elder daughter,
were at the Queen's concert at Buckingham House; Miss
Mary Linley, being ill could not attend. The King and
Queen were particularly affable; his Majesty told Mr Linley
that he never in his life heard so fine a voice as his daughter's
nor one so well instructed; that she was a great credit to
him, and presented him with a £100 bank note. No one
attended the concert but their Majesties, the children and
one lady. It continued five hours, yet no one sat except the
two performers who played the harpsichord and the violin-
cello.

If that irreverent chronicler, Horace Walpole, is to be
trusted, the decorous monarch George III ogled Miss
Linley "as much as he dares to do in so holy a place as
an oratorio and at so devout a service as 'Alexander's
Feast.'"

To this period of success and fashion must be attributed—
if indeed it can be accepted as genuine at all—a letter which,
together with Miss Linley's alleged reply, was published in
The Bath Chronicle of 15th of April. This epistle, which
begins "Adorable Creature," must be presumed to have
come from a married man, since it declares that its writer

H

" has it ever to lament that the laws will not permit me to offer you my hand "; he offers therefore his heart and fortune instead, and flatters himself that " Lady A——, who will deliver this and who obligingly vouchsafes to be my mediator " will obtain permission for him to throw himself at her feet. In momentary expectation of which he remains her devoted admirer, G——R. Her answer—and it reads like hers—runs as follows:

MY LORD, Lest my silence should bear the most distant interpretation of listening to your proposals, I condescend to answer your infamous letter. You lament the laws will not permit you to offer me your hand. I lament it too, my lord, but on a different principle—to convince your dissipated heart that I have a soul capable of *refusing* a coronet when the owner is not the object of my affection—despising it when the offer of an unworthy possessor. The reception your *honourable* messenger met with in the execution of her embassy saves me the trouble of replying to the other parts of your letter, and (if you have any feelings left) will explain to you the *baseness* as well as the *inefficacy* of your design.
L——Y.

The covering letter is signed " Horatio," a circumstance which suggests that the two others may possibly have been sent to the *Chronicle* by Elizabeth's indignant young bridegroom.

On the 8th of April the bride-elect and her sister sang in the chapel of the Foundling Hospital, and the announcement of the performance requested that gentlemen would come without swords and ladies without hoops. On the 12th she appeared for the last time at one of the united family performances, when she sang at a concert for her brother's benefit at the Haymarket Theatre.

Meanwhile some decisive meeting must have occurred, either between the young people, or, more probably, between Sheridan and Mr Linley, who, it may be remembered, had already announced an intention of going "immediately to your lodgings." Now, whenever Mr Linley and his daughter's persuasive suitor came into personal contact, the elder man it was who was talked over; and perhaps on this occasion he may have gone to Waltham (or to the Bedford Coffee-house, which seems to have been the young man's resort in town) resolved to ban, and may have remained to bless. The exact details can never, in the absence of Alicia's four pages, be known, and Moore's generalised statement that "after a series of stratagems and schemes which convinced Mr Linley that it was impossible to keep them much longer asunder he consented to their union" is decidedly tantalising. Whether the picturesque tale of Sheridan's disguising himself as a hackney coachman to drive Miss Linley home from the theatre is well founded is equally impossible to determine; but since the gregarious habits of the Linley family would prevent any chance of private speech with any one of them on such an occasion, and since those habits must have been perfectly well known to Sheridan, we can scarcely imagine him likely to adopt so futile a device. The variant, which describes him as driving a coach for his friend Ewart when that young man was engaged in eloping with the wealthy Miss Manship, is at least more credible. But while these things remain obscure, the solid testimony of a church register assures us that upon the 13th of April—the very morning after her brother's benefit concert—Richard Brinsley Sheridan and Elizabeth Ann Linley were married at Marylebone Church, and that the witnesses who signed that register were Thomas Linley and John Swale. The friendly Ewart and his heiress, back from

France, were married, or remarried, at the same time and place.

Thus was the romance that had begun on 18th of March, by that imprudent flight from Bath, closed in the most decorous and conventional manner on 13th of April of the next year. The bridegroom, not yet two and twenty, had meanwhile declared that to hope for happiness from his attachment was and must be impossible; the bride of eighteen and a half had, but a few weeks earlier, vowed, "in the most solemn manner," that she would never, with her own consent, be his; her father had assured her that he would rather follow her to the grave than see her married to Sheridan. Yet, upon this Tuesday morning of the appropriately variable month, behold them assembled joyfully and hopefully at Marylebone Church! Nor, so far as I can learn, did any one of the three ever express regret for the morning's work.

CHAPTER 5. THE YEARS OF HOPE

THE young Sheridans must have begun their married life with a very small income. Upon the bride was settled a sum of ten hundred and fifty pounds, the trustees being her father and John Swale; the income of this fund would be about one pound per week. Another twelve hundred pounds or thereabouts remained in the hands of Thomas Linley, and had perhaps been invested in the chapel in Brock Street. Presumably the income of this sum also would be handed to Elizabeth's husband, and would represent another sixty pounds or so per annum. It is possible that upon coming of age Sheridan may have inherited some small portion from his mother—with the capital of which he would doubtless be able to deal as he chose. Of course there was also the gold mine of Eliza's voice ; but Sheridan (besides any objections that his own pride might make to the appearance of his wife as " a public performer ") knew well how profoundly she disliked her profession, and was firmly resolved that she should exercise it no more. Various offers were made to him, the songstress being now the property of her husband, as formerly of her father, and the terms proposed give an idea of the income that she must have been earning. " No less than £3200 for various performances were declined," says Mr Sichel, who must have seen many of the original documents.

To Mr Linley, we may be sure, the refusal of engage-

ments so remunerative would appear as a flying in the face
of Providence; evidently he wrote urging that the decision
should be reconsidered, for on the 12th of May Sheridan
is found replying in the following terms:—

Yours of the 3rd instant did not reach me till yesterday,
by reason of its missing us at Morden. As to the principal
point it treats of, I had given my answer some days ago to
Mr Isaac of Worcester. He had enclosed a letter from
Storace to my wife, in which he dwells much on the nature
of the agreement you made for her eight months ago, and
adds that "as this is no new application but a request that
you will fulfill a positive engagement, the breach of which
would prove of fatal consequence to our meeting, I hope
Mr Sheridan will think his honour in some degree concerned
in fulfilling it." Mr Storace, in order to enforce Mr Isaac's
argument, showed me his letter on the same subject to him,
which begins with saying "We must have Mrs Sheridan
somehow or other if possible! the plain English of which is
that if her husband is not willing to let her perform, we will
persuade him that he acts *dishonourably* in preventing her
from fulfilling a positive engagement." This I conceive to
be the very worst mode of application that could have been
taken; as there is really no common sense in the idea that
my *honour* can be concerned in my wife's fulfilling an engagement which it is impossible that she can ever have made.
Nor, as I wrote to Mr Isaac, can you who gave the promise,
whatever it was, be in the least charged with the breach of it,
as your daughter's marriage was an event which must always
have been looked to by them as quite as natural a period to
your rights over her as her death. And in my opinion, it
would have been just as reasonable to have applied to you
to fulfil your engagement in the latter case than in the former.
As to the imprudence of declining this engagement, I do not
think, even were we to suppose that my wife should ever
on any occasion appear again in public, there would be any

at present. For instance, I have had a gentleman with me from Oxford (where they do not claim the least right as from an engagement) who has endeavoured to place the idea of my complimenting the university with Betsy's perform-ance in the strongest light of advantage to me. He likewise informed me that he had just left Lord North who he assured me, would look upon it as the highest compliment and had expressed himself so to him. Now, should it be a point of inclination or convenience to me to break my resolution with regard to Betsy's performing, there surely would be more sense in obliging Lord North (and probably from his own application) than Lord Coventry and Mr Isaac; for were she to sing at Worcester, there would not be the least compliment in her performing at Oxford.

Mrs. Oliphant, commenting upon the tone of these passages, remarks that "the most arbitrary husband nowa-days would think it expedient at least to associate his wife's name with his own." But Mrs Oliphant was probably not very well acquainted with Elizabeth's disposition and senti-ments; any reader who really knows the facts and the persons concerned will understand how painful "Betsy" would have felt it to place herself in direct opposition to her father, and how much more conducive to her comfort it must have been that Sheridan should take upon himself the whole responsibility of a refusal that in fact fulfilled her wishes. She did sing at Oxford on the occasion of the installation of Lord North as Chancellor of the University, at which time degrees were being conferred *honoris causâ*, and, accord-ing to Jekyll, Lord North told Sheridan that he deserved one *uxoris causâ*. As for Linley, however many may have been his head-shakings in private, and however many the lamentations poured into Mrs Linley's sympathising ear, he bore no grudge against his son-in-law, and indeed another passage in the same letter shows how friendly was the relation between them:

There is but one thing that has the least weight upon me, though it is one that I was prepared for. But time, while it strengthens the other blessings we possess, will, I hope add that to the number. You will know that I speak with regard to my father. Betsy informs me you have written to him again. Have you heard from him?

The elder Sheridan had received with the most violent anger the news of his son's marriage. In communicating the event to the absent Charles, he wrote: "I consider myself as having no other son but you. . . . Your sisters know of no other brother, and would therefore naturally expect an increase of attention." The interposition of Linley, far from appeasing this anger, appears to have inflamed it, and some years elapsed before Mr Sheridan would permit himself the possession of a second son.

On the 14th of May, when his marriage was just a month old, Sheridan wrote to his friend Grenville an account of his abode and condition which presents both in the rosiest light:

My dear Tom, I know not whether you will reckon me tardy in writing to you or accuse yourself of some little delay in not having written to me. Were I to plead the seducing avocations of what folks call the honeymoon, perhaps you would seize the same plea, and say that you imagined that even the voice of friendship would sound ungrateful were it to intrude upon that ambrosial month of love. But as I am now four days gone in a simple twelfth part of a year,[1] I give up all excuse myself and demand the

---

[1] Sheridan was no arithmetician. Reckoning by the calendar month he was but one day " gone in a simple twelfth part of a year." Reckoning by the lunar month the fraction would be not a twelfth but a thirteenth.

same of you. You must not conclude from this that this moon sheds less honey on me than the last; yet I would never wish my love to have his wings so clogged with sweets but that I could borrow one quill from them for the service of friendship. Were I to venture this style much longer I am afraid that you would think the moon had another more serious effect upon married men.

To write then like a married man, I should inform you that I have for some time been fixed in a grand little mansion situate at a place called *East Burnham* about two miles and a half from Salt Hill, which, as an Etonian you must be acquainted with. Had I hunted five years I don't believe I could have hit on a place more to my mind, or more adapted to my present situation: were I in a descriptive vein I would draw you some of the prettiest scenes imaginable: I likewise waive the opportunity of displaying the rational and delightful scheme on which our hours proceed.

On the whole I will assure you, as I believe it will give you more pleasure, that I feel myself absolutely and perfectly happy. As for the little clouds which the peering eye of prudence would descry to be gathering against the progress of the scene, I have a consoling Cherub that whispers me, that before they can threaten an adverse shower, a slight gale or two of fortune will disperse them. But when a man's married, 'tis time he should leave off speaking in metaphor. If I thought it would be entertaining to you, I would send to you an account of my household, which I assure [   ] is conducted quite in the manner of plain mortals, with all due attention to the bread and cheese feelings. I have laid aside my design of turning Cupid into a turnspit wheel, and my meat undergoes the indignity of a cook's handling. I have even been so far diffident to my wife's musical abilities as to have carrots and cabbages put into the garden ground: and finding that whatever effect her voice might have upon the sheep on the common, the mutton still continued obstinately at the butcher's, I have deigned to become indebted to the brute's abilities. . . .

The *solitude à deux* of Sylvio and Laura at East Burnham was not entirely unbroken. In June Mr Linley and his eldest unmarried daughter stayed with them, and after reaching home Linley wrote (on the 26th) that he had found nothing during his journey to give him pleasure " but the reflexion of the happy hours I had so lately passed with you and Betsy." So great had now become his confidence in his son-in-law that later on in this letter he wrote: " Do, my dear Sheridan, give young master " (*i.e.* Tom Linley, now just eighteen) " a little wholesome advice."

In the latter part of 1773 the pair came to London and lodged for a little time in the house of the Mr Storace mentioned in Sheridan's letter of the 12th of May. Storace, whose name was originally Sorace, and who inserted the " t " into his patronymic for reasons now inscrutable, was a Neapolitan who played the double-bass at the Opera House, and had married one of the Misses Trusler of Bath. The brother of these ladies was Dr Trusler, a " chronologist," and they themselves were famous as makers of a peculiar kind of cake. Mr and Mrs Storace lived, Kelly tells us, in Marylebone; Mr Rae and Mr Sichel, on the authority doubtless of addressed letters, add that their residence was in Orchard Street. Stephen and Nancy, their children, were musical prodigies; at fifteen years old, the girl was *prima donna* of the Comic Opera House at Leghorn; while the boy became that composer whose charming melodies, lingering in old music books, modern performers might find it worth their while to revive. Of young Stephen Storace, Kelly had often heard Mr Sheridan say that if he had been bred to the law he thought he would have been Lord Chancellor. The

name of Storace recurs at intervals throughout the Linley letters; Mrs Tickell (Mary Linley), who evidently did not admire the singing of Nancy Storace, speaks somewhere of her "brazen throat," and Jane Linley, in letters written from 1798 to 1800, speaks often of Mrs Storace, who must have been Stephen's widow, and of Mary Storace, who must have been his daughter.

Early in 1774 Sheridan and his wife were living in their "own hired house" in Orchard Street, and at that house they resided until after he became chief proprietor of Drury Lane Theatre. It is a curious coincidence that their first London home should have been situated in a street of the same name as that in which they had first known each other in Bath. Since, however, the Storace household was already located in Orchard Street, we must suppose that that circumstance, rather than any romantic associations of the name, determined their choice. It is declared by various biographers that the house was furnished by Mr Linley: a statement which may either be literally true or may mean that he and his fellow-trustee permitted a certain expenditure out of capital for the purpose. The house had a music-room in which Mrs Sheridan gave semi-private concerts at regular intervals. The dates were advertised in a manner that suggests the admission without special invitation of any members of "the nobility and gentry," but no charges were made (Egerton MSS.).

A letter written by Sheridan to his father-in-law, in November 1774, is full of interesting information as to his doings and intentions:

If I were to attempt to make as many apologies as my long omission in writing to you requires, I should have no room for any other subject. One excuse only I shall bring forward, which is, that I have been exceedingly employed, and I believe very profitably. However before I explain how, I must ease my mind on a subject that much more nearly concerns me than any point of business of profit. I must premise to you that Betsy is now very well, before I tell you abruptly that she has encountered another disappointment and consequent indisposition. . . .

I have been very seriously at work on a book, which I am just now sending to the press, and which I think will do me some credit, if it leads to nothing else. However, the profitable affair is of another nature. There will be a comedy of mine in rehearsal at Covent Garden within a few days. I did not set to work on it till within a few days of my setting out for Crome, so you may think I have not, for these last six weeks been very idle. I have done it at Mr Harris's own request; it is now complete in his hands and preparing for the stage. He, and some of his friends also who have heard it, assure me in the most flattering terms that there is not a doubt of its success. It will be very well played, and Harris tells me that the least shilling I shall get (if it succeeds) will be six hundred pounds. I shall make no secret of it towards the time of representation, that it may not lose any support my friends can give it.

The play in question was *The Rivals*, which, on its first night, 17th of January 1775, was by no means decidedly successful, and after being performed a second night was withdrawn for alterations. Mrs Sheridan was at Slough and her husband many years afterwards told Creevey that when he brought her the depressing news she declared it to be not depressing at all, since she would return to her profession, and soon make them both rich.

Curtailed, and with a different actor in the part of "Sir Lucius," *The Rivals* reappeared on the 28th of the same month, and, being at once successful, was very soon acted

in other parts of the country, and among other places at
Bath, where naturally it aroused especial interest. Several
letters from " Polly " Linley describe its advent and reception, and incidentally show the writer to have been just as
warm-hearted, just as gay, and just as much of a theatrical
critic at sixteen as we find her to be some years later. On
the 18th of February she wrote:

What shall I say of *The Rivals !*—A compliment must
naturally be expected; but really it goes so far beyond anything I can say in its praise, that I am afraid my modesty
must keep me silent. When you and I meet, I shall be
better able to explain myself, and tell you how much I am
delighted with it. We expect to have it here very soon:—
it is now in rehearsal. You pretty well know the merits of
our principal performers. I'll show you how it is cast. . . .
There, Madam, do you not think we shall do your *Rivals*
some justice? I'm convinced it won't be better done any-
where out of London.

The play was duly produced, and on the 9th of March
the delighted sister wrote again:

You will know, by what you see inclosed in this frank,
my reason for not answering your letter sooner was that
I waited the success of Sheridan's play at Bath; for, let me
tell you, I look upon our theatrical tribunal though not in
quantity, in quality as good as yours, and I do not believe
there was a critic in the whole city that was not there. But,
in my life, I never saw anything go off with such uncommon
applause. I must first of all inform you that there was a very
full house; the play was performed inimitably well; nor did
I hear, for the honour of our Bath actors, one single prompt
the whole night; but I suppose the poor creatures never
acted with such shouts of applause in their lives, so that they

were incited by that to do their best. They lost many of
Malaprop's good sayings by the applause; in short, I never
saw or heard anything like it; before the actors spoke, they
began their clapping. There was a new scene of the North
Parade, painted by Mr Davis, and a most delightful one it is,
I assure you. Everybody says, Bowers in particular, that
yours in town is not so good. Most of the dresses were
entirely new and very handsome. On the whole, I think
Sheridan is vastly obliged to poor dear Keasberry for getting
it up so well. We only wanted a good Julia to have made
it quite complete.

Encouraged by his success, Sheridan worked diligently in
his new vein, and was soon demanding the assistance of his
father-in-law and brother-in-law for the setting to music of
the songs in a comic opera—*The Duenna*. Despite the hint
of idleness conveyed by his father's request that wholesome
advice might be administered to him, Tom Linley had been
extremely industrious since his return from Italy. Not only
was he considered " one of the most eminent violin performers of the age," but he was already making his mark as
a composer. An anthem of his, " Let God arise," was
performed, in September 1773, at the Worcester Musical
Festival; and between that time and 1775 he wrote no less
than twenty concertos for the violin, with full accompani-
ments, " many of which were performed at Drury Lane in
the oratorio season, and received with unbounded applause."
The songs of *The Duenna* composed by him were: " Could
I each fault remember," " Tell me, my lute," " Friendship
is the bond of reason," " Sharp is the woe," and " My
mistress expects me." On the published score of *The Duenna*
only the name of the elder Thomas Linley appears, though
Tom composed these five songs. The letters of guidance
that passed from the dramatist in London to the composer

in Bath culminated on a date in October with an "important petition":

> You may easily suppose it is nothing else than what I said I would not ask in my last. But, in short, unless you can give us three days in Town, I fear our Opera will stand a chance to be ruined.
>
> Harris is extravagantly sanguine of its success as to plot and dialogue which is to be rehearsed next Wednesday at the theatre. They will exert themselves to the utmost in the scenery, etc., but I never saw any one so disconcerted as he was at the idea of there being no one to put them in the right way as to music. They have no one there whom he has any opinion of. . . . He entreated me in the most pressing terms to write instantly to you, and wanted, if he thought it would be any weight, to write to you himself. Is it possible to contrive this ? . . . .
>
> Every hour's delay is a material injury both to the opera and the theatre so that if you can come and relieve us of this perplexity, the return of the post must only forerun your arrival; or (what will make us much happier) might it not bring *you* ?

Mrs Sheridan adds her entreaty:

> DEAREST FATHER, I shall have no spirits or hopes of the opera unless we see you.   ELIZA ANN SHERIDAN.

On the 2nd of November the petition is renewed:

> Our music is now all finished and rehearsing, but we are greatly impatient to see *you*. We hold your coming to be *necessary* beyond conception. You say you are at our service after Tuesday next; then I conjure you by that you do possess, in which I include all the powers that preside over harmony, to come next Thursday night (this day se'nnight) and we will fix a rehearsal for Friday morning. From what

I see of their rehearsing at present I am become still more anxious to see you.

It is to be presumed that Mr Linley did come, and that he was therefore in London when his first grandchild, to whom the name of Thomas was given, was born, in Orchard Street, on the 16th of November.[1]

On the 21st of the same month *The Duenna* was produced with great success. No doubt it was much assisted by the music; Linley thoroughly understood the human voice, and songs of his setting were agreeable to sing and to hear sung— which is not always the case with composers even of very great distinction.

In Sheridan's petitioning letter to his father-in-law there is a reference to Garrick, which shows that nine months before his actual retirement he was disposed to pass over to Sheridan, whenever that event should take place, the reins of management and his own moiety in the property of Drury Lane theatre. Sheridan hailed the opportunity, and offered to his wife's father the chance of sharing it. Linley, as we know, had for some years had in his mind the desirability of securing a share in one of the Patent theatres, and had also an eye to the management of the oratorios that were produced every spring at Drury Lane. Garrick's price was thirty-five thousand pounds; between them they took up four-sevenths, and the remaining three were purchased by Dr Ford. Thus Sheridan and Linley each paid or promised to pay ten thousand pounds. Linley's share, says Mr Sichel, upon the authority of a MS. *précis* in the British Museum, evidently more comprehensible to him than to me, was raised at four per cent., " by a bond to Garrick and also by

---

[1] The Tickell pedigree gives his name as " Thomas Linley," but the register at Marylebone Church has only " Thomas."

a charge on part of his Bath estates." As the scheme involved his coming to London and taking an active part in management, he would of course let his house in the Crescent, of which he was, almost certainly, the leaseholder. He possessed also his share, whatever it may have been, in Margaret Chapel in Brock Street, Bath; and at the time when he made his will, in 1788, he owned a farm and lands called Oldbury in Didmarton. How this estate came into his possession has not yet been ascertained; he may have bought it, for he had certainly saved money; or it may have come to him through his wife; or even, conceivably, from the family of his mother, but hardly from his father, who was still living in 1788. For his services at Drury Lane he was to receive five hundred pounds per annum, and to this salary his teaching and his composing made additions. Mrs Linley acted for many years as wardrobe mistress, a post in which her natural turn for economising had full play—although Mrs Siddons did have to be allowed forty yards of purple satin for her dress as Lady Macbeth, in addition to a petticoat of gold tissue.

A letter from Sheridan brings out very neatly the difference of spirit in which the two men entered upon their new venture—a difference not to be accounted for by the depression of age on Linley's part—he was after all less than twenty years the elder—but by some inherent despondency of disposition, perhaps physical in its origin. In any case it is worth noting that in the year 1776, when his prospects were at their brightest, when his handsome and brilliant children were all still living, when Sheridan's success was a delight to him, and when he himself was but forty-four years old, he was already something of a desponder. Perhaps he had worked too hard and from too early an age; perhaps the constant companionship of that voluble and often angry

woman, his devoted wife, had exhausted his nervous powers.
It is easy to see how great a comfort and support to him
must have been the buoyant hopefulness of his son-in-law.
Again and again was Sheridan the David to Linley's Saul;
and often during their partnership must the younger man have
applied to particular cases the general sermon which he now
preached:

You represent your situation of mind between hopes and
fears. I am afraid I should argue in vain (as I have often
on this point before) were I to tell you that it is always better
to encourage the former than the latter. It may be very
prudent to mix a little fear by way of alloy with a good solid
basis of hope; but you, on the contrary, always deal in
apprehension by the pound, and take confidence by the grain
and spread it as thin as leaf gold. In fact, though a metaphor
mayn't explain it, the truth is that, in all undertakings which
depend chiefly upon ourselves, the surest way is to determine
to succeed.

During the first few months in London of the young
Sheridans it was to the talents of the wife rather than to
those of the husband that they owed the possession of
fashionable friends; but after *The Rivals* and *The Duenna*
the vogue of Dick became as great as that of Eliza; and
she, who had never given him cause for that jealousy which
was aroused by the veriest trifle, began to taste the bitterness
of seeing his attentions given to others. Women of far
higher birth and standing than herself began to " run after "
the popular and witty dramatist, and he was flattered by
their adulation. Not one of them was so lovely, so gifted,
or so fundamentally sincere as she, but they were what the
tongue of their day denominated " fine ladies "; and
Sheridan, it is to be feared, much as he really loved his wife,

had a lurking notion that fine ladies were of a race superior to the daughters of musicians.

Nothing could be more truly herself than the candour with which she acknowledged the fascination of these lovely ladies, the justice with which she allowed for her husband's temptations, the profundity of her own affection and her pathetic trust in the fundamental truth of his. If ever there came a deeper estrangement, the fault—as, to do him justice, Sheridan well knew and acknowledged—was not hers.

With the taking over of the theatre shares comes a fresh epoch in the history of the family; henceforth they cease to be the Linleys of Bath; and the sister who had first taken flight was now rejoined in London by her parents, and by the sister and brother who were nearest to her in age and in affection.

CHAPTER 6. THE LINLEYS OF LONDON

MR LINLEY presently took a house in Norfolk Street, Strand, and from this time forth the headquarters of the family were in London. The Norfolk Street of those days ran down to an unembanked Thames, and up to a leisurely Strand. How comparatively peaceful was that now roaring avenue of traffic may be judged by the fact that even a good many years later—in 1806, to be precise—a careful ancestress of my own who inhabited the adjacent Surrey Street used to let her six-year-old daughter trot across, unaccompanied, to her day school in Newcastle Street. The church of St Clement Danes, which Mrs Linley no doubt attended with regularity, as we know that she afterwards attended that of St Paul, Covent Garden, was surrounded by the churchyard, which remained until some seventy years ago. Not one of the Norfolk Street houses that were standing when the Linleys lived there still exists; but some of us remember those that were last left untouched; they were of the familiar Georgian, flat-fronted pattern, with graceful Adam canopies over some of their doorsteps and beautifully framed fanlights above some of their doors. Compared with the amplitude of Bath's famous Crescent, the new abode must have been almost cramped, and even Mrs Linley can hardly have found room for lodgers. Probably there was some little expanse of garden behind, across which the southern winds blew from the river; and, quite certainly, the skies were less bedimmed with smoke and the whiteness of window curtains less

116

transient than to-day. No doubt it was entered upon, that house in Norfolk Street, with hopes and schemes in which the elder sons and daughter largely figured. Not even the temperamental pessimism of the father could foresee that in some sixteen or seventeen years' time he would quit that house, a man broken in health, in mind and in heart, having buried during his sojourn there two out of his four sons and all but one of his remaining daughters.

One result of the removal to London was the renewal of companionship between Elizabeth and Mary: a companionship that filled their letters with all those little human details of everyday life that alone make old letters good reading, and to which we are indebted for the delight of knowing that charming woman, Mary Linley, across the gap of over a century.

The first event of primary importance in the history of the new management at Drury Lane was the production, in May 1777, of *The School for Scandal*, the success of which was immediate, and which not only brought both fame and money to its author, but also brought money to the theatre. No letters about it to or from any of the Linleys seem to exist, no doubt because all who were grown up sat among the audience and made their comments by word of mouth to one another. With the acting of this admirable play Sheridan came to the highest achievement of his life, and the Linley family to the zenith of their happiness. There were as yet no gaps in the circle.

Tom Linley's work was attracting more and more attention; in 1775 a chorus of his writing, "Arise ye spirits of the storm," had been introduced into the performance of *The Tempest*; and in March 1776 Lawrence's "Ode on the Witches and Fairies of Shakespeare" was produced with Tom's music in the oratorio season—that is, during Lent. Next year, on 20th of March, his "Song of Moses" was heard at Drury Lane, and is pronounced, in an account of him in the Egerton MSS. (2492), to be one of the "finest specimens of the Simple, Affecting, Grand and Sublime styles that was ever produced by the pen of a Musician." One chorus: "All Canaan's Heathen Race," is declared equal to and almost indistinguishable from the work of Handel. Of the "Song of Moses" the British Museum possesses no score; perhaps none now exists. His glee for five voices, "Hark, the Birds melodious sing," is in the British Museum, and no doubt was sung by five Linley voices. My cousin, Miss Patten, who is, as I regret I am not, a competent judge, has kindly examined the MSS., and confirms the very high opinion expressed by his contemporaries of the younger Thomas's talent. It seems plain that by his early death English music did unquestionably lose a composer of the very highest promise.[1]

In August 1778, when he was twenty-two years old, he was on a visit to the Duke of Ancaster, at Grimsthorpe, in Lincolnshire, and on the 5th of that month was, with other young people, in a boat on a lake or canal in the grounds. The boat was overturned and Tom Linley, who was wearing the high boots of the time, was drowned, although he was said to be an expert swimmer. Some accounts say that one of his sisters was present; but I think it improbable that if this were so the fact should not be recorded more definitely

[1] Parke, who knew him, says that he was a great favourite with the public ("Musical Memoirs," vol. i., p. 7). Busby, in his "Concert Room Anecdotes" (vol. i., p. 171), has a story of "the younger Linley" at a rehearsal with Madame Catalani being so impressed by the grandeur of her voice that he forgot his part, played wrong, and, on being reproved by her, fainted and "dropped from his seat." The circumstance that Madame Catalani was born the year after Tom Linley's death may be taken to decide the anecdote's authenticity.

and unmistakably. These sisters mourned his loss and cherished his memory while they lived. Elizabeth's feelings were partially expressed in some verses, headed: " On my brother's violin."

Does it perhaps still exist, that violin? Was it among the many musical instruments of different kinds that used to hang upon the walls of Ozias Linley's room at Dulwich— and into what hands did all those instruments pass? That it was a fine violin we may be sure; neither father nor son were persons likely to be mistaken in such a choice. That none of the Linleys would have permitted its sale I am convinced; and if at some later date Ozias had given it away its history would surely have descended with it.

The second of the sons who survived childhood was Samuel, four years younger than Tom. Sam, trained like his brother and sisters to music, decided when he was some seventeen or eighteen years old that he wished to abandon his oboe and to go to sea. He became a midshipman and sailed with Captain Walsingham in the *Thunderer*. Gainsborough painted him in his blue uniform before he went away, and the portrait hangs at Dulwich. The lad is so like his sister Elizabeth that if he had acted Sebastian to her Viola the mistake of Olivia would have appeared inevitable. In the autumn or winter fever broke out on board the *Thunderer*, and Samuel Linley caught it. The ship put into Portsmouth to land the sick; his father hurried down to fetch him home; and there, in the words of Angelo, "after remaining some time in a dying state, his disconsolate parents were left to deplore his loss." Angelo, Sheridan, Tickell (probably by this time engaged to Mary Linley), Dudley Bate, and Richardson, the faithful friend of Sheridan, were the pallbearers at Samuel Linley's funeral, and his burial register, dated 6th of December 1778, may be seen at St Clement's

119

Danes Church. He was eighteen and a half years old.

A romantic incident belongs to the story of the poor boy's death. Mrs Linley had as a servant, at that time, a beautiful, illiterate young girl, called Emma Hart, who in later years was destined to be known as Lady Hamilton. She helped to nurse Samuel, and waited on him with assiduous attention; but when the end came, she could no longer endure to remain in the house. Mrs Linley told Mrs Angelo, some days afterwards, "that Emma was so attached to her son and her affliction made such an impression upon her mind that no entreaties could prevail on her to remain, not even a day." Young Angelo saw her lingering about the streets of Soho, and made an appointment to meet her, but she did not keep it; and when he next saw her she was already the mistress of Charles Greville. The death of Samuel Linley was thus the turning-point of her strange career; if he had recovered and returned to sea, Emma Hart might have remained in her respectable occupation, have made by-and-by a humdrum marriage with some man of her own rank and have lived and died unknown to history. Sam himself, however, would have lived in that case but a few months longer, since the *Thunderer*, in her next cruise, went down with all hands.

Thus the year 1778 had deprived Thomas Linley of both his elder sons; there were left only the boys: Ozias, thirteen years old, and William, nearly eight. One by one the "nest of nightingales," as Dr Burney called it,[1] was losing its tenants. To the bereaved father any chance allusion was anguish; in the "Memoirs of Mrs Crouch,"

[1] Mr Green is in error in supposing the word "nightingales" to be a modern substitute for "linnets." Dr Burney was probably sufficient of a naturalist to be aware that the vocal abilities of the linnet are strictly limited.

written by her niece, there is a striking (though singularly ungrammatical) account of his uncontrollable grief: " After the death of one of his sons, when seated at the harpsichord in Drury Lane theatre, in order to accompany the vocal parts of an interesting little piece taken from Prior's Henry and Emma by Mr Tickell and excellently represented by Mr Palmer and Miss Farren, the tutor of Henry, Mr Aickin gave an impressive description of a promising young man, in speaking affectionately of his pupil Henry; the feelings of Mr Linley could not be repressed the tears of mental agony rolled down his cheeks; nor did he weep alone, the cause of his distress was too well known not to obtain the tears of sympathy from many who beheld *his* flow so fast.— The writer of *this* was in the pit close to the orchestra and witnessed his paternal woe, and the effect which it had on those who perceived it."

The name of Richard Tickell, which has now appeared twice in connection with the history of the family, was before long to be more closely associated with it. Precisely where, how and when Mary Linley became attached to him cannot now be determined; but, since his family appears to have resided for a time in Bath, it was probably there that the Linleys and Sheridan made his acquaintance. It is clear that his earlier ancestors belonged to Cumberland, where the family property, Thornthwaite, is still in the possession of a Tickell; and Mr Sichel says that the father of Richard died at that place in May 1771, but a pedigree that has been kindly lent me gives a different account. According to this, Richard was a grandson of Addison's friend, Thomas Tickell, and of his wife, Clotilda, a co-heiress of the great Eustace family who claimed descent from Eustace Plantagenet, brother of Henry II. If this pedigree be right, his father was the eldest son, John, to whose unsatisfactory and

unsettled disposition it must be confessed that that of Richard
showed some resemblance. This John died at Aix-le-
Chapelle in 1782, and to him are attributed three sons, of
whom Richard is the second, and two daughters. That
Richard Tickell had at least two sisters and one brother is
certain. To a brother called John, the Dean of Norwich
is said by Mrs Tickell to have given a living in Norfolk ;
and the few facts recorded of the beneficiary suggest that the
transaction was less advantageous to the parishioners than
to the Rev. John Ambrose Tickell. The owner of a certain
quack medicine called the Ethereal Anodyne Spirit (or
Elixir), who also lived in Bath, is often confused with
Richard, and may possibly have been a relative. His
Christian name was William; he was a surgeon, and lived
in Queen's Square.

If Richard Tickell was indeed the son of John, son of
Thomas and Clotilda, he must have had the misfortune of
missing any settled family life in his youth; and the habits
of his maturity are such as might have been fostered by such
a lack. His conduct was irregular and spasmodic, and his
talents, which somewhat resembled those of Sheridan, were
on a smaller scale. Unlike Sheridan, he was coarse in his
witticisms, and his passion for practical jokes made him
sometimes unfeeling. He was certainly the father of an
illegitimate boy (whom he cared for very properly), and
perhaps also of a girl, since it is constantly stated that the
mother of John Arthur Roebuck was his daughter, and it
is beyond question that no daughter of either of his wives
was Roebuck's mother. Though he often irritated her,[1]
Mary Tickell was warmly attached to her husband, while
he—as long as she lived—loved her genuinely enough.

---

[1] " T——, who is of all God's creatures the most provoking,"
she remarks parenthetically in a letter to her sister.

When she died, indeed, he believed himself inconsolable, and desired to inscribe on her tombstone the impossibility of his marrying again. From this intention he was judiciously dissuaded, and within two years he eloped with a flighty and beautiful girl of eighteen, his marriage with whom seems to have been unsatisfactory to both parties.

Probably, however, his unstable temperament was steadied by the influence of his wife, who, if at times she found her marriage disillusioning, kept her disappointments to herself. She was the last woman in the world to demand too much of her neighbours; moreover, to have gone about proclaiming dissatisfaction with the husband who was certainly of her own choosing would have been to present a figure ridiculous in her own eyes. Her short life, marred as it was by much ill-health, was assuredly one on the whole of much enjoyment; her circumstances might be narrow, but her heart was wide, and she rejoiced more in the prosperity of her sister and her sister's husband than she would have done in her own. She was devoted to her three babies, and was the best though by no means the blindest of daughters and sisters. The passage of years had drawn her closer to her father, and through all her letters runs the undertone of her constant preoccupation with his happiness. For her mother she had, I fear, not very much love, and less esteem; there were, indeed, qualities in the mother that both exasperated and—even worse, perhaps—bored the daughter. Yet there were points about Mrs Linley by no means despicable, one of which was the firmness of the bond between her and her husband. "Baucis and Philəmon," "Phillis and Corydon," their slightly irreverent daughter calls them; and behind the nicknames we perceive the inseparability of the older pair. That, considering their respective tempers, Thomas Linley and his wife must sometimes have quarrelled, even in these days, is certain, but in Mrs Tickell's picture of them but little dissension appears.

The Tickell marriage did not take place until July 1780, by which time the bridegroom's operetta, *The Camp*, had been acted at Drury Lane, and various verses, of which the best known is the political forecast, "Anticipation," had appeared. The first year of married life was spent at Wells; in the second, Tickell was appointed to a Commissionership of Stamps, and then, or not long afterwards, rooms at Hampton Court were allotted to him. Such rooms were, at this time, given in very odd ways, and sometimes without any royal sanction; but we have no reason for supposing that the grant to Tickell was in any respect irregular. Hampton Court being in those pre-railway days more distant from town than now, Mr and Mrs Tickell had also an abode in London, at one time in Brook Street, at another in Queen Anne Street. It is likely that while she lived with her parents Mary had given assistance in various ways to the manifold activities of the theatre, which now formed so large a part of the family's business, and with which her letters are so much occupied. Tickell, who had a valuable talent for newspaper puffery, acted as a kind of amateur Press agent.

The history of the younger Linleys during the first five or six years after the family removal remains obscure. Maria, in the former year, would be thirteen, and presumably already singing in public. Her voice was considered to be almost, if not quite, equal to that of her eldest sister; and the coloured print in the British Museum, from a portrait by Westall, of which no other record has come to light, confirms the opinion of her contemporaries who called her beautiful. The face is most attractive, full of intelligence, character and spirit, but without that tragic quality that belongs to Elizabeth's and to Samuel's. At Dulwich there is a little

124

portrait, attributed to Lawrence, and catalogued as that of Mrs Tickell. Careful comparison, however, with the portraits of both sisters, shows this to be Maria's, and a letter from William, quoted in the gallery catalogue of 1880, states plainly that it represents " Miss Maria Linley." Some later cataloguist clearly supposed Mrs Tickell and Maria to be the same person. The hair and eyes are dark, but the complexion fair, the dress white, with a rather eccentric arrangement of bright blue ribbons, and the figure that of a slim, apparently rather tall girl. At the same place and by the same artist are portraits of the two younger boys, that of Ozias being evidently the earlier in date. The curly locks of that pretty boy are brown, and brown too are his bright eyes; the face is animated, and just a little whimsical —and whimsical Ozias remained to the end. William, who in his picture is some twelve or thirteen years old, is the darkest in complexion of them all, and is a remarkably handsome lad, but neither so interesting-looking nor so distinguished as Tom and Sam; it is true that he had not the good luck to be painted by Gainsborough.

William, when his parents quitted Bath, was but six years old, and apparently they left him behind, in the charge of Mr and Mrs John Symmons, the latter of whom his sister Jane describes as having been almost a mother to him. In 1785 he became a pupil at St Paul's school, and either there or elsewhere he acquired an excellent education. Ozias would seem to have lived with his grandparents until he went to college. Jane also lived until she was thirteen away from London, and in some country town—not apparently Bath. She was not at boarding-school, but resided with a grandmother and aunt; and since Mr and Mrs William Linley lived, we know, in Belmont, Bath, this grandmother must have been the mother of Mrs Linley.

The town may very probably have been Wells, of which place Kelly declares Mrs Linley to have been a native. The history of Jane's twin sister Charlotte is uncertain. From 1784 or so onward Jane was generally with either the one or the other of her married sisters, by whose superior talents, she says, she was so much overawed that she became permanently diffident and rather silent. She sang, evidently, very well, her voice resembling Elizabeth's and blending admirably with it.

By the time of Mary's marriage Sheridan was not only the most successful of living dramatists, and a full-blown man of fashion, but also a politician. Unlike most men who when they rise from poverty after marriage find themselves hampered by unpresentable wives, he had the good fortune of having won, while he was yet obscure, a wife whom "the great" already idolised. In various leading Whig houses she was a welcome guest, and might enjoy for as many weeks as she chose the pleasure of losing money at cards to some of the most admired and popular of her contemporaries. The friend of her heart, however, the woman whom next to her sister Mary she loved best in the world, was one who cared little either for fashion or for cards, Mrs Stratford Canning, by birth Mehetabel Patrick. Mrs Canning, whom, following their habit of nickname, the sisters called "Sister Christian," was a deeply religious woman, as good as she was delightful, and her quiet but strong influence must have been a kind of anchor to Elizabeth Sheridan amid the levity and moral irresponsibility of the world in which she now lived. On her part Elizabeth was the steadying influence in Sheridan's existence. To her his political associates and his theatrical subordinates alike appealed, whenever absolute necessity arose for the immediate doing of something which he was likely to procrastinate. She kept the accounts of the theatre—they are still preserved in her handwriting; she and her sister read the plays that were offered, and passed on to Sheridan only those that were really worth his consideration; she wrote out his notes and speeches; she was ready at need to adapt songs; her voice was always for retrenchment and a simple life. With all their brilliancy her married years must have been years of the experience of Sisyphus, so greatly did the task to be achieved always exceed the achievement. The root of the evil was of course that Sheridan undertook work and responsibilities beyond the limits of human power. He was a circus-rider attempting to stand on three horses at once. To be the successful autocrat of a great theatre demands nearly the whole working time of a methodical and experienced man; to be a successful Member of Parliament, without private means, difficult enough in our day, was even more difficult in his; while to play the man of fashion, sharing the diversions and the irregular hours of a rich idle coterie, was to cut himself off wilfully from the possibility of fulfilling properly the business upon which he depended for his livelihood.

That Sheridan should have dreamed of succeeding in an enterprise so impossible can be attributed only to the fatal desultoriness of his after-school education. Having no experience of regular work, he had never learned, among other things, the limits of what even regular work can do; he lived, mentally, from hand to mouth, and was always expecting some miracle to ensue from a sudden burst of industry. Once, for a couple of years, his feet were upon the right track, and of those years the two comedies that still survive are the milestones: it is too much the custom to write as though in them the whole harvest of Sheridan's literary talent had been gathered—at seven and twenty!

My own belief is that these plays were but the first-fruits of a genius the maturity of which might have been very great indeed. True, feeling does not run very deep in them—nor did it, we may remember, in the youthful plays of Shakespeare —but even in feeling the work of this young man was far more alive and human than that of his predecessors on our stage. Except those of Addison (whose comedy failed) and Steele (whose comedies furnish good reading still in spite of their *longueurs*), the famous English dramas of humour before Goldsmith are unfeeling in quite an incredible degree; they lack not merely ordinary human kindliness, but even such kindliness as we daily see cats and dogs render to one another. Compared with the comedy personages of the preceding century Lady Teazle and Sir Peter are models of good feeling, good manners, and above all of decent speech. When we consider the frittered life of Sheridan, the saddest reflection is not that the opportunity of being great in politics never came to him, but that in pursuing that opportunity he threw away a greater one. It is for the plays that might and, I believe, would have been written between 1778 and 1798 that I lament. By 1798 it was too late: the man who could write *Pizarro* had retained nothing of his early promise but his incomparable stage-instinct.

Other and even greater things were sacrificed in his wild effort to live three men's lives at once. There was certainly an interval during which the patience and devotion of his wife were worn out; and no doubt her physical strength was worn out too. Delicate she had always been, but a quieter and more regular life—the peaceful country life for which she was always craving—might have prolonged her existence by another ten, if not, indeed, another twenty years. It would in any case have made her a happier woman, and have spared her husband many an hour of bitter remorse.

128

Let us remember, however, that he might have had every
one of those solid virtues that distinguish the hundreds of
prosperous gentlemen who stream from the suburbs into the
city every weekday morning, and yet have made his wife less
happy than on the whole she was. For that which saps the
happiness and alienates the affection of a wife is far less the
occasional grave fault or even the serious habitual failing
than the absence of daily kindnesses and courtesies, the habit
of daily disrespect; and these were not lapses to which
Sheridan's temperament was prone. I do not believe that he
ever caused Elizabeth to feel—as many wives of better men
habitually do—relieved by his absences and chilled by his
returns.[1]

Although both sisters were now residents in London,
Mrs Sheridan was often away on long visits, and Mrs Tickell
occasionally on jaunts with her husband; and when they
were apart they exercised freely that admirable talent for
letter-writing which was one among the many gifts of their
race. Both of them also wrote pretty frequently to Mrs
Stratford Canning, and she, like the sensible and discerning
woman that she was, carefully preserved their letters. Thus
for a certain number of years we are able to follow in their
own words—so much more vital than those of any later
comer—the course of the family's life for weeks, sometimes
for months, at a time. The dating of these letters is sadly
inadequate; but, judging from the allusions that occur in
them, those of which portions follow were written by Mrs
Tickell from some time in 1783 onwards. By that year she
was the mother of two children, Elizabeth Ann, born
probably in the end of April 1781, and Richard, a year or

---

[1] In a letter to her elder sister-in-law Mrs Sheridan writes : " So
Mrs —— is not happy. Poor thing ! I daresay if the truth were
known he teazes her to death. Your *very good* husbands generally
contrive to make you sensible of their merits somehow or other."

more younger. The precise sequence of the letters is difficult
to fix. There are, however, occasional pegs—the production
of this or that play, the birth of Mrs Siddons' baby, remarks
upon this or that political proposal, by which the approximate
date of one or another letter can be decided. Those which
immediately follow belong probably to the winter of 1783–
1784:

I have not yet seen S. but he sent me to-day a Pidgeon
Pye and a Sucking Pig and promised to call to-night if he
could. He will come at a most curious time for my dear
Betsey is to be inoculated to-night at nine o'clock by which
time we hope Bess will be asleep and so know nothing of the
operation which Mr Pratten says will be so trifling that
perhaps he may not wake her. They are to go to my
Mother's next Wednesday and when they are well enough
recover'd I shall send them to Hampton Court for a fortnight. I hope you approve of all my proceedings about
them and will join your prayers to mine for their recovery.

Ozy [Ozias] went with T—— on Friday [to the House
of Commons] but had not Courage to stay till five in the
morning without Dinner, so got away about six, he heard
a very fine speech from Sir Charles Fox, he said the Editors
seemed very busy taking it down in short hand round the
Table—so I found that some of [   ] members who were
taking notes he took for Editors—he is with me at present
as the children are in the Street [*i.e.* Norfolk Street].

Ozy is, at present writing, reading Ferguson's Optics at
the same Table with me, he is with me instead of the Young
Ladies, Maria rather choosing to take a Bed at her Friend
Miss Troward's—and tho' I am much better pleas'd with
my present Guest I was very hurt at her Behaviour—however it's all over for I did not intend mentioning it to you
only you asked me about them. She wrote me an assuaging
fine letter and we are at present very good Friends, for I
think she is quite old enough to judge of Proprieties for

130

herself even if I thought she would be guided by me—but
we all know how much " She is herself the Guardian of her
Honor."—We are all sitting for our *Shades* to a young man
that Birch recommends—I have sat for mine and it will be
very like tho' incomprehensibly ugly. I don't say this to
draw a Compliment from you, for I assure you I am not
blind to the *Charms* of my Front but Jane and I don't happen
to think so well of your *Profiles*—T—— has sat for his,
and we are to have the Philosopher's [Ozias is the philosopher]
I shall have Tom's and yours the instant you come home and
so put them all in a string (?) and put Bess and Dick in the
middle if we can contrive to make them sit.

For some ten days after the inoculation, not only the
mother and grandmother in London, but also the aunt, in
the country, suffered continual anxiety about the little
patients. From the fact that it was considered safe for them
to be with their grandparents, but not with their mother, it
may be inferred that Mr and Mrs Linley had had the
small-pox, but that Mrs Tickell had escaped that scourge of
our ancestors. The operation was successful, but the moral
effects of Betty's visit in Norfolk Street were less satisfactory
The little creature appeared at breakfast " with Grandmama's watch at her side " and nobody was permitted to
contradict her:

I'm told she is now compleatly spoil'd between Nurse and
Grandmama. She is no Favourite of her Aunt Maria's, nor
indeed will be of anybody's if she is suffered to grow up so
headstrong—we are to turn over quite a new Leaf when she
comes home.

Maria herself was by no means free from the failing which
she reprobated in baby nieces; indeed, it may be said of nearly
all the Linleys—as of most really able people—that they
liked and took their own way. Even Mrs Sheridan, whom

every contemporary describes as "gentle" and "angelic," could write to her husband: "You know me well enough to be sure that I never do what I am bid, Sir."

My Shade is come home, but oh *che figura* and as to T——'s it's as like Hare as anything you ever saw. . . . Maria still sleeps with Miss Troward tho' the Room that T—— and I used to sleep in is now meant for Her. I ventur'd to expostulate with her yesterday but She answer'd very violently "I don't chuse to sleep in the Garret, Mrs Tickell," and I was silenc'd at once. Ozias is on the verge of going to Bath and regrets very much that he has only seen you twice since he has been here, however we have all agreed that he shall come up every holydays to get a polish and to be at my house—he has never written a line to Belmont since he left it at which Grandfather is very wrath, and has more than once hinted in his letters to my Father that he might stay where he is. I believe Ozias would desire nothing better for he says they grudge him every meal he eats—he has no place to sit in but the Kitchen and breakfasts on 6/ Bohea[1] with coarse moist sugar, notwithstanding my Grandfather is paid very handsomely for his Board—but the Spirit of the Linleys is rouz'd in Ozias and he threatens great Revolutions in their domestic Concerns.

We din'd yesterday at my Mother's and had both the Children as all fear of infection was quite over, they are both thin and delicate, otherwise quite well. . . . Maria din'd with us yesterday but afterwards went to Mrs Freeman's, I know nothing at all of her *System*. She sleeps in with Miss Troward still, and I believe my Father does not know it—so don't take any notice of it when you come, for it would only teaze him and be of no use.

---

[1] In the latter part of the eighteenth century, six shillings was a low price for a pound of tea. As lately as about sixty years ago ordinary household tea cost five shillings per pound, and all considerate people saved and dried the tea leaves for some poor woman who could never afford to buy tea.

Yesterday evening at half-past eight the accomplish'd Miss Linley[1] set off for the Metropolis or in other words (that you may not think Maria has elop'd with the well-timber'd Troward) Betty embark'd on board the Sheffield fly with a lyght heart and a heavy Purse—for S—— din'd with us and very contrary to my inclination would give her two Guineas—I was very angry—because I had before given her half a Guinea over her wages and two Guineas for her Passage which had left me pennyless, and then it *did* vex me to think he should give *two*. . . . However she is off with a great deal of good advice which I bestowed very plentifully upon her. She left a great many *Duties* to you—Poor Girl I wish her Success with all my Heart, but I'm afraid she is too pretty, too foolish and too lazy to be made an honest woman of soon—To my great astonishment when I called [her] to give her my last farewell Lecture She approach'd me with powder'd Hair, two large Curls, and a fly Cap so I took the liberty to expostulate a little and I believe the Curls were taken down before she set out.

There were sometimes gay doings in the neighbourhood of Hampton Court, and various letters speak of balls that were to take place. A certain Miss Boss, who had " self-invited " herself to stay with Mrs Tickell, and who seems to have held some sort of Court appointment, intended to be very fine on some such occasion, " and has actually dispatch'd a messenger for Mrs Snow and her rose-coloured Tabby that she may strike all beholders at once." A " tabby," it should perhaps be explained, is a waved, or as it is now called a " watered," silk; Queen Charlotte once presented to

[1] This young woman, who had for some time been one of Mrs Tickell's maids, was probably a distant relative, since she came from the same district as William Linley. She may conceivably be the original of that portrait in the Glasgow Municipal Gallery which bears the name of Miss E. Linley, and which certainly does *not* represent Mrs Sheridan or any of her sisters.

Miss Burney a dress of "lilac tabby." On the morning
before the dance, Mrs Tickell wrote, how "the Herberts
and North and Townshend came" and "we got through
an evening of Miss Boss very well which was some comfort."

The men stayed last night or rather this morning till four
or five tho' I entreated T———. to think of to-night's fatigue
for me and let them go, but 'twas all in vain, for the moment
my back was turn'd off they march'd into the other room
with their Bottles and Glasses and order'd Stephen to bring
the fire after them—so at least they had the grace to think
of not disturbing me, for you are to know since the cold
wether we dine and sup in the Drawing Room. However
unfortunately my ears were quick enough to reach to
Stephen's Pantry where I heard every cruel Pop of that
odious five shilling claret which entirely hindered my closing
my eyes, so here I am at half past one just after breakfast
and thinking of my evening's dissipation. Don't you think
that I should cut a figure in the great world?

．　　．　　．　　．　　．　　．　　．

But now for our ball which to be sure you must be quite
dying to hear about. The Cannings came according to
promise and Miss Boss's red Tabby struck upon us about
four, for she din'd with us with a Spanish hat and feathers,
faux Diamans—in short everything that could dazzle and
surprise. We all arrived at the Toy about half past seven.
All the Waiters ranged in the Passage to receive us and the
Staircase hung with blankets to keep us warm, but I will not
say a word to ridicule our Ball, for I assure you it was a very
good one and the Drawing Room a very spacious one and
well lighted—and what *if* it was over the Stables, we were
not the worse for that. . . . Mrs Canning and I of course
were not dancing so we retired to the card room with Mrs
Storer and played some whist, I was indeed to have play'd
vingt-e-un with Miss Boss, to whom I was Chapron for the

night, but the *giddy thing* gave me the Slip and upon being unexpectedly asked to dance with Captain Bowater was at the top of the room in a minute tucking up her Tabby—so we Matrons retir'd to our whist. As for T——, he danced the whole night—the redoubtable Mrs Arabin was as handsome as ever yet I did not feel at all uneasy about her tho' like a good wife I staid most of the evening in the other rooms—but then I knew I had a precious little spy in Jane and that I should have a true and particular account of all their flirtations—however I have heard nothing that gives me the least alarm, so at present I can think of her great black eyes and broad brows with tolerable patience. After our whist we return'd to look for our *Girls,* for Miss Jeffries was likewise under our care, and when we had *caught* them we all went to vingt un with Lady C. Herbert and two or three others. Here we staid till supper was ready, for as it was all agreed that we were to be monstrously *lively* and *agreeable then,* Miss Jeffries had brib'd the Waiter to give due notice that we might be the first at the door. Our Vingt e un was well enough. I won four fish, which Miss Jeffries *owes* me, so you may congratulate me on my Turn of Fortune. We all play'd in pretty good humour till unfortunately there was a Pool made for Vingt e un which when it came to near three guineas and all our hearts beat high with hopes of Sweep, Miss Boss laid down *her* abominable Red Fan with " Vingt e un, I protetht, so give me my winnings." I wish you could have seen Bet's[1] Face, 'twas quite Purple with Spight—in short up she flounc'd and refus'd playing any more . . . we return'd to the Dancing Room to partake of a great treat indeed this was no less a sight than Miss Boss's agility which she exerted to Mr Storer —oh, how I wish'd for you. She was so herself in every motion and when she gave hands, oh! 'twas such a Pane-Tidde—'tis impossible for any Description to do justice to the swimming and sinking of this tender Virgin. . . .

[1] Miss Jeffries.

Yesterday we passed a very quiet comfortable Day by our own fireside with Books, Work, the Children &c—all as it should be. This Day is not fated to turn out so pleasant, for Storer is just gone and made us promise to go there in the Evening to meet Miss Jeffries who always invites herself. It's very odd People won't let one enjoy the Comforts of one's own Fireside in Peace. I know it will end in our losing our money and passing a most unpleasant Evening. . . . Adieu I must put on my Cap for these boring People. I am as cross as two sticks to be so thwarted. Good-bye— Wish us success from these Harpies, but I know we shall be pick'd to the bone.

And picked to the bone she accordingly was, as she duly reported a few days later. Nor even Mrs Linley, an inveterate player of cribbage and whist, was a match for those expert practitioners of Hampton Court whom Mrs Tickell designates collectively "the Tabbies." Mrs Sheridan to some extent partook her mother's taste, but neither Mrs Tickell nor—except for a very short time—Jane cared for cards: and during the visits of their insatiable parent the evenings were to their minds spoiled. Mrs Tickell's boredom cries out on one occasion:

For my part I am doing penance for all my sins, I believe, or shall before my Mother goes. Think of her nailing me down to two-handed Loo last night at a halfpenny a Fish till my Faculties are all numb'd or *doos'd* as she says. . . . She is worse than ever I think. No intermission from 5 o'clock until near eleven, think o' that by way of passing one's evening in a pleasant domestic way.

On Friday Mrs Linley went; Mrs Tickell in reporting her departure declared that, "tho' as good as a daughter ought to be," she shall find herself glad of some breathing space; and by the next day had leisure enough to remark that: "Jane and I are as fix'd here as any two evergreens in the Gardens."

Here is a pleasanter aspect of Mrs Linley:

My Mother made me laugh by describing how Reid took my Father in on his return from Salt Hill, with a long face he began making Apologies for S—— that he had not sent what he promis'd him but really he had not been at all well since he left Town, but that he (my Father) might depend upon having it from him very soon and receiving it all Compleat. "Ah I thought so," (says my Father). "Well then, there's an end. I never indeed thought it would come to anything, but it's something vexatious after all our trouble." "My dear Sir" (says Reid) "I daresay you'll have it sooner than you expect——." "Pooh," (says my Father) "I give it up, I *give* it *up entirely*." Here Reid very judiciously drew the precious manuscript from his pocket with a letter and my Mother says it would have rewarded S——. for all his Pains about it to have seen the Brightness of my Father's Countenance at that moment.

The little narrative, showing, as it does, Mrs Linley in her lighter mood and perfectly able to appreciate Reid's joke upon her husband, gives us the happy assurance that the mother had something of the daughter's sprightliness and that at least a comprehending glance could pass between them at moments of diversion.

The next extract comes from a time when the Tickells were in Queen Anne Street, and belongs, I believe, to the spring of 1784. Evidently Tickell, if provoking, could also be conciliatory; probably he had learnt that "the spirit of the Linleys" was dangerous only when opposed. She was "afraid T—— and I should have quarrelled about Lawrence" who had taken "possession of the room I was sitting in at 10 o'clock," had "din'd with us of course," and remained with Tickell when she and the Storers went to the theatre, whither Tickell promised to follow her but never came.

So when I came home after eleven half angry with him for not coming—to my utter horror and astonishment there was *Snaggs* stretch'd before the fire repeating his horid Verses in a Voice scarcely Human. Temper I own quite left me. All the Mother rose indignantly in my soul—I was sure I should be too rude and retir'd to my own room for the night. However I soon heard my gentleman decamp and T—— came up and we had a pretty warm Debate tho' he was very good natur'd and forgave me all my impertinence—but do tell me do you think it was in mortal patience to bear with that odious wretch *twelve hours round* who if he had been encourag'd I am convinc'd he would have stay'd.

The " odious wretch " is not Sir Thomas Lawrence, with whom also the Linleys were well acquainted. This bearer of the name was a Member of Parliament and writer of clever political verses, who belonged to the Sheridan-Tickell-Richardson-Reid group of able and unmethodical men. Upon the origin of the nickname " Snaggs " I can throw no light, but its intention was not probably a complimentary one.

Whether Maria Linley consented to return to the house of her unsuspecting father does not appear; but her mocking sister presently reports having seen her at the play:

in an old black bonnet and her own common Cloaths and a Man's Great Coat over all. This is quite a new Stile. I suppose she thinks her natural Charms shone through the Surtout.

The poor pretty young creature never had time to out-grow these little eccentricities. She was taken ill at her

grandmother's house in Bath of what is described in one
account as brain fever and in another as " an inflammatory
fever " and died in a few days.   In her delirium shortly
before her death she sat up in her bed and sang: " I know
that my Redeemer liveth " with all the beauty of voice and
of expression that marked her singing when in full health.
Her brother William, who was probably in the house,
testified to this fact.   She died on the 5th September 1784,
when she must have been almost exactly twenty-one.   " Her
death," said a writer in *The Gentleman's Magazine*, " is a
loss almost irreparable to the musical world. . . . The
union of a sweet voice, correct judgment, extensive compass
and above all beauty of mind and person distinguished the
much lamented maid."   She was buried in the churchyard
of Walcot, Bath.   *The Bath Chronicle* printed two sets of
verses about her, the earlier and shorter of which I suspect
to have been written by William Linley, who, although he
was not yet fourteen, was already poetising.   " Beauty,
innocence and wit " are attributed to her—and the last
quality looks more like real knowledge than conventional
compliment.   Another effusion, published in *The Cabinet*,
and reprinted by Mr Green, was written by Charles Leftley,
whose sonnets and odes were published (posthumously) in
the same volume with William's.   He too was doubtless
acquainted with Maria, but his description has no individuality.   She is:

> Sweet as opening buds,
>   Mild as the hours of May,
> Bright as the sunbeams on the floods
>   And constant as the day

—lines which may be accepted as an assurance that, like all
the rest of the family, Maria was exceedingly attractive.
   No account of her death occurs in the letters; probably

the sisters were together in London at the time. Somewhat later, however, Mrs Tickell acknowledges some verses sent by her sister which have, she says, brought tears into her eyes. They seem to have been an epitaph, and were perhaps inscribed upon Maria's tombstone, about which some particulars are given. No tombstone now exists, nor can the place of her grave, in which her grandfather and grandmother were subsequently buried, be identified.

By the death of Maria, Thomas Linley lost the last of his children who was pursuing his own profession, and his grief was bitter. Mrs Crouch has recorded how when she sang with him songs that his daughter had been accustomed to sing "his tears continually fell on the keys as he accompanied her." No doubt his "glooms" were deepened and the constant care of his elder daughters more necessary than ever. We may be sure it never failed him.

The next letters belong, I believe, to the autumn and winter of 1784. The first of them dated "Norfolk Street Sunday morning, 10 o'clock" is a little perplexing. Tickell's appointment (as a Commissioner of Stamps) is described as having been made in 1781; yet here, on some Sunday in 1784 (or at the very earliest, 1783), are he and his colleague Fawkener, fulfilling a necessary preliminary to holding that appointment:

You'll be surprised to find us here so much sooner than I expected and at so very early an hour—but so it is that we were obliged to rouze ourselves with the Sun this morning and to set off from Hampton Court by seven—at least we were up at that hour and actually off before eight. To explain this sudden manœuvre you ought to know that I received an express from Mr Fawkener yesterday to say it was absolutely necessary they should qualify themselves for holding their places to-day, and part of this Ceremony consists in their receiving the Sacrament which they are now at St Martin's for the purpose of doing. T—— was just in time for Crawford's coach which stood at the door as we came along the top of Essex Street so they are gone, I'm afraid ill-prepar'd for so solemn a business. You know what a (——?) I am about these matters and (I) did not fail (   ) giving T—— a long Lecture on the Subject all the way in the Chaise, till he said if I frighten'd him so much he would not go at all. We shall be here some days till my Baggage Cart comes to Town and all my matters are comfortable at Home. I was afraid we should have incommoded S——., who I took it for granted slept here, but I find my Gentleman prefers a bed at the Hummums, I take it for granted I am making no mischief in mentioning this; as you know he always tells me everything himself. Here is no sign of the Lady of the House, tho' it is now eleven. . . . I have been peeping into the accounts[1] by way of amusing myself—bad, bad, very bad indeed. If I can get to speak to S—— I shall use my influence to persuade him not to be too cruel—but I suppose we shall see little of him. Charlotte and Amoret, Amoret and Charlotte,[2] hey? But Lord, Lord, what Treason am I scribbling. You must burn this directly for fear—I know for once he won't read it or I should not be so daring—however joking apart I daresay he has honour enough to be very particularly prudent in your absence. I hear my Mother's voice so I must bid you Adieu for the present.

Monday Morning. Well, Ma'am I've seen the Man of Men. He is just gone and left me, a Trump. He promises to see me every day and give me an account of himself for I told him I should report him accordingly to you. I laugh'd at him a good deal about his Hummums—indeed, we had a few jokes. I said how comfortably I could now write all my secrets without the fear of his seeing them—but I must tell you what I believe his Chief Business here was—truly, to

[1] Of the theatre.
[2] " Amoret " is Mrs Crewe, " Charlotte " probably Mrs Love.

get my Mother's box for Mrs Crewe—who he said stayed in town on purpose for the play, and could not get a side box, so I suppose they will be very snug. . . . I don't know whether I shan't peep in upon them about the third Act. However I made no jokes about this, because I was afraid he might suspect you of having betrayed him.

He (*i.e.* Tickell) found my Mother in the most violent agitation in the World. "Oh! Tickell, I am fretted to death. Those Devils, but it is all Mr King's fault." "Why what's the matter, Ma'am." "Matter! Why, do you know they have hir'd a whole regiment of Guards amost for Arthur and for what? as I said, for you know there's a plenty of common men in our house" (that is, in the theatre) "that always come on as Sailors and why should they not make as good *soldiers*. What, because forsooth they can't march in Time, Ma'am, but my husband is such a fool."

I am not in the best Spirits to-day—My dear little brat looks pale and thin. I have allways fancied her exactly like poor little Charlotte who if you remember was all Spirits and animation without strength of frame to support it. . . . Please God I have a good getting up as the old women say will take a trip to the Sea for she is dearer to me than ever her little darling prattle is the prettiest thing in the World and indeed she is my Doating Piece. . . . I assure you the Family Wit begins to appear. She makes paragraphs in the papers about Mr Luard and the *Bloos* and rhymes at a great rate. . . . My poor dear Father I quite suffer for him and the only hope I have of seeing him at all cheerful is the success of the farce. T—— and he have both promis'd to write a great deal about it and T—— is to be at the Rehearsal to-morrow. You would think with all these disappointments we had reach'd the ground of my Father's Glooms. But no—a much more dreadful cause remain'd behind, and he might have well cry'd out with Laertes The King, the King, the King. The King (I wish his great wooden head was stuck on Temple Bar) goes to-morrow night *again* to Covent Garden—he told us so himself at last in thoro' vexation of Spirit. My Mother had kept up pretty well till this last Stroke of Fate, and then "indeed she could not blame Mr Linley, what *could* be the reason. She would have an *audience of the King* and ask the *Cause.*" So they went on groaning and scolding to the very great Disquiet of my Spirits. I beg'd a candle and have written this to you since, but I hear a knocking at the Door which I hope will relieve us all—The knock was Tickell who is gone out again with Richardson. My Father brighten'd up with their coming and seem'd quite reviv'd by the prospect of a little Society. We have tried to account for the King going to Covent Garden as well as we can and have persuaded him we shall certainly have him twice at Drury Lane in return. So now he is gone to teach Miss Phillips and I hope he will return in tolerable Spirits. I must go to my evening task of Cribbage for my Mother would not go to the House and dreads opening the accounts. I shall go to bed o'er early to rest my poor bones which at present ache very much.

The family are down as you foretold on Tuesday morning and by the Provision of Music Paper my Father has in his Bundle, he does not seem to have any *distant* idea of removal. . . . We had prepared King William's Bed for them and T—— was very Comical in the morning in his enquiries. They dine at Mr King's to-day and I trust will stay too late to make our usual Party of Whist necessary, for it is impossible to tell you how bad it is—and I believe poor Jen had rather go through any operation than be Father's Partner which she generally is and her stupidity which to be sure is astonishing makes a fine Subject for his Passion to work upon.

As for Jane she is growing quite a Card Player and takes her place at the Commerce Table with as much *sang froid* as any Lady—as there are a good many young people here they generally make a low Table—tho' even then it is very

143

much against my inclination that she plays so often. However, we have now fixed her an Establishment as my Father doesn't allow her a farthing for Pocket Money . . . we advance her a shilling a week for her Pin Money with which she is highly delighted. It is really a great shame in my Mother not to send her *Things* when they cost her nothing. I'd venture to lay any wager, she means to cribbage some of poor Maria's things for herself, but I shall make (a) great *noise* if I find that to be the case when we go to town.

My Mother and I have had a warm debate about Jane. You know this is the eighth Sunday of our first mourning, and I am really worn to a rag in my old Bumbazeen. Yet, because hers is tolerably good she discover'd that I was very unfeeling and not like a sister to wish to wear deep mourning less than three months and I gave her a very good Lecture loud enough for my Father who was standing at the window to hear, for the affectation of such a reason, quite put me out of patience. So now we are to have the black Silk directly that it may be got ready for a Subscription Ball which I told you was to be at the Coffee House to-morrow Sen'night.

As to my Lady Georgina's[1] embroider'd shoes I don't mind them—My Bet has a remarkable pretty Foot very like her Mother's.

My forte was never Letter writing, that is, I mean making something clever out of nothing and my Events here are few indeed.

Just as I had sent Bill [her brother William] in the Study for the sixth volume of Shakespeare in came T—— with the Sieur Reid and Henry the Sixth was laid on the Shelf once more. I was made very happy by having a very favourable account of my Father. T—— says he sup'd in Norfolk Street Friday night, having previously dispatch'd a Brace of Partridges to prepare his way and took Richardson

[1] The Duchess of Devonshire's little daughter. Mrs Sheridan was staying at Chatsworth.

and Reid with him by way of helping off the Evening—but
Ma'am when they came instead of finding my Father and
Mother as usual at opposite Sides of the Fire, groaning
against one another, the first thing they heard as soon as the
Street Door was open'd was a Roar of Laughter from below
and on entering the Parlour they found a very jolly Party
at Supper, consisting of Mr Cobb and his brother, Mr Shaw
and my Father in very good Spirits and my Mother quite
gay—in short T—— says he never saw my Father in better
Spirits, or ever pass'd a merrier evening. . . . Mrs Leigh
has sent a set of Dissected Maps and I find great Amusement
in tracing you on your Northern Tour—I suppose you'll see
Liverpool and as it is a Seaport which I did not know till now
will probably get a dip.

So Ma'am T——, Jane and I arrived at Mrs March's
about four, and I walked directly up to the School—I was
afraid at first the little Fry were *all out* as I walk'd quite thro'
the House without seeing a single Boy—however, in the
Garden there was such a Swarm and *such* a noise (as they
were all at Play) that it was some time before I could make
Enquiries for my worthy Nephew, but I believe I was taken
for *you*, for in an instant all their little Voices set up at once
a Hollow for "Sheridan! Sheridan!" Tom was at the
other end of the Garden but the Moment he heard himself
call'd, came running to me like a little Lapwing—the
picture of (I may say) *beautiful Health* for I never saw him
look so well—it is the greatest Satisfaction to me, my dear
Betsy, to be able to send you the most Satisfactory Account
of him in every Respect and he is, I think very much
improv'd in his Looks (I mean as to *beauty*) and in the most
florid rude Health, I assure you it did my Heart good to
look at him—and all the little tribe about him looked so
clean, so happy, and so healthy, that it quite put me in good
humour with the School. I saw Mrs Cotton (her husband
was out) who said Tom had behav'd extremely well since his

return to School and comes on very well with his Latin. Willy Canning and John Bouverie we beg'd Mrs Cotton to send to us after Dinner. Tom of course came *with* me, but before we left school he beg'd to introduce his *bosom* Friend to me, *Clarke*. So he was likewise included in the invitation to fruit, Tea and Supper. Tom says he has written to you every Sunday, but his Master he supposes took your y for a g, for he has constantly directed to Winstage. His companions came to their appointment, and till tea-time the noise of the four together has really been tremendous, as you will easily imagine when I tell you *Clarke* is not at all behindhand with his Friend for Noise and Riot. Since I have been writing, however, they have been tolerably quiet, as I have supplied them all with Paper, Pen, and Pencils. Tom and Clarke have been amusing themselves with writing anonymous Letters. Tom's is a Love Letter addressed to his "charming M." in which he is at the Point of Death, and that if she doesn't release his Pain he must put both her and himself out of their Misery!!—the other's is a Challenge and both excellent in their way. Poor Will is drawing ravenous Bulls and I think the genius of John Bouverie seems all to be devoted to the raspberry jam that is bespoke for their Suppers—if you write to Mrs Canning soon you can tell her that nothing can look better than Willy—and to Mrs Bouverie, the same. I have been taken for you by everybody. Mrs March is but *just now* undeceived—'tis now about 8 o'clock—I shall keep Tom *till ten* as we are obliged to go off early in the morning to Town. . . . I have got all your journals with me to entertain my Father and have read some to Tom to-night to his great delight. He stumbled over the Chair just now in their Play and then exclaimed "Pho! I thought I had been as foolish as my Father and hurt my Leg." . . . I must leave you now as the Raspberry jam and Bread has made its appearance and my little Crows are already pecking. . . . I wish I could conjure you here for a moment to see the four little mouths

(but perhaps you may not think *Tom's* included in this
Description) that are all moving at once opposite me I
believe they have had all the Tarts in the Larder.

Tuesday morning, Norfolk Street. . . . We pouch'd the
four with half a crown apiece and Tom had the odd sixpence
of the half-guinea—I would have wished to have divided it
more in his favour but as they were all such dear Friends
T—— thought it was more to Tom's wish to treat them
pretty equally. . . . Here is nobody but poor Charles and
Will in the House, my Mother having discharg'd Sally, and
before she had provided herself with another Servant. So
poor Charles is cook, Lady's Maid, and Valet. It is more
disagreeable than I can tell you, and my Mother is so stingy
she does not even get a Charwoman to wash the dishes.

A few days later Mrs Tickell is found awaiting a hair-
dresser "to frizzle me" in pity to poor Charles; somewhat
later "our Charles" is in all the panic of being a new
performer—apparently in the Jubilee show at Drury Lane,
in which, doubtless, a large number of persons were wanted
to "walk on." Later still "Charles" has come back from
Margate and "she" looks no better; Dr Ford sees her and
says she ought to go to Margate again. Mr Sichel believes
that "Charles" is Charlotte, the twin sister of Jane; but
there are difficulties in the way of this view. Mrs Tickell's
reference to "poor little Charlotte" who, "if you remember," was a child whose bodily strength was never equal
to the energy of her mind, reads not like the memory of a
living person's childhood, but like the recalling of a dead
child. Nor can I find a single reference to "Charles" as
a partner in any of the family's junketings. The name may
have been applied to some relative in poorer circumstances
than themselves, who (like Betty Linley) acted as maid-
servant in the Linleys' house; if so Mrs Linley must, when
she first lived in London, have kept two maids, as indeed

147

Jane's letters of much later date make it certain that she did
even when her family—and probably her income also—was
smaller. It is clear from the reference to Charlotte's childhood that she was not in any way afflicted, so that the "poor
Charles" upon whose shoulders the weight of the Norfolk
Street household rested after the too hasty discharge of
"Sally" was not, as one might have conjectured, a slightly
feeble-minded youngest daughter. Further evidence may
some day present itself; in the meantime it can only be said
with considerable certainty that Charlotte Linley did not
live beyond 1788 at the latest; and with absolute certainty
that she was not alive in 1798, when Jane writes of herself
as the only daughter her mother had left. My own impression is that Charlotte died as a child, but probably away
from Bath.

A few glimpses of William occur at this time He had,
somewhat earlier, written a poem upon Westminster Abbey
that had led Mrs Tickell to foretell (most erroneously) that
he would become the genius of the family. She now reports
a further development of his talents:

Bill continues to be the *Genius* of the Family. Miss
Farren has asked my father to reset the song in "The way
to keep him."——"I assure you, if you don't like it I have
an offer from a very (　) pretty fellow to compose it for
me."——"By all means, Ma'am, I beg you'll use no
ceremony with me" (thinking it was Shield or Shaw or one
of her acquaintances) but it was Master William's gallantry.
. . . Don't you think our young Genius *Sores*.

It must have been an agreeable thing to hear Mr Linley's
laugh when he discovered the name of his rival.

CHAPTER 7. THE YEARS OF SORROW

NONE of Mrs Sheridan's letters to her sister seem to be in the hands of those descendants who have piously preserved the correspondence from which I have been quoting, and it is only too probable that they have long since been destroyed. Many, however, which she wrote to her husband and to Mrs Canning are in existence, and indeed a good many have been wholly or partially printed already.   Some of them are so like in tone and turn of phrase to Mrs Tickell's that many a passage might be interchanged—and it may be added that the letters of Jane Linley, written years after the death of both sisters, are emphatically of the same type.   Jane, however, did not employ the little family phrases, the " ee," the interjected " ma'ams " and " sirs," and the quaint coined words not current beyond the Linley circle.

The next group of extracts comes from letters all but one of which seem to have been written during a visit to Mr and Mrs Crewe.

Thank 'e Dearest Love for not disappointing me.   Never —no not once have 'e missed writing, 'e dear good boy. When I see 'e I will kiss 'e up as never 'e was kiss'd before.

My idea originally you know was to give up our house in Town entirely, and then the money we should get for our furniture there, would pay for what we should want here, and when you were oblig'd to be in Town, a ready furnish'd house would do as well as another for us, and would be a trifling expense in comparison with Bruton

Street. I wish to God[1] you would reconcile yourself to this. Suppose people should say you could not live in so large a house, where would be the Disgrace? And what *can* they say more than they do at present, you never will persuade People you are very rich if you were to spend three times as much as you do, and the World in general so far from condemning you for retrenching would applaud you for it. Do think of this, my dearest Dick, and let me have a little quiet *home* here that I can enjoy with Comfort.

I do think it is very odd my Dear Dick that you never say a word of my poor Father and Mother. Surely you and my Father have had no quarrel in settling your affairs. I really begin to be uneasy at your Silence for 'tis very odd if you have been so often with Wallis[2] without calling upon them.

God bless thee my Dear Soul. Thank ye for the good News of Politics. I hope it is all really good, but 'e are such a sanguine Pig, there's no knowing.

Thank 'ee my Dearest Love for your nice comfortable charming Letter. . . . I did not mean to lecture ee my soul in my first Letter, me only vex that you should ever fret yourself or be unhappy without the Shadow of a Cause and indeed, indeed my heart's own one you never shall have any, but if you have Confidence in me you will not wish to make me do anything remarkable or studiously avoid every person whose Society happens to be more agreeable to me than Mr R. Wilbraham's or such People. . . . Won't you see Dear Mary or Sister Christian? I am more interested in their Good Looks than in all the Dukes and Lady's in the World. God thee for ever Love and preserve my Dearest. Your own E.A.S. I forgot to tell you how delighted every

[1] This expression and similar ones were used as commonly in England in Mrs Sheridan's day as *Mon Dieu !* still is in France.

[2] Albany Wallis, a solicitor concerned in the affairs of the theatre. He lived in Norfolk Street.

body here was with the parts of your Letter that I read to them and how I was envied by them all for having such a kind, Good-Natur'd attentive little Bodye of a husband, but I told 'em ee didn't love me a bit better than I deserved, for that I car'd for nothing in the world but 'ee.

With this letter may be compared one that belongs to the same subject though not possibly to the same period:

MY DEAR DICK, though I do not yet despair of seeing you to-night, I write for fear you should be unavoidably detained again, for I fretted very much last night that I had not done so, as I thought that you would have liked to have received a fiff[1] from me this morning when it was too late to send you one. Your note from Sevenoaks found me alone in very bad spirits indeed. It comforted me a little, but I cannot be happy while you are otherwise, whatever you may think to the contrary. Whilst I live in the world and among people of the world, I own to you I have not courage to act differently from them. I mean no harm. I do none. My vanity is flattered, perhaps, by the attentions and preference which some men show towards me; but that is all. They *know* I care for nothing but *you*, and that I laugh to scorn anything that looks like sentiment or love. I feel naturally inclined to prefer the society of those who I think are partial to me. Lord F. and H. Grenville both appear to like me, that is to say as far as laughing and talking goes. As to anything serious, even if they were inclined to think of it, they know me too well to risk being turned into ridicule for the attempt. I never miss an opportunity of declaring my sentiments on the subject, and I am perfectly convinced

---

[1] This word is often used by Mrs Sheridan to mean " a short note." Her husband also employs it ; but I have not found it in any of Mrs Tickell's letters. Mr Sichel suggests that since the word is used in Austria for a small measure of wine, it may have been acquired by Tom Linley from his friend Mozart, and adapted to this secondary signification.

they have no other views in seeking my society than that of amusing and being amused.

However, I am not sorry, as you are so foolish about them, that they are gone. They went Monday morning, meaning to return to the Prince's ball Thursday for two days, when Lord F. goes to Scotland.

I trust, my dear Dick, that matters are going better than you expected in Town; but let what will happen, do not despair. It is in times of trouble and distress that the real feelings of the heart are known. You, who think me given up to folly and dissipation, put me to the proof. Say, " Betsy, I am ruined; will you prefer going with me to the farthest part of the globe and to share with me there the misery of solitude and poverty, to staying in the world and to be still flattered and admired? " and see if I hesitate a moment. Believe me, my dear Dick, you *have* a resource if you really love *me* better than your ambition. Take me out of the whirl of the world, place me in the quiet and simple scenes of life I was born for, and you will see that I shall be once more in my element, and if I saw you content, I should be happy. . . . God bless you, my dear Dick, and depend on it I should not say all I have done in this letter if I did not feel it.

One day she writes how she thought, when she was kept awake the night before by a bad headache, that if " my poor Dick " had been there " he would speak to me and Comfort me up and I should be well directly. But I am very well to-day, Sir, so don't frighten eeself and think I am ill."

Sheridan was not the only person whose mind was haunted by a terror of her being ill. The dread seems never to have been quite absent from that of her sister and often does that sister report the anxiety and apprehension of their father.

Do, my dear Betsy, write me one word about yourself for Sheridan frightened me a good deal this morning.

I was excessively alarm'd to find you had again been taken suddenly ill when I hop'd to have seen you so soon—and poor Mrs Bouverie too to be depriv'd of nursing and comforting you by illness . . . I shall poke up S—— to fetch you on Saturday for indeed my dear Soul you *shall not* be sick any more.

Once when Mrs Sheridan was setting out for a journey in winter she sent her a pair of *Sabots* for her " Petty toes," sighed over the thought of her sister's driving " in this Snow," and assured her that " they are a great Treasure. God bless and preserve thy little feet, for 'tis main cold."

You frightened me with your Cough and Fever. Good God, what horrible words they are. What does S—— say about them; for Goodness sake drink Goat's Whey when you get into Wales and keep good hours. Do you hear, you Mr Sportsman and mind that while you have your Dog and your gun you have also a wife and take care to nurse her up and make her wear Flannel across her breast, and above all keep decent hours.

And with what a cry of rejoicing does she welcome her return from an absence:

Oh, Ma'am, I'm glad I've got ee once more within our reach. . . . Father and Mother daily expect and long to see you.

The affection of Mrs Sheridan was equally warm: she is disturbed when her husband cannot report from personal observation how her sister and the babies are; " perhaps you will contrive. I should be sorry not to know how she looks and the dear little Minikins." " The Minikins," by the way, were increased in number in 1785 by the birth of Mrs Tickell's youngest boy, Samuel, through whom alone the line of her descendants is continued. Both the sisters

153

loved children and there are pleasant allusions to those of Mrs Canning, of whose daughter Mrs Sheridan was god-mother, as Sheridan was godfather of one of her sons. At one time during the absence of Mr and Mrs Canning in Ireland her children were in the care of her friend who writes: " Your boy and I are got a little better acquainted," but she fears that " the attraction lies in a pair of very pretty avadavats his godfather sent me as a present last week." To Sheridan she wrote about the same time the pretty letter reproduced in facsimile at page 21 of Mr Fraser Rae's second volume:

Here we are, Sir, return'd to our Cottage, and my avadavats are very well and send their duty to you—so how do e do sir? What's your History as Mrs C. says? Am I to see e Eyes to-night—or is there faro or anything going on in town? I send George for some Books—so send me a fiff if e are at home—but don't keep him—I am very well—God thee bless my dearest. E.A.S.

Unfortunately this excellent state of health on the part of the avadavats did not remain unbroken; Mrs Tickell is presently found writing that she has seen Edwards—the faithful old servant of the Sheridans, who no doubt was in charge of their house during their absence—and has inquired after " the little family." One avadavat is " but poorly " although Edwards takes most tender care of them. Evidently his ministrations were of no avail, for among the verses preserved by Mrs Sheridan is an " Elegy on the Lamented Death of an Avadavat " from the pen of Sheridan.

Two sets of letters were written by Mrs Tickell while she was away from home. On one of these occasions she visited the eastern counties with her husband, whose errand seems to have had some connection with oyster fisheries. From

Norwich where she saw a much bepraised young actress[1] she wrote, in one line and a half, a really profound bit of criticism. She begins by remarking that Mrs Siddons has no reason to be afraid of this young lady.

She is too much an actress already ever to come to real greatness upon the stage. I daresay Harris will make her worth fifteen guineas a week. I see no real genius about her at all.

Presently she must have received a letter very similar to that which Mrs Sheridan wrote to Mrs Canning after having revisited East Burnham.

I visited our old House at East Burnham the other day, and I wished for you [Mrs Canning] to keep me in countenance. I wept so pitifully at the sight of all my old Haunts and the ways of Happiness and Innocence. But though I have tasted the forbidden fruit since that time, I have gained the knowledge of good and evil by it.

Mrs Tickell wrote, sympathising:

I could not help wishing myself with you at poor East Burnham. It would to me have been the greatest Delight in the World to have stroll'd over all our old haunts and recollected our former pleasant Days of quiet Comfort. I should have had *my* feelings too for *you* and for myself. We should have sympathised very well together. Jen could not help to bring back any ideas of last time *there* so well as I could. Ah! *my Dear Friend* you were not *then* a Parliament Man or a Member of Brooks's and yet I question if you have *ever* known happier hours than those we passed at East Burnham. . . . Cox [her maid] brought me a letter

---

[1] Her excellent letters about Mrs Siddons and Mrs Jordan having been reprinted more than once, I reluctantly abstain from repeating them. It is to be regretted that she did not write much more about contemporary actors and actresses.

which frighten'd me a good deal till I open'd it as it was directed by S—— it prov'd however only a good natur'd letter from my Mother, with the most Melancholy note from my poor Father. I'm afraid he never will get the better of the infamous behaviour of that ——. One part of his Letter however made me amends for all the rest as it mentioned his having heard of "Socrates"[1] and Sam and Bet, and that they were all as well and happy as Health, Beauty and Innocence could make them.

Oh! my dear, dear *Cuddykens* how your Mother longs to see you, with what Delight do I look forward to next week when I hope to [   ] at Hampton Court with the darlings of my Heart.

The children were staying with Mrs Sheridan who wrote about them to Mrs Canning:

I have had the Care of her little ones in her absence and anxious enough I have been about them you may suppose. They are beautiful and engaging Creatures. Her Girl makes me such a fool that I am sometimes persuaded I never loved Tom so much.

To Betty came in a postcript a little moral, maternal warning over which I am sure the writer must have smiled:

Miss Perceval is the Sweetest Girl in the World and always does as her Mama bids her, for nobody would love her if she was naughty which would be a sad thing you know.

Another expedition was made by the two sisters and their two husbands after due preparation; Mrs Tickell's part in the shape of a new gown and two yards of plain gauze for handkerchiefs. The party stayed with Lord and Lady Palmerston and apparently prolonged the visit a little, since Mrs Tickell announced to Mrs Canning that " Lord Ralph

---

[1] Socrates is little Dick Tickell.

and Lady Payne and a little Million of Earwigs were the Temptation that kept us at Broadlands till Wednesday."

They went to Weymouth among other places, and on the way there was a little scare and nearly a dissension, reported by Mrs Sheridan to her friend:

having reason to suppose our Gentlemen were gone on some frolick and had left us to our own discretions, we thought proper to proceed on our journey without them.

So having left a letter of instructions the sisters went on to Wimborne and waited "with great patience till eleven o'clock," when Elizabeth's courage began to fail her:

For having discover'd by this time that they were gone over from Lymington to the Isle of Wight, and that from thence they meant to coast it to Christchurch my horror of the Water with all the dreadful circumstances that first occa-sion'd it[1] acted so powerfully on my busy mind that I was completely wretched, and notwithstanding Mary's remon-strances (who felt nothing but resentment at their ill usage of us) at one o'Clock I sent off an express to Christchurch to gain some tidings of them, thank God, my fears were soon remov'd as the man return'd in a quarter of an hour having met a Servant coming to order Supper for them at that hour. As my fears subsided my anger *rose* and as I had nothing agreeable to say, I went to bed and left them to eat their Supper by Daylight. This is the only *Rub* we have met with and this as you may suppose was soon forgot.

From Weymouth Mrs Tickell wrote two or three gay letters to Mrs Canning, although her state of health was such as would almost have justified a complaining tone; and

---

[1] These words probably refer to Tom's death; but it is possible that the "dreadful circumstances" were those of her flight to France, when, as we know from a letter of Sheridan's, there was some fear of her dying on the crossing.

in the very act of declaring that it was impossible to write produced a good number of sprightly pages.

If I half boil myself in warm sea-water, all the blood is drawn from the Head, the hand relaxes and the pen becomes an oppressive weight. The Cold dip contracts the diameter of the veins and then the blood is check'd in its accustom'd Career and if one tries to circulate ink, the black juice moves as slowly as the red, so that the whole Sea Philosophy is against good writing. Sometimes small testacious fish adhere to the joints mistaking the knuckles of the hand for points of rock and the crevices of the fingers for creeks. How can one write well in this shelly state?

I suppose Betsy told you what a rheumatic poor Soul I have been for these six weeks past, last night was the first I have Passed without taking opiate in some shape or other for the last month. And I wonder I don't sprout at my finger-ends Daphne-like with the loads of Bark I have Swallowed. But now I think the Monster is overcome.

During this jaunt they heard that Mr Linley, who had been at Exeter (on a visit no doubt to that old friend, Jackson, the musician), was in the neighbourhood. " In a moment," says Mr Sichel, " they resolved to surprise him. They were told that he would be returning from a friend's house through a lane under the moonlight. They stopped their chaise, changed their clothes and voices, and accosted him in loud and forward tones, to his shocked surprise and eventual joy when he found that the supposed minxes were his own dear daughters."

It was I think soon after the return of the party to London that Mrs Tickell wrote the next letter to Mrs Canning:

I contriv'd to be at Mrs Sheridan's Ball the other night, where your Son Harry I assure you footed it away at a great rate and was one of their Smartest Beaux. It was really a very pretty sight. Every mother was in such a fuss and thought nobody's Child Danc'd half so well as hers that it was quite Comical. The Duchess (   ) as anxious as anybody that Georgina should be admir'd, a little thing a month younger than my Dick. But still she danc'd, and of course amazingly well. . . . But I have not mentioned my little Bet and I'm sure I wasn't the least anxious Mother in the Room, but without Partiality, Lud, you know, why how could one be partial to one's Children! She perform'd very well considering she had never had the advantage of a Dancing Master.

Previous letters have shown how unfailing was the care and attention of the two sisters for their father, and there are plenty of indications that they wrote often to him whenever they were away. Not very many letters to him seem, however, to remain; only papers that were in the hands of Sheridan or of Mrs Canning were sure of preservation. But here is one from Mrs Sheridan, written when Linley was about to visit Brighton with Mr and Mrs Birch, whose names appear frequently in Mrs Tickell's letters.

My DEAR FATHER, I have just been scolding Sheridan well for depriving me of the Satisfaction I should have felt at receiving a cheerful letter from you, but he says in his own defence that he kept it from me purposely as he was sure that it would not have had the effect upon me you perhaps intended. As he wrote to you himself, I hope he told you of this trick, otherwise I fear I must have appear'd very unkind and neglectful towards you, when really I was suffering a great deal of uneasiness at your silence.

She speaks with pleasure of his going to Brighton and of the companionship of the Birches, who

will save you the trouble of seeking Society among new Faces which I know you are not fond of. You will find that Theatrical affairs are going on very well. Sheridan has had a great many consultations with Mr King and the Pantomime promises to be very successful. By Sheridan's desire too Mr Cobb has been for some time engag'd in writing an opera which is finish'd, and Mr King thinks highly of. Sheridan has a great opinion of Cob as a Comic Writer and means to give him every possible assistance in his Power, but he has been particularly anxious to have this Opera finish'd on your account as he thinks (with me) that such an Employment will occupy your thoughts and assist the Sea air to dissipate all your Glooms and bring you back to us as well and happy as we wish you to be. . . . So you see my dear Father the Theatre has a good Prospect.

. . . I am only anxious for this [a plan for Linley's taking up the Oratorios which were being given up by the persons who had carried them on at the Pantheon] as it will amuse you and occupy you, for the profits is not an object. I insist upon it to affect your happiness and Comforts for as I told you before I'm sure we shall all be Croesuses very very soon. Mr Pitt will be routed next Sessions and then we shall get something substantial that cannot be lost again. In the meantime Sheridan is settling all his affairs very Comfortably and he has interested himself a great deal about the Theatre in order that you may have the less to prevent your going to the Sea and taking care of your Health, which is as dear to him as to any body in the World.

Though he was now well over fifty Linley would appear to have remained as eager—and as impatient—as ever in musical matters. In 1786 or thereabouts Mrs Tickell sent to her sister the following vignette:

Ozias was drag'd by my Father to learn the second of one of his Elegies. Bill had gone through the fiery ordeal, but luckily for him his voice was broken so as not to reach a note, so he was joyfully dismissed with a "Stupid Scoundrel."

At breakfast on this same day she had been informed of her father's pleasure in a "fine Scholar," a Miss Clarke, "who is instructed on the Score of Friendship, a system my Mother abhors."

Another time she finds her father weeping and wondering whether he was worth sixpence "in the world." On one occasion she writes that he had rheumatism; again he suffers from excruciating headaches, and leeches and blisters are applied. Mr Pratten, the friendly apothecary who inoculated Betty Tickell and her little brother, wished him to shave his head, so that a blister might be applied on the crown, and Mrs Linley had a wig prepared, but says Mrs Sheridan "when he saw the formidable Grizzle display'd upon my hand his heart fail'd him and he was as unprevailable as ever." From which it may be concluded that at the age of fifty-five (the letter belongs to the year 1788) Linley retained the thick hair shown in the Dulwich portrait, and was still but "grizzled."

His habits of travel remained with him. We hear of his going not only to Bath, where his parents were living until the latter part of 1792, to Exeter and to Brighton, but also to Margate, and "into Essex" with that unclerical clergyman and industrious journalist, Dudley Bate, of whose company he seems to have been fond, and who, on one occasion, "whisked him over to France" in his yacht. From every holiday he seemed to return better, but the improvement was never lasting. Cheerful company, too, was always beneficial, as were good accounts of Mrs Sheridan's health. So much did his state appear to depend upon such external conditions that Mrs Tickell was once moved to declare a conviction that his ailments were half vapours; and perhaps there was truth in that diagnosis. Perhaps also the other half might have been summed up as too much industry for too many years working upon a temperament naturally disposed to be anxious. Moreover, without going so far as Miss Elizabeth Sheridan, who declared that his wife's " eternal prate " was enough to account for his head-aches, we can hardly deny that Mrs Linley was the wrong companion for a nervously irritable man. At a later date it is pretty clear that some definite malady did affect his brain; and although at the time of which his daughters write he was evidently entirely sane, it is possible that the balance of his mind was ceasing to be perfectly steady, and that the veil of stoicism with which throughout his earlier years he had succeeded in concealing his real self had dropped away. In truth he was very far indeed from being a Stoic—nor, probably, was there ever any genuine musician who was one. He was a creature quite unusually sensitive to every impres-sion, capable of being engrossed by a game of cards, or by a pupil's lesson as though a matter of life and death; capable of feeling over and over again with an anguish ever new the loss of a dead child. Indeed the Thomas Linley revealed by these later letters would show us very plainly, if we had ever doubted, from which parent his highly strung daughters derived their delicacy of perception. To such a man as we now behold the delight of music must have been nearly a pain, and the nervous fatigue of his continual teaching enormous.

He was curiously composite, too; generally apt to dis-regard appearances, and too fond of wrapping himself in his " woollen cap and Persian robe," he could sometimes awaken to a desire of being in the fashion. In November 1786 Mrs Tickell informs her sister that their father is going to Bath, but not until the amusements begin. " What do you think of that ' for a change,' as Betty says. I assure you he is growing rather Beauish, thinks his Coat shabby, finds fault with his hair, and desires to have long Cravats ' as they wear 'em.' "

Not many more of the laughing, tender letters were to reach the sister who so prized and preserved them. The dear companionship which had but grown closer with the years was drawing to its end, and she whose apprehensions had always been for her elder was to depart the first.

On her birthday, 4th January 1787, Mrs Tickell wrote to her sister:

Will you spare one corner of your mind in the midst of your fine doings to think on this momentous Day. Oh, such a Day to me, my Dear, brings me to such a dreadful O, at least in the road to it, that I shall be more cautious than you could wish in future as to the matter of times and Dates.

The " dreadful O " to which she saw herself approaching was no doubt the second figure of the number 30, since she was now twenty-nine years old, but that " dreadful O " of which she pretended to be frightened never reached her; and when the fourth of January came again, she had been more than five months dead.

The sad story of her last days was recorded by her sister in a paper dated 24th August 1791:

In February 1787 my Dear Sister came to Town in a bad state of Health. On the 15th of May she return'd to Hampton Court without having receiv'd any benefit from the various Remedies prescrib'd for her. The three last letters were written between the 15th and the 25th when she was once more brought to Town dangerously ill of a Fever which turn'd to a Hectic that never afterwards left her. On the 13th of June she was carried back to Hampton Court where I remained with her, and on the 19th we went by slow stages to Clifton Hill near the Hot-Wells with a faint Hope that the air and waters would restore her, but

after struggling with this most dreadful of all diseases and
bearing with gentlest Patience and Resignation the various
pains and Horrors which mark its fatal Progress. On the
27th of July she ceased to suffer, and I for ever lost the
Friend and Companion of my youth, the beloved Sister of
my Heart whose loss never can be repaired, whose sweet
and amiable Qualities endear'd her to all who were so happy
as to know her. She died in the 29th[1] year of her age
universally regretted and lamented, and was buried in the
Cathedral at Wells where she spent her Infancy and where
she enjoyed Happiness in Poverty the first Year of her
Marriage. In less than two years afterwards Mr Tickell
married again a beautiful young woman of eighteen!!! The
dear Children remain'd with me till that time, the boys were
then taken home by their Father, the Girl, the dying Legacy
of her ever Dear and lamented Mother is still mine and
constitutes all my Happiness.

Several touching letters written at this time to Mrs
Canning remain; they have the straightforward simplicity
of profound feeling:

Indeed my Dear Woman however I may have laugh'd
in our Giddy Hours as you call them, there is nobody has
more true Religion *at Heart* than I have though I profess
to think less seriously of some forms and Ceremonies than
some do. I know and feel that it is the only Comfort in
Affliction, and am Confident in my belief we shall meet all
those we love in a better World. This is a Subject I could
talk of with Enthusiasm but I dare not trust myself to write
more at this time for my Hand and Heart are both aching.

You perhaps would have thought it right to undeceive
her, but I trust it is better not. She has no need of preparation. Her Life has been so actively virtuous, and as free
from Sin as human Frailty will allow. I do not think the

---

[1] The thirtieth.

Supreme Being whatever is its Nature can be influenced by our vain Supplications to reward or punish. The first and greatest of his attributes is Mercy and I can never bring my Heart to believe that foreknowing he could create us poor Wretches to Doom us to everlasting Punishment in another World. I am convinced Mary will be happy eternally. I have confidence and faith in the goodness and justice of God therefore why give her the pain of knowing her Situation. She has too many dear ties to attach her to this World to make the thought of leaving it indifferent to her. I hope therefore you will think I have acted rightly in endeavouring to make her last moments as Calm and free from Mental Pain at least as possible. Probably before you receive this I shall have lost my more than Sister, and you a tender and affectionate Friend. God knows how I shall bear the Shock, for you know too well I daresay that bitter as it is to expect it, when it comes it is not less dreadful. . . . I am not bless'd by Nature my dear Hetty with that calm angelic Resignation with which you have submitted to the Decrees of God. My Passions unfortunately have too much command over me and I must wait till they have a little subsided before I interrupt the Composure I hope you have regain'd . . . he (Sheridan) is sadly taken up in managing us all here in our distress. My Father and Mother and Ozy have been here since last Week. It is indeed a House of Mourning. God bless you, my dear Woman.

The choice of Wells as her place of burial may have been Mrs Tickell's own; or it may have been a consequence of the differences of opinion about the tombstone of Maria that seem to have arisen between the family in London and the grandfather in Bath; in either case it decided that of her sister and of her father, who now purchased a vault in the cathedral. An aged verger informed me that when the vault was dug " they found it wasn't empty "; in other words the diggers came upon an ancient stone coffin, belonging, if I remember right, to the thirteenth century. It was not disturbed, and still bears the Linley coffins company.

Mrs Sheridan, who had written verses upon the death of Maria and upon that of Tom, wrote some also upon that of the even dearer sister who had followed them—but she did not write at once, for a time her grief must have been too acute for utterance. But as months went by she acquired calmness; her good sense and her good feeling taught her the duty of showing a cheerful face. Nothing more characteristic of her deeper nature could possibly be written than her own words to Mrs Canning, who in the year of Mrs Tickell's death had lost her husband; the letter belongs to the next year.

You mistake me, my Dear Woman, if you supposed I congratulated you on recovering your tranquillity, and that I had an idea that you had ceased to cherish that right and tender sorrow so dear to the memory of your dear Stratty. Everybody who knew him who was acquainted with his kind good Heart and amiable qualities must lament the loss of such a man, such a Friend—how much more strongly then must you, the Partner of his Heart feel. But time and the conviction of his Happiness *ought* and I trust, *has* restored you to that tranquillity which will enable you once more to find Pleasure in the Society of your and his Friends, and to fulfil the many Duties of your Situation in this Life with cheerful resignation. This is all I meant and all that was imagined by those who told me that you were more tranquil. It is what I feel myself—though I do not think our Misfortunes equal—yet I am sure you will own, mine has been very bitter, the severest I have ever known. God forbid I should live to experience greater affliction! But though I never shall forget or cease eternally to lament my Dear Mary, I can now find amusement in my different occupations

which I could not in the first Passion of my Grief, and can
mix in the Society of my Friends without wrapping them in
the gloom of my Sorrows.   In my solitary Hours I am more
selfish, but my reflections are calm though sorrowful, and
I can think and talk of my beloved Sister very often with
Composure and without Tears.   It will grieve me to find
you have not acquired this Repose from Misery, and I think
it a duty which we owe all the dear connections which
remain to us, to attain by every effort both of Reason and
Religion.

The words have the nobility that comes of looking
sincerely at the facts of human life—a distinction that
belongs alike to the letters of Mrs Sheridan, of Mrs Tickell
and of Jane, and that oddly enough seems to have belonged
to none of their three husbands.

The lines that she wrote for an epitaph upon her sister
are probably the most perfect ever composed by her.   There
is indeed something almost classic in their simple directness.

> You who have mourned the sister of your Heart
>   The dear companion of your youthful years,
> Pass not regardless.   Drop ere you depart
>   On this sad spot your tributary tears.
> For here the sweetest friend for ever lies,
>   The best, the kindest, lovely and beloved,
> Whose cheerful spirit brightened in her eyes
>   And graced those virtues which her life approved.
> Modestly wise and innocently gay,
>   She lived, to my grieved heart a blessing given,
> Till God approving, from its beauteous Clay
>   Called the pure Spirit to its native Heaven.

When the first sharpness of her anguish had worn away
Mrs Sheridan must have found herself left terribly lonely.
In losing her beloved Mary she had lost the one person who
knew her completely, the one confidant by whom her every

hope, fear and thought would have been understood. Mrs Canning was dearer than any other woman now remaining—but Mrs Canning was not a Linley. Jane, who had much more of themselves than her elder sisters ever saw, was in their presence silent and reserved, and moreover was ten years Mary's junior. Her father was rather a burden than a support and her husband was no longer as dear to her as he had once been. Slowly, insidiously some alienation had crept in. She must have felt him often neglectful, and believed him perhaps indifferent. She had forgiven him what she regarded as passing aberrations, while she was still able to believe that

> Though fairer objects tempt thy view
> That heart is *mine* alone,

but even in order to forgive she had to teach herself to think such aberrations pardonable. As Emerson truly says: "We sink as easily as we rise, through sympathy." She could hardly have gone on living in the circle of which she was now a member if she had not brought herself to tolerate a moral laxity very different from the faithful companionship and steady industry of her father and mother. Miss Sheridan (Elizabeth), writing at the end of 1788 to her sister Alicia, says:

Mrs Sheridan, always amiable and obliging, has adopted ideas on many subjects so very different from what mine must be, that we can never converse with that freedom that minds in some sort of the same kind indulge in. She told me last night she had converted Mrs Canning who was *uncommonly rigid* in her notions.

From the moment that a woman of Mrs Sheridan's well-nigh irresistible charm began thus to accept a lowered standard, it is clear that she stood in the utmost peril. And in 1789, probably early in the year, some act or letter of hers (or possibly some letter to her) caused a brief estrangement from her of her best and truest friend Mrs Canning. The precise facts are not known, nor is it necessary to pry into them. But they were known to Sheridan, and, all his petty jealousies now dropping away, he intervened to restore Mrs Canning's friendship. His letter is one among the three or four instances that show how far nobler was Sheridan's fundamental self than the external doings of his hurried unpunctual, disordered existence.

Dear Mrs Canning, Altho' I do not think it likely that I shall miss you to-morrow morning, yet I am so anxious to prevent any accidental engagement interfering with my seeing you that I send this to reach you very early, hoping that you will give me a leisure half-hour about twelve.

I wish exceedingly to speak to you about your friend and your answer to Mrs B. I am confident you do not know what her situation is or what effect may arise, or has indeed taken place on her mind from the impression or apprehension that the *Friend she loved best in the world* appears, without explanation even, to be cool'd and chang'd towards her. She has not seen your letter to Mrs B., and I would not for the world that she should. My dear Mrs Canning, you do not know the state that she has been in, and how perilous and critical her state now is, or indeed you would upbraid yourself for harbouring one altered thought, or even for abating in the least degree the warmest zeal of Friendship, of such friendship as nothing in Nature could ever have prevented her heart showing you. Pray forgive my writing to you thus; but convinced as I am that there is *no chance of saving her life* but by tranquillising her mind, and knowing as I do, and as I did hope you knew, that God never form'd a better heart, and that she has no errors but what are the Faults of those whose conduct has created them in her against her nature, I feel it impossible for me not to own that the idea of unkindness or coldness towards her *from you* smote me most sensibly, as I see it does her to the soul. I have said more than I meant. When I have the satisfaction of seeing you to-morrow, I am sure you will enable me to heal her mind on this subject, or real love, charity, and candour exist nowhere. Yours most sincerely,

R. B. SHERIDAN.

The intervention was, as it deserved to be, successful; not only was the friendship of Mrs Canning restored but the hearts of husband and wife were once more drawn together and not even in the days of their early romance had they been so truly united. But the apprehensions that spoke so plainly in Sheridan's letter were but too well founded, and the approaching shadow darkens her letters. As ever her thoughts and cares were less for herself than for those whom she loved. The following letter, so characteristic of her in many ways, comes however from some time earlier than the threatened alienation of Mrs Canning:

London is absolutely forbidden and change of air and Scene strongly recommended. This advice except on yours and my poor Father's Accounts I should not be displeas'd at, for God knows London has no Charms for me, and if I could draw the very few left to me that are Dear to my Heart around me, I should like to rest in some quiet Corner of the World and never see it again. But when I think I should be a resource and comfort to you and my Poor Father, who in a letter yesterday tells me he is a " perfect outcast of Society " and impatiently awaits my return, I cannot but grieve that my health will not permit me to follow my inclinations in returning to you both directly. I wrote to my Father and ventur'd to tell him that I was sure you would supply my place to him. As you will not see many people you will not find his Society unpleasing

I know, and it will be a great comfort to me to know that he has *one* house in London where he may amuse and be amus'd himself. I do not think he was in Town at the time you sent to him but you know he is the shyest of all Creatures and wants a great deal of Encouragement to be put at his ease.

In the spring of 1792 Mrs Sheridan's dearest hope, more than once disappointed, was fulfilled by the birth of a daughter. Need I say that the name given to the child was Mary? But this event, though it filled the mother with new hopes, and even tempted the better-informed father to fly, as he says, from his fears, was no point of arrest in her decline. "Since Friday when the infant was christened, she has been rapidly falling back." The disease was but too clear; and the story of the younger sister was repeated almost step for step in that of the elder. She too was ordered to the " Hot Wells," that Davos of our ancestors; and once more Sheridan accompanied the melancholy pilgrimage. She was eager to arrive and "sanguine of the Event " but he did not deceive himself. " Her friend whom she loved best in the world, Mrs Canning, I have prevailed on to accompany her, and she is now with her. There never was in the world a more friendly act than her doing so. She has left her daughter and all her children whom she dotes on for this office." Jane Linley, too, seems to have been with her sister, as she had been with Mary, five years earlier.

On the 8th of May Mrs Canning reports to her daughter their arrival, and the verdict of Dr Bain (who many years later was to attend Sheridan in his last illness) that the case was not yet beyond hope. " To-morrow," she adds, " we go into a charming house, the white bow-windowed one that overlooks the strawberry garden."

Within a very short time, however, Dr Bain saw reason

to change his favourable opinion.   On the 13th Mrs Canning was writing that he pronounced Mrs Sheridan's to be really " a *lost case* and that she could not live for six months." As for Sheridan:

It is impossible for any one to behave with greater tenderness and attention than he does.   His whole time is devoted to her; he reads us a sermon every evening and does everything in his power to sooth and comfort her, keeps up his spirits wonderfully before her, but when she goes to bed then he is low and dejected.   He does not say much, but grief is depicted on his countenance.

On the same day he was writing to the Duchess of Devonshire and her sister:

Ever since she has been brought to bed, she has turned her head almost wholly to think and talk and read on religious subjects, and her fortitude and Calmness have astonished me. She has put by any other contemplation.   I am confident if she can recover, there never was on earth anything more perfect than she will be; and to be different she says, to me for ever from what she has been makes her so seriously eager to live.   But she cannot be deceived about the Danger of her situation. . . . Last night she desired to be placed at the Piano-Forte.   Looking like a shadow of her own Picture she played some notes with the tears dropping on her thin arms.   Her mind is become heavenly, but her mortal form is fading from my sight, and I look in vain into my own mind for assent to her apparent conviction that all will not perish.

Sheridan also wrote during this sad month of May: "This morning I rode to a place where I remember she made me drive her when poor Mrs. Tickell was dying here. It is a spot on the side of Brandon's Hill where she and her sister used to play when they went to a boarding school close by.   And I remember how bitterly she cried here and lamented her sister's approaching fate." [1]

The fluctuations that belong to the disease enabled him presently to entertain a gleam of hope, but Mrs Canning, probably more experienced in illness, had no such illusion.

Mrs Sheridan wrote a whole sheet of paper yesterday of directions which she sealed up and gave to me, having written on the outside " To be opened after my death and to be considered as my *last will*."   She gave it to me with great composure, and smiling said, she hoped there would be no reason to open it, but as her disorder was of a very deceitful nature, she thought it best to be prepared for whatever might happen.   She read sometimes to herself and after dinner sat down to the piano.   She taught Betty a little while, and played several slow movements out of her own head, with her usual expression, but with a very trembling hand. . . . It was so like the last efforts of an expiring genius and brought such a train of tender and melancholy ideas to my imagination that I thought my poor heart would have burst in the conflict, it did not strike Mr S. in the same light; he was pleased to see her able to amuse herself, and augured everything that was good from such favourable appearances.

The instructions contained in the paper thus written are summarised as follows by Mr Sichel: " To Eliza Canning, her god-daughter, she left her watch, chain and some jewels; to Jane Linley, her pearls.   The ' fine linen which she had lately made up ' was ' so far as suitable to be reserved for her dear little infant ' the rest to be divided between the beneficiaries just named.   To a maid she left much of her wardrobe and she specially requested that her mother might not interfere.   The £50 or more in a brown silk pocket-book at Isleworth " (where Sheridan had taken a house)

---

[1] Sichel, "Sheridan," vol. ii, p. 432.

" was to be disposed of in mourning rings for the Leighs and the Le Fanus; while the 'fausse montre with my dear husband's picture,' she left to 'my dear and beloved friend, Mrs Canning,' also a portrait of herself, to be painted by any one but Cosway, and a ring both to her and her daughter. She desired that 'the picture of my dear Mary' should be 'unset and one copied of me joined to it, and the hair blended, and this, I trust, Mrs Tickell will permit my dearest Betty to wear in remembrance of her two poor Mothers.' To her own mother she gave, 'a new black cloak which will be comfortable for her in the winter.' She disposed of all her ornaments and desired that twenty-five pounds should be settled on George Edwards (Sheridan's butler), and on the woman-servant—'Faddy'—already benefited. 'There are other circumstances,' she concludes, 'which I have mentioned to Mrs Canning, which I hope will likewise be considered as my earnest wish—I am now exhausted.' "

While Mrs Sheridan was fading gradually away at Clifton her parents were in Bath, whence they came over to see her. William was by this time in India, where he held a post in the East India Company's service; and Ozias, who had taken his degree in 1789, was a minor canon of Norwich and probably unable to leave his charge. On the 27th of June the relatives were summoned to what was evidently a death-bed. Mrs Canning, writing three weeks later to Alicia Le Fanu, in Ireland, says:

They were introduced one at a time at her bedside, and were prepared as much as possible for this sad scene. The women[1] bore it very well, but all our feelings were awakened for her poor father. The interview between him and the

---

[1] Probably Mrs Linley and Jane. Mrs Philpot may have been with them.

dear angel was afflicting and heart-breaking to the greatest
degree imaginable. I was afraid she would have sunk under
the cruel agitation—she said it was indeed too much for her.
She gave some kind injunction to each of them, and said
everything she could to comfort them under this severe
trial. They then parted in the hope of seeing her again in
the evening, but they never saw her more. Mr Sheridan
and I sat up all that night with her—indeed he had done so
for several nights before, and never left her for one moment
that could be avoided. About four o'clock in the morning
we perceived an alarming change, and sent for her physician.
She said to him, " If you can relieve me, do it quickly; if not,
do not let me struggle, but give me some laudanum." His
answer was, "Then I will give you some laudanum."
Before she took it she desired to see Tom and Betty Tickell,
of whom she took a most affecting leave. Your brother
behaved most wonderfully, though his heart was breaking;
and at times his feelings were so violent that I feared he
would have been quite ungovernable at the last. Yet he
summoned up courage to kneel at the bedside till he felt the
last pulse of expiring excellence and then withdrew. . .
For my part I never beheld such a scene—never suffered
such a conflict—much as I have suffered on my own account.
While I live the remembrance of it and the dear lost object
can never be effaced from my mind. . . . She talked with
the greatest composure of her approaching dissolution assuring us all that she had the most perfect confidence in the
mercies of an all-powerful and merciful Being, from whom
alone she could have derived the inward comfort and support
she felt at that awful moment, and she said she had no fear
of death, and that all her concern arose from the thoughts
of leaving so many dear and tender ties and of what they
would suffer from her loss.

The outward beauty that seems but the natural expression
of her exquisite personality remained to the end. " You

never saw anything so interesting as her countenance," wrote Mrs Canning, " even with death depicted in it, it is still lovely." The funeral must have been a horrible ordeal; crowds of persons " lined the road all the way from Bristol," and in the Cathedral at Wells the crush was so great that Mrs Canning almost fainted. All this was undesired and distasteful; Sheridan wrote afterwards that he looked back with pain to the " gaudy parade and show." The little inner circle of real mourners consisted of Sheridan and his son, Mr Linley, Ozias, Jane, Richardson, Mrs Canning and " poor little Betty " together with Mr Leigh, an old friend, who read the service.

Before the close of the year the grandparents in Bath had both passed away in ripe old age. Only five Linleys were now left: the bereaved father and mother; Ozias, fixed by his duties in Norfolk; William, away in India; and Jane, now twenty-four years old, who alone, after their forty years of married life, remained with her parents.

CHAPTER 8. THE SURVIVORS

SHERIDAN'S grief for his irretrievable loss made him cling the more eagerly to those survivors who had belonged to his wife; he idolised the infant daughter, who already was so like her, and devoted himself to his forlorn father-in-law.

Poor Mr Linley, wrote Mrs Canning,

is very much broke, but is still an interesting and agreeable companion. I do not know any one more to be pitied than he is. It is evident that the recollection of past misfortunes preys on his mind, and he has no comfort in the surviving part of his family, they being all scattered abroad.[1] Mr Sheridan seems more his child than any of his own, and I believe he likes being near him and his grandchildren.

Tickell, with characteristic negligence, had delayed writing to Sheridan, until he heard that the latter had felt his silence unkind. Yet evidently a bereavement so parallel to that which he had himself suffered had drawn closer the bond between him and his old friend, and the letter that he wrote has a note of warm sincerity. Variable, unsettled, perhaps unprincipled, though he was, this letter shows what it was in him that won and kept the love of Mary Linley.

I was shocked to find that my long silence had offended you. Could you doubt, my dear Sheridan, the keen sufferings of my heart on such a subject? Who in the world, next yourself, had known so long, so entirely, her goodness, her tenderness to my children! I am sure my heart bleeds for

---

[1] This seems as though Jane were staying away soon after Mrs Sheridan's death. She may have been in Bath, where her grandfather and grandmother both died this year.

your sufferings under this heaviest affliction, nor can I think of words to justify my thoughts, or in any way express my sympathy. . . . Yet still I should have written, and have now only to entreat you to forgive my silence, and to believe that I partake your affliction not as a brother only, but as a friend more and more attached to you by increasing esteem for your worth that every new occasion proves and establishes, and devoted to the restoration of your peace and your service by every tie of gratitude and love. . . . It would indeed be presumptuous to give counsel to a mind correct and manly as yours, yet let me express to you that I rely upon every exertion of your understanding to constrain the imagination from dwelling with too fond indulgence on a calamity too heavy for almost reason to submit to, unless sustained by principle. My dear Sheridan, let this dreadful affliction cement our friendship more closely than ever.

The next woe in store for Sheridan and the Linleys was the death, in October 1793, when she was about eighteen months old, of the child upon whose head rested so many hopes. Born at a time when her mother's life was already doomed, she had never had more than a very frail hold upon existence. "The dear babe," says Mrs Canning,

never throve to my satisfaction: she was small and delicate beyond imagination and gave very little expectation of long life; but she has visibly declined during the last month. . . . The dear babe's resemblance to her mother, after her death, was so much more striking that it was impossible to see her without recalling every circumstance of that afflicting scene, and he was constantly in the room, indulging the sad remembrance.

Just a fortnight later came the death of Tickell, who fell from a parapet outside his rooms in Hampton Court, upon which he had been in the imprudent habit of sitting.

Perhaps he threw himself over intentionally; but Sheridan used his influence to prevent any official inquiry, and the matter was treated as an accident. Be the truth upon this point as it may, the event must have been a severe shock for Mr and Mrs Linley, and for Jane, who, in former years, had so often been an inmate of Tickell's house. Sheridan interested himself in the welfare of the children, and so did other friends; the elder boy by-and-by entered the navy, and the younger the service of the East India Company. Betty was placed at school with Miss Sophia Lee, at Bath, who, I strongly suspect, received her without payment and who was the truest and kindest of friends to her.

Of the life of the Linley household during the six years that intervened between Mrs Sheridan's death and Jane Linley's engagement to Charles Ward, in 1798, only scattered scraps of information have been discovered. It is not even certain at what period the family removed from Norfolk Street to No. 11 Southampton Street, Covent Garden, although a letter, now in the British Museum, from a Mrs Beaver of Dorchester to Mrs Linley speaks of a removal as being in contemplation as early as two years before the date of her letter, which was written in April 1791. She had met Mrs Linley in Wells. I do not think the removal took place, however, much, if at all, before Mrs Sheridan's death. Nor have I succeeded in learning at what date Mrs Linley's superintendence of the Drury Lane wardrobe came to an end.

The two remaining brothers were oddly dissimilar in character and temper. Ozias lived his own eccentric life, oddly unclerical in non-essentials, and calculated to furnish parishioners with abundant material for mild gossip—thrummed strange musical instruments, composed occasional hymns and anthems, asserted boldly that he had seen a ghost, disputed warmly when he could secure congenial opponents, and made dryly humorous observations to himself or to a likely hearer as happened. The opinion held of him by his neighbours was evidently a matter of the profoundest indifference to Ozias Linley. It was by a happy appositeness that the quaint Christian name had been assigned to him whom it suited so well rather than to his brother.

Even as a boy, "Ozy" was "the philosopher" to his nicknaming sister, Mary; and there are indications in her letters that, like other immature philosophers of his sex, he was at times less attentive than could be wished to details of personal appearance. His college at Oxford was Corpus Christi, and a vivid vignette of him as an undergraduate is to be found in a letter of Mrs Tickell written in the last days of December 1785. She mentions that her company to dinner will be "Mr Palmer, Mr O. Linley and Mr Snagg Lawrence," and that "our first Christmas Turkey will acknowledge the force of its assailants. . . . Ozy is here now tormenting the children in his old way." Efforts were made by Tickell and his wife to convince Ozias that it was allowable for him to be acquainted with fellow-undergraduates who were gentleman commoners, he having "a notion . . . that none but Gentlemen Commoners herded together." The next morning her letter was continued. "Ozy" had stayed late "and I think I never laughed so much in my life." Tickell gave a representation of Lawrence for the benefit of Ozias, and then acted "a young gentleman's first appearance in 'Young Meadows,'[1] I thought he [Ozias] would have been choak'd for he was eating his supper of toasted cheese. I'm sure you never saw him laugh as he did last night."

[1] The hero of the favourite operetta *Love in a Village*. Michael Kelly had recently made his appearance in this character, and was probably the original of Tickell's performance.

I ask'd him how he contriv'd to read his lessons (which he is oblig'd to do every other week) with a tolerably grave face. " Why, by my faith (says he) I was very near laughing out once." How so, Ozy? " Why, it happened to be a most ludicrous Chapter indeed, upon my Word, I never read anything so extremely ludicrous." Why, what was it? Can't you recollect what Book it was in? " Oh, I don't know, 'twas something about the Woman, then, that went to wash her Feet in the Bath." Oh, what, you mean Susannah & the two wicked Elders? " Aye, aye, that was it sure enough—upon my Word I wasn't at all prepar'd for such a ludicrous affair, and then they kept such a tittering about me that I was as near as anything bursting out in the middle of it. God bless me, 'tis astonishing to me how they can put such Nonsense in the Holy Scriptures." This is word for word, I assure you. I'm sure I laugh'd till my Jaws ach'd to see his Face while he was telling it.

Several odd tales of Ozias's Norwich days were told of him, by himself and others. His absence of mind was proverbial, and the Rev. John Sinclair, afterwards Archdeacon of Middlesex, who consecrates to Ozias Linley a chapter in his " Sketches of Old Times and Distant Places," declares that Sheridan used to invent incidents illustrating this characteristic and to narrate them in the presence of their subject. On one such occasion, Ozias, after energetically repudiating the fiction, proceeded to relate how he had, in fact, gone into the shop of " my tobacconist " to replenish his snuff-box, and—" I know not how it happened" —had taken up and was walking away with " the two brass candlesticks that were standing alight on the counter " when their owner intervened with the expostulation: " Surely, Mr Linley, you do not intend to carry off my candlesticks! "

One Sunday, when it was his turn to preach in Norwich Cathedral, he " well knowing my own infirmity " rang for his landlady, handed her the key of his study, and begged her to lock him in and undertake the duty of fetching him at the right time. The woman demurred and returned the key, which he put in his pocket, and, sitting down to read over his sermon, immediately forgot the circumstance. The bells began to ring. He put on his surplice, and awaited his landlady, who, of course, did not appear. He began his sermon again, and had gone half through it, when he heard " the great bell begin to toll, as it always did when the Dean and Chapter were about to form into procession." Still no landlady appeared to release him from his supposed imprisonment. " In this extremity " the anxious minor canon threw up the window and, with the aid of the water-butt and water-pipe, climbed down in his surplice into the street. " Happily I was so late that comparatively few of the congregation witnessed this exploit." His sermon on this agitating occasion was one that he had copied *verbatim* from Bishop Hoadly " whom the Dean and Chapter looked upon as an execrable heretic, but who was an especial favourite of the Bishop, Dr Bathurst. After the service as we were going in procession to the vestry, the Bishop turned to me with a gracious smile and said, ' Mr Linley, I am much obliged to you for the excellent sermon you have *selected* ' " —an observation which must have delighted the recipient.

On yet another Sunday he rode out to go and preach at a village some few miles from Norwich, and presently arrived with a whip in his hand and a bridle trailing upon the ground at a turnpike, where he inquired of the keeper what he had to pay. " You have nothing to pay, Sir," replied the man, " you must have left your horse behind you." So, indeed it proved; turning back, he found the animal not far off, grazing quietly at the side of the road.

A very different person was William. Nobody, we may

be sure, ever said of William, as of Ozias, that he was the same odd creature as ever; and we may also be sure that while Ozias would have heard the description with perfect indifference, his brother would have been seriously hurt by it. An extremely susceptible young man was William Linley, always in love with some charming lady; but, though with his dark hair, blue eyes, and fine features, he must have been a handsome fellow, though he was well-mannered, something of a poet, and one moreover who could set and sing his own verses, the only lady apparently disposed to care about him was one for whom he cared nothing. To have been really profoundly in love with some woman who returned his affection would have been the making of him, but that good fortune never befell him. That it should have befallen Ozias is almost unthinkable; Ozias seems to have been a born old bachelor, quite happy in his solitude, and falling naturally into the rôle of an uncle. There is no hint in any of the Linley letters or in any of the records of Ozias that he was ever in love.

As for Jane, she was not without suitors; in 1790 Mrs Sheridan had written :

Jane has had two lovers with decent names since I saw you last but neither of them will do. One is old enough to be her father without the advantage attending disparity of years. The other would do but unluckily he is only now going to the East Indies to make a Fortune. He flatters himself that at his return in about ten or twelve years time the amiable Miss Linley will reward his passion. Here's a proposal for a Miss turn'd of two and twenty, who seems to think she is already approaching to old maidenism. Poor Jane is very unfortunate in her conquests. Better have no offer at all than be so tantalised.

At some time before her father's death, Jane became engaged to a Mr Gordon, who was in some distant part of the world, and who may very well have been the lover to whom Mrs Sheridan referred. Our only direct knowledge of the matter comes from her own later letters. That the match was broken off by Mr Gordon is clear, and the cessation of the engagement took place after William's return to England, which occurred in the summer of 1796. Jane, a perfectly straightforward woman, informed Charles Ward of this previous engagement, at the time of his proposal to her, and the fact rankled in his mind. That she should speak of "a disappointment" led him to protest; but she maintained that she *had* felt disappointment, although she now rejoiced that she had been disappointed; she also maintained that she had felt something approaching to love for her distant suitor—what opinion, she asks, could be entertained of her if she had been capable of accepting him without it? She admits, however, that the discomforts of her home and the violent disputes between her father and mother weighed with her in her decision. The admission suggests that the last years of Mr Linley's life were not only melancholy, but discordant; on the other hand it seems to contradict those reports of his death which describe him as having fallen into imbecility. That the temper of Mrs Linley had not grown milder with years there is ample evidence in Jane's letters; and I am afraid that in the inactivity of their ageing days the pair who had lived so long and so faithfully together were rather a torment than a comfort to each other. The release of Thomas Linley from a life already bereft of happiness came suddenly on the 19th of November 1795; he had lived long enough to see that second marriage of Sheridan's which had taken place in the previous summer and which must surely have added another drop of bitterness to his already bitter cup. He was buried in Wells Cathedral with his daughters and his grandchild, the little Mary Sheridan; and a tablet to his memory may be seen there in the cloisters.

Mr Linley's will, which had been made as long before as August 1788, is summarised by Mr Green, who, however, does not mention that Sheridan was his executor. He left to his daughter Elizabeth all his music-books, printed and manuscript, and his harpsichord; his other musical interests to Ozias and William. His property at Didmarton he left to Ozias and, if Ozias should leave no children, to William. To Jane he left £100; and he desired that the Drury Lane shares should be kept in the family (or sold only to a member of it) as long as possible. It must be remembered that this will was made while the father of the testator was still living; and the fact that no alteration was made in it after the death of that father seems to show that William Linley of Bath must, by his own will, have decided the descent of his property to his grandchildren. His house in Bath was left to William and Jane, and a letter still in existence shows that after Jane's death her husband was receiving pew rents from the chapel; therefore she must have had some share in these. Ozias, who inherited Oldbury at Didmarton, had a share in the chapel, but not, perhaps, in the Bath houses. These various bequests show how entirely false are any statements that Linley died in a condition of indigence brought about by the extravagance of his famous son-in-law. The granddaughter to whom two-thirds of his property— that is to say, everything left by William and by Ozias— eventually descended, left £12,000 and it is safe to say that his property must have exceeded that figure by at least £5000. Now in the year 1795 money had a higher value than it has at present, and the fortune accumulated by Thomas Linley must be considered no small one for a man who had, in all probability, begun his career forty-three years earlier with nothing.

That a year and a half later his family were distressed
for money is true; and that they held Sheridan responsible
for that distress is also true. It is plain from a letter now in
the British Museum that their income from the theatre was
not being paid to them; and for this failure it is difficult not
to hold Sheridan responsible.

William, whose health had suffered from the climate of
India, returned in 1796 to England, where he hoped to earn
enough, by means of his musical accomplishments, to enable
him to live at home. He obtained some sort of post at the
theatre, where it seems clear his presence was unwelcome to
persons already in employment there, and where a sort of
organised passive resistance prevented him from remaining
or his works from being successful. Who these enemies
were I am not able to say with certainty; but I feel pretty
sure that Sheridan was not one of them. To neglect the
interests of the Linleys, to fail in keeping voluntarily-made
appointments with them, to leave their letters unanswered—
nay, even perhaps temporarily to appropriate their income—
all these were misdemeanours of which it is easy to believe
Sheridan capable; but to have been deliberately malicious to
them either in act or speech would have seemed to him
shocking. With all his appearance of recklessness, he was
not a man who said what he did not mean to say; he was
master of his own temper and early in life had taught himself
to keep his wit from ill-nature.

A year later William was still in England writing and
composing for the stage, and Mrs Linley was still inhabiting
the Southampton Street house and employing at least two
servants. It may therefore be presumed that the family was
now receiving some support from the theatre ; and it is
certain that in the year 1798 the Bath property was bringing
in an income.

CHAPTER 9. JANE AND CHARLES

In 1798 the records of the family begin again. In May Jane became engaged to Charles Ward, whom she subsequently married, and whose family received her with warm and lasting kindness.

There was brought up to my house one evening by a descendant of that family a little old square wooden box that had once been painted either black or dark green. On its lid was nailed a bit of card, inscribed in faded ink: " No. 4. Mr Ward. Passenger to Iver." Its lock, still fastened and hanging by the hasp, had long ago been broken open. Within were four packets of letters, besides a good many loose papers. The four packets contain over two hundred letters exchanged between Jane Nash Linley and Charles William Ward during the two years and a quarter that intervened between May 1798 and the end of August 1800; and the correspondence enables us to reconstruct very accurately the life and doings of three out of the four Linleys still living. Of Jane herself these letters, taken together with the two portraits still in possession of the Ward family, give a very clear impression. This last survivor of Thomas Linley's daughters, though less brilliant and less beautiful than her elders, was made of the same stuff; and just as her eyes and her voice reminded contemporaries of them, so do her letters recall their temperament, their turn of thought and their subjects of interest. She had Mary's sincerity of mind, seeing facts and persons as they were, and never pretending, either to herself or to others, that they were anything different—a quality that always gives distinction to the written or spoken word of its possessor. Naturally therefore her letters are entirely free from the taint of sentimentality. Her affections, like those of her sisters, were strong, and she was genuinely and firmly in love with the man whom she married, knowing her mind upon that point as decisively as ever did Elizabeth or Mary. She was a regular churchgoer, and seems to have been sincerely, though not at all enthusiastically, religious; music she loved like a Linley, playing the "piano-forte" fairly well and singing much more than fairly well; for the theatre too she had a taste, and wrote both of plays and acting with judgment and discrimination; cards she disliked and played badly.

In person she was but a little creature, thin and generally pale, her cheek showing a hollow of which Charles Ward, in imitation of Rousseau, declared himself an admirer; her eyes both she and he describe as grey, though her miniature, according to the reprehensible practice of miniatures, has eyes as blue as sapphires. The hair in both portraits is dark brown, like the hair of Mrs Sheridan and of Mrs Tickell, but the locks plaited at the back of the miniature—which one would naturally assume to belong to the subject of it— are at present flaxen. Cut hair sometimes becomes bleached in course of years; while paint on the other hand sometimes darkens. Allowing something therefore for each of these changes, we may conjecture the hair of the living Jane to have been of a light, but not very light, brown. In both portraits, the poise of her head and neck is particularly graceful; graceful too is the figure shown by the miniature, although slender across the shoulders to a degree that suggests delicacy of constitution.

Mrs Linley and her daughter were still inhabiting South- ampton Street; and there seems good reason for supposing that Mrs Linley, though often talking of removing to a smaller house and of being unable to support the expense of this one, remained in it to her death. William was still living with them and, after experiencing the failure of *The Honeymoon*, was now engaged in writing and composing *The Pavilion*. The whole family frequented the theatre pretty constantly (Mrs Linley still had her box) and enjoyed a good deal of quiet and friendly social intercourse with a fairly intimate circle. The names of the Irelands, Barnards, Parkes, Angelos, Storaces, Cockers, Porchers, Howards and Prattens recur continually, in addition to those of Mrs Linley's whist-playing cronies, Mrs French and Mrs Lonsdale, both of whom lived near. Of the Angelos and Storaces mention has already been made; in both families the fathers were now dead, and " the Storaces " stands for Mrs Stephen Storace, a widow, and her daughter, or perhaps daughters. Henry Angelo, who has recorded Samuel's death, was now married and was living in 1800 at Windsor. Mr Pratten may be remembered as an apothecary who inoculated Mrs Tickell's children and gave some advice to Mr Linley; he and his wife seem to have lived in Bond Street, and their daughter Mary was suspected of a *tendresse* for William Linley. Some forty to fifty years later Mr Sidney Pratten was a flautist who had Fred Walker among his pupils, so that we may suspect a musical strain among these friends of the Linleys. Mr Cocker was a solicitor, and seems to have acted on Jane's behalf in the financial arrangements that preceded her marriage. He lived at one time in Nassau Street. Mr Parke is the author of certain volumes of recollections already quoted in these pages; he was a member of the orchestra—I think the leader of it—at Drury Lane, had known all the Linleys and had a high opinion of both Thomases, but not apparently of William.

189

The most intimate friend of Jane Linley was Jane Ireland, whose family history was an uncomfortable one. Her father, Samuel Ireland, was an engraver of some distinction, whose passion for art must have made him an interesting person although he was comparatively uneducated and of an irritable temper. For the last sixteen years at least of his life, Mrs Freeman kept house for him and was treated by his friends as a member of his family. She acted as his amanuensis and had some pretensions to authorship; some very successful private theatricals by children took place under her direction at Ireland's house, and Mrs Tickell reports that the prologue and epilogue were of her writing. She has been supposed to have been Ireland's mistress, but a passage in Jane Linley's letters seems to show that she was his daughter's aunt, therefore either his sister, or more probably his wife's sister. Another daughter, whom Jane Linley calls Anne, was married to Mr R. Maitland Barnard, who seems to have held some post under the East India Company and wrote a letter on Miss Tickell's account from the East India House probably in the year 1816. In his daughters, Ireland was happy enough, but a son of his, William Henry, produced, while still little more than a lad, a series of forged documents which he succeeded in imposing upon some judges, who should have known better, as genuine works of Shakespeare. One of these, a tragedy called *Vortigern and Rowena*, Sheridan brought out at Drury Lane in 1796. It failed conspicuously and deservedly; and young Ireland was entirely discredited. His father was suspected, but pretty certainly not with justice, of being a party to the fraud, and probably suffered in pocket as well as in reputation. Jane Ireland was a painter of miniatures and it is reasonable to suppose that it was she who produced Jane Linley's.

Having been born in January 1768, Jane was over thirty

years old when she engaged herself to Charles Ward, but it
is clear that she looked a great deal younger, small and slight
as she was, than her real age; and neither her mother nor
her brother seem to have been willing to regard her as
qualified to decide her own affairs uncontrolled. Precisely
when and how the Linleys became acquainted with Charles
Ward does not appear.[1] He came of a family that had been
for more than two hundred years connected with Staple Inn,
Samuel Ward having been master of that Inn in 1679,
Thomas Ward (who held the office for four terms) in 1734
and William Ward in 1763. In November 1756 a fire
broke out beginning at No. 1, which entirely consumed the
premises of five residents. "It was with the utmost difficulty that Mr Sackvill, Mr Ward and Mrs Ward and several
others saved their lives; but Mrs Ward's sister (a young lady
who came out of the country upon a visit the night before),
two of Mr Ward's children and their nurse perished in the
flames." Charles Ward had two brothers: William, a
lieutenant in the army, and Edward, a chaplain in the navy,
as well as two sisters, who were living with their widowed
mother at Lymington. His own calling is less definite;
he had been in the East Indies, had written a comedy, which
does not seem to have been ever accepted, and was at this
time engaged with some plan that had to do with the
manufacture or amalgamation of minerals. He was living
at 10 Staple Inn, in a house that has been described by
Dickens, who made it the residence of Mr Grewgious in
The Mystery of Edwin Drood.

Of the two hundred and twenty odd letters that passed
between these lovers and that have been preserved, a few

---

[1] From the Register of St Paul's School it appears that Charles
William Ward entered the school in April 1785, aged fifteen ; and
William Linley in February 1785.

are mere undated scraps, passed from the hand of the writer to the hand of the recipient—a suggested chance of meeting, a change of hour, a whisper as it were from loving lips to loving ears. The larger number, however, are communications of some length conveyed by the post when one or the other of the correspondents was away from London— epistles whose existence is largely due to Mrs Linley's custom of making a long annual visit to Bath. Jane usually spent her time during such absences in those prolonged sojourns with friends that were in her day habitual, and of course wrote regularly to her Charles. Sometimes it was he who, in pursuance of his mysterious business schemes, went to Birmingham, to Sheffield and into the wilds of Wales, whence, in a hand even more illegible than usual, he despatched long accounts of his adventures. Jane on her part had an admirable handwriting, clear and full of character —a writing that bears a family resemblance to those of her eldest sister, of her father and of William. Her grammar is seldom at fault, her vocabulary extensive and precise, and her spelling not often erroneous. True she invariably writes " chearful " and almost invariably " melancholly " but upon these points the current orthography of the period agreed with her; she also sometimes writes " teize "—as Samuel Richardson also did—and at least once I regret to say " neice." Other peculiarities seem to suggest that she had had a French teacher; thus the word " circumstance " always has an " o," and she tends to reduplicate consonants that English use leaves single. For her period, however, hers is the orthography of a well-educated woman; and although ladies of ours may possibly spell better, few of them ever write such good letters. In the prime duty of dating their letters both correspondents often failed; Charles was the greater sinner as to omission, but Jane, on the other hand, not infrequently dated wrong, conjoining a day of the week and a day of the month that did not occur simultaneously in the year of writing. Fortunately, the post-mark in those pre-envelope days was printed upon the letter itself.

The very first letter of the series, which comes from Charles, bears no post-mark, and is headed merely " Sunday 5 o'clock." We learn, from a later sentence of hers that it was " snatched from his hand while William was pacing the little parlour " in Southampton Street. It must have been written within a day or two of their explanation, which had taken place on the 17th of May 1798, and is chiefly occupied with his raptures. Already the disapproval of her family is being expressed. William has written a letter of advice to his sister, which she had forwarded to her lover.

Oh, Jane, my Lovely Jane, what a novice is your Brother! His whole Letter is one friendly caution, is it not too late? He begs you to use your discretion, reminds you of the treachery of Mr Gordon. . . . You are next warned against indulging in a partiality for one, who by his own confession, is not at liberty to decide upon his union with you. . . .

Though not possessing at the moment, the necessary independence. . . . I have every moral certainty of possessing it.

At the time of writing thus, Charles was apparently upon the point of leaving London, but perhaps it was before his departure that a little scrap of paper, now worn at the folds as though it had been long carried about, was handed to him; its contents run thus:

Past one o'clock. I will not sleep nor recommend you in my prayers to heaven my dear Charles before I repeat all I have *looked* & all I have *said*—I love you! I hope you *did* get some dinner to-day tho', for after all, you know, Love is but spare diet—Wm has desired me to rise early to-morrow on purpose to make his breakfast before he sets out for the

O

Lodge[1]—God bless you *dearest* Charles. Your sincerely affectionate Jane.

His next letter (with a post-mark of Birmingham, 23rd June) speaks of his fifteen hours' journey on a cold night, and bids her direct to him at " Brozeley, Shropshire," the spot whence, very probably, Jane's remote ancestors came, and from the immediate neighbourhood of which their surname originated. Neither Charles nor Jane, evidently, knew of such a connection; she finds a difficulty (and no wonder!) in reading the name and he, if he had heard or discovered that a place called Linley was in existence, would certainly not have failed to mention it, and to find a good omen in the fact. In a postscript he added: " Best Love to Mother and Brother " and then corrected himself: " Best Love! oh no...."

Jane answered rejoicing in his safe arrival and assuring him that indeed her eyes were not, as he chose to suppose, closed in sleep throughout the night. *" I often waked to think how it might fare with you,"* and her first question was whether rain had fallen in the night.

William, evidently dissatisfied with the small result of his letter to Jane, and in all probability urged on by Mrs Linley, now wrote to Charles, remarking that, since there was no prospect of his sister's hearing reason, he was trying her lover. This letter Charles forwarded to her, and on Monday, 2nd July, she replied:

Oh Charles, how I have been watching the Post all this last Week & it has brought *odious* Letters from every place but Birmingham, this is not meant as a reproach to you, but a

---

1 " The Lodge " seems to have been situated at Dartford and to have been the headquarters of a club, called, perhaps, " The Bowmen's Club," by which plays, dances and concerts were organised. William was a member ; and Jane considered his membership an extravagance.

proof of the undiminished affection I have acknowledged for you. I confess however that I have felt a little uncomfortable as I knew my Brother had written to you & all the confidence I have in your love could not entirely divest my mind of some degree of anxiety. Think then my dear Charles how happy I was made on Saturday when your Letters arrived. . . . I don't know what you have said to William but he seems still doubtful and makes me very angry indeed! had you seen me the day I replied to your first Letter Charles! *I'm afraid* I was in a great passion and the tears I shed were those of Indignation, at the accusation of *forwardness* for answering you so soon, and at the Injustice done you in supposing *you* would be of their opinion! If the candour for which you have praised me dear Charles were to meet with *such* a return what would you deserve? why what of course you would wish, and my pride would readily grant! . . . My Mother has fixed this day fortnight for her journey to Bath in a new opposition Coach which will carry her there for fifteen shillings! a temptation not to be resisted.

Charles, who had been at Sheffield, had left that place before this letter reached, and was writing to her at " four of Clock Morning, 3 Miles from Sheffield " on a scrap of paper afterwards stuck to his letter.

Dearest Jane, sweet Love that thou wert with me to injoy this Morning & this Prospect! Or rather that I might have thy Company Dearer to my Heart than all the World contains.

He was a good deal disturbed by not getting the expected letter from her and on the 5th she explains the delay:

I should have written Saturday but shall I tell you that I thought I should respect my *Mother's* opinion so far (altho' so opposite to my own) as to put in practice the necessary virtue of *self-denial* for one day, but not even that

motive should have actuated me, had I had an Idea that you
would be made uneasy by it, & I got no credit for my pretty
behaviour after all, for I heard William say to my Mother
" I haven't a doubt but she has answered his Letter again
by the return of the post! " Well, Master William—another
time " I won't be suspected without a *cause* I assure you! "
—Sheridan. How I laughed at Dr Pangloss last night.
Mamma & I were at the Haymarket tete a tete, for it was
a sudden frolic, & we could not get a Beau for love nor
money—however you see we took very good care of ourselves, and for my part there is but *one* in the World I would
have given three straws for.

William is off at last for Southampton, he went at six in
the Morning on Tuesday, & the preceding Evening, he
favored me with a farewel Sermon poor dear Fellow! I
should forgive him if his advice did not imply a doubt of my
beloved Charles for I know that he gave it from motives of
brotherly affection. . . . Only think of your passing by
Ashbourne, there it was I first heard of Mr. C. Ward;
little did I imagine that that flirting Gentleman who amused
himself with running away with Ladies' Necklaces would
obtain such an Interest in my heart. I was at that time
vowing eternal Indifference to you all, no, never would
I listen to any professions nor give you credit for any sincerity.
I had made up my mind to a state of blessed singleness and
defied ye all! How soon were these resolutions destroyed
when this pilferer of Necklaces made his appearance in
Southampton Street & made me hope at last that there *was
one* exception. There, I have not told you a bit of News,
now! Lord, I've no News for you my dear Sir! what care
I whether Buonaparte goes to Constantinople or not, or
whether France goes to War with America, or—Mr Pitt's
spasmodic affections are in his head or his heels, or—in short
I *did* read the newspaper with an audible voice to my good
Mother this morning but I met with nothing so interesting
to me as my own thoughts were, consequently you know

the sentences were no sooner pronounced than they were gone.

On July 11th Jane is found employed "about a thousand things" by her mother who was shortly leaving town. For her own part she will go for a week to the Cockers', and then to the Lewins' at Eltham, who have asked her to make a "very long" visit, and, Eltham being not too far from London to make it possible to see Charles when he returns, she is disposed to consent. She adds in a phrase rather unexpectedly modern that she is "tempted to cut the Birchalls altogether."

A gap of a fortnight now occurs; no doubt Charles was back in Staple Inn, and Jane at Mr Cocker's. On the evening of Thursday, 26th July, having parted from him but a few hours before—for he had seen her off—she wrote from Eltham:

Welcome as rest will be to me, I will not take it 'till I have told my dearest Charles how much I regret this second separation from him, how constantly I think of him, and how fervantly I shall pray for every blessing to him till I see him again! As I feared, you see Mr Lewin was blind and deaf to all our hints, I think he could never have been thoroughly in love with Mrs L—— or he would not have been so stupid. . . . We got here to tea without encountering any Highwaymen, tho' we have been informed that three Gentlemen were robbed Yesterday Evening at the same hour we were on our way here, about a Mile & a half from hence, so I think we are in luck. Mrs L—— and her Daughter received me very cordially and I daresay my time will pass as much to my satisfaction as it is possible for it to pass absent from you my Charles. Good Night—God bless you!

Friday Morning.—well Sir I have had a very comfortable Night & am risen as bonnily as can be. I tell you the truth by all that is *dear* to me Charles! They have got a sad stick of a Piano Forte here, but they have a tolerable Organ upon

197

which I mean to *improve* myself in old Handel nor shall the Lute be neglected you may be assured, for though I shall not be much delighted myself with the performance I shall hear upon it, if I can impart the slightest pleasure to you, your praise will give harmony to every note, and I shall be proud in spite of myself—by the bye the female Lewins do not know of the *treat* I have in store for them—they will be quite surprized.

Life at Eltham was cheerful but monotonous; music, mild parties and drives with Mrs Lewin in the buggy form the main events of the record. Jane also rode and wished that Charles could have seen her.

I don't know whether you would have recognized me in my borrowed Accoutrements, for I was dressed up in a habit of Miss Lewin's (who is almost twice my size) with a prodigious green shade over my face to save my complexion, but I found on my return that it was ornamented with a plentiful sprinkling of freckles notwithstanding.

She proudly reported that she had ridden nine miles, although she had not mounted a horse before "these three years." Mr Lewin took her through "a beautifully romantic country" (alas! poor Eltham! what has now become of that beautiful and romantic scenery?) and she reflected that *she* could live there in a cottage and rise at five in the morning "which is more than some People will say." They had a distant view of "Woolich & the Shipping," and the short-sighted, but evidently not *very* short-sighted, Jane saw St Paul's without the assistance of the "smart glass" Charles had given to her. "Oh, thank-you sir for it, but it was very extravagant of you to have it rimmed with gold!" There had been a fine dinner-party too:

twelve of the Eltham Noblesse, & seven or eight more in the

Evening. I played shilling Whist with the grave people &
cut the Youngsters & their noisy Vingt'un.

One Mr Pott was "mightily facetious and witty" at
dinner and made a pun about "chilli sauce." Does it not
all sound like a party in one of Miss Austen's stories?
Charles Ward, however, like some of Miss Austen's contemporaries, regarded the history of such doings as too
trivial for the dignity of pen, ink and postage; and with the
odd love for the systematic that belonged to the eighteenth
century presently urged the desirability of turning their
letters into what was termed by people of their day "a
regular course of correspondence." Subjects upon which
information could be given were to be introduced and
discussed, and he was to "*praise* with *pleasure* and *correct*
with *candor*." Fortunately for those later readers whose
applause he complacently forecasted, the excellent directness
of the Linley mind in her, and nature in both of them were
too strong for the execution of this scheme. Jane frankly
declared that she should grow tired of "a detail of sensations
and reflexions, and *sentiment*, you know, I have a decided
aversion to." Moreover she is a less meditative person
than he thinks her.

You have frequently observed me musing & perhaps have
thought I was making useful reflections on some book I had
been reading, or forming an opinion on what might have
been said or done at the time; but on the contrary my
Imagination has been wandering back to past times, &
dwelling on the memory of Objects for ever lost to me.
I feel a peculiar pleasure in this sort of contemplation, but
it is very idle, as it is productive of no one advantage to
myself or anyone else. I am very apt to indulge myself in
this foolish habit when I am in a mixed society where the
Conversation becomes so confused that I find my attention

199

tire, & then instead of trying to discriminate characters, or making any observations on the topics under discussion, my whole mind becomes alienated, and I am as much lost to what is going forwards as if I were not in the room.

Her memory must indeed have been full of many scenes far more interesting than anything likely to be furnished by the society in which she now lived. It is a pathetic picture that she draws of herself, the last sister, sitting " alienated " amid a buzz of society chatter, her mind back in the past hearing the voices and seeing the faces that were gone—and the more pathetic for the complete absence of pose.

At some time before this last separation, Jane had given her lover a ring, and now, sad to say, a misfortune had befallen this gift, " a rude fellow, in the warmth of his gratulations, broke my poor favourite ring " (whence we may conclude that Charles, with characteristic imprudence, wore this cherished ring on his right hand) " which is now confined like an invalid, to my drawer." Jane, though sorry for the misfortune, consoled herself and him with the reflection that to have lost it would have been a greater one.

In a letter on the 8th of August she gives an interesting and evidently accurate account of her earlier life.

How truly you have accounted for my slowness in conversation! It has been exactly as you say; when I was very young & living with my elder Sisters, I felt so sensibly their superiority that I scarcely ever spoke. My silence was often noticed by them, & in a way so discouraging to me that, half offended, & at the same time mortified by the consciousness of the dulness and Insipidity of my character, at least in their eyes, I have grown indifferent even to the wish of improving, & never felt perfectly happy but when I co^d converse by Letter with my young friends, then it was that all reserve was thrown off and I spoke freely the senti-

ments of my heart. My Sisters knew this, & were hurt at
the preference I gave to the conversation of School Girls.
Had I lived with them from my Infancy, I don't think that
the disparity of Years would have produced the distance
between us, but at the awkward age of thirteen, I was
suddenly brought from a country Town where I had been
residing with a Grandmother & great Aunt, with no other
advantages of education than going to a day school &
receiving a twelvemonth's instruction in music from the
Organist. Think what a change it was! I must indeed
have had a boldness & confidence unheard of, if I could have
been devoid of diffidence in the presence of such superiority
of mind & Talents, tho' possessed by Relations who were
only my equals in point of consanguinity. To those dear
Sisters I owe what little accomplishments I may possess.
Oh, if you had known them, Charles, You would find that
their Sister still falls very short of their perfections.

Now I'll tell you of a fault then my Charles! You are
like a spoilt Child that don't know what it would have, at
one time you want a fine sentimental Epistle, then you must
have a Journal, & now forsooth, you would have both. I'll
tell you what my dear? suppose I should send you neither,
how should you like that? . . . Not a creature has knocked
at the Gate to enliven the humdrum of a *family party*, nor
have we left the House the whole day. Mr Lewin, you
must know is going a long Journey to-morrow, first to
Southampton, & from there into Devonshire, so there has
been a great packing on the occasion & other preparations.
He is as cross as an old Cat about it, as he hates leaving his
home, but it is a case of necessity, I understand. After Tea
I proposed our having a little Concert together, for I have
found out he is not a little fond of accompanying on the
Violin. Mrs Lewin & her Daughters were at their Needles,
& he was sitting grumpily in a corner from which my
proposal rouzed him immediately, the Fiddle was uncased,

tuned, and down we sat. I must inform you (entre nous) that my kind Host is a very so so Performer. *I* am not a very capital hand at *execution* (tho' I know a crochet from a quaver as well as most folks) & yet we had the *audacity* to play Clementi, & Pleyel, at *first sight* oh what scraping and scrambling it was! poor Lewin was so eager in *his* part of the Concert, that (not being a very correct *Timist !*) he got the start of me several bars, & made such a doleful noise (looking all the time as if he were a second Gionavichi) that I could not proceed for laughing, and so left him in the lurch! however he took it all very good naturedly & says he shall tell his Brother, & mine, in what a superior style we play together.

Charles, who either really had, or made for himself, occasion to go to Woolwich on business had constantly talked of coming to call at Eltham on the way; and the absence of Mr Lewin raised this project from the region of dreams into that of possibilities. So strict were Mr Lewin's notions of propriety that he had hardly yet forgiven a lady who, while "visitting" at his house, went out in an open chaise with a gentleman to whom she was at the time engaged and whom she shortly afterwards married. It is scarcely surprising to find that from such a parent his own eldest daughter was concealing her engagement with (apparently) quite an eligible suitor, nor that the painting of her miniature for him by Jane Ireland was an affair of the profoundest secrecy. The general social life of the household, however, does not seem to have been in any way altered by the absence of its head.

A small party came to Dinner, & of course the *young Ladies* made themselves a little smart on the occasion & the *eldest* of these Misses (being grown particularly vain & fond of admiration since the 17th of May) must needs fancy she would make herself vastly charming by the addition of a little Rouge. "Well," exclaimed one of the company, "Miss Linley has done great credit to Eltham upon my word! she looks so well & has got such a *nice bloom!*" This is not the first time *you know* that I have been so *justly* punished, but if I had been among friends I should have owned the cheat immediately as I did at the Barnards'; now here, I was obliged to take the Compliment so *undeservedly* bestowed upon me, & before the company had departed my nice bloom was *all my own*.

Presently among her jaunts with Mrs Lewin in the buggy, to visit the "Lions of Eltham" Jane was taken to call upon an old and nearly blind Sir John Boyd, who at once inquired:

Is that *young* Lady any Relation to that Charmer that used to sing so divinely? "Only sister, Sir!" Then another exclamation broke forth and the old Gentleman asked me so many questions about my late Brothers and Sisters whom he remembered before *I was born* that I grew quite distressed and confused: at last he observed that I was not quite so young a thing as he took me for, for that if I was in being when Mrs Sheridan married I must be *past twenty* to which I owned very *honestly*. I think there is a melancholly sort of pleasure in talking of those near and dear Relatives you have lost & I look upon it as a respect due to their memory to think frequently of them, & not, from mistaken feeling, to endeavour to banish the remembrance of them.

Charles Ward's visit to Eltham is indicated by an unposted letter which he must have handed to Jane on Saturday the 17th or 18th of August. On the Sunday after he wrote very prettily:

Oh my Love, when I compare the velocity of time when we are together with its tardiness during absence I feel apprehensive that our Union will shorten our Lives very

203

much ; at least we shall think them short & Heaven forbid mine should extend a moment beyond yours.

The dread hinted in this and in some other passages can never have been entirely absent from Charles's mind; and in a letter written early in September 1798 it finds a fuller expression. He had been calling upon a young lady " a sort of relation " who was " fast advancing in a consumption," and was on her way to Bristol with her mother. The spectacle recalled to him how ill Jane had been on the 20th of May, and his imagination

put the dear object who then was ill upon a sick couch with the pillows and all the preparation of a Bristol journey. . . . Oh then what a pang did my foolish imagination give my heart, but your constitution, tho' not strong, is good, the evenness of your temper, the serenity of your mind all concur to insure you many years of happiness.

She replied that his account of his " poor young friend," brought very forcibly to her remembrance

similar scenes which I have witnessed when my dear Sisters were dying. Bristol could not save *them* nor I fear will this young Lady be restored by it. 'Twas my anxious Ozias that put so many dismal notions in your head about me; don't you know that it is said *little* People are the longest lived, by which rule I expect to hold it out to fourscore at least, so you see what you have to expect!

To readers who know within how few years the story of her sisters was to be repeated in her own case, and how short a span of married life lay before these lovers, her cheerfulness is almost sadder than his terrors.

She goes on to relate gaily how she and Mr Lewin rode over to breakfast with a very pleasant family at Blackheath and

got there by ½ past eight when you Londoners were hardly
out of your first Naps. . . . It was a beautiful morning &
I heartily wish it was more generally the fashion to rise early.
You talk of becoming " a great man," it is within the reach
of possibility then that I may become a great Lady & if
I am you will see what Reformations I will plan for the
good of the Constitution.

She remarks upon the speed with which her summer had
fled and upon how happy a one she had found it.

I believe it is not a new observation I have made that
when your time is uniformly spent in a regular succession
of occupations & amusements unmarked by any particular
Incident & with the Blessing of a contented mind, it passes
with great rapidity.

Clearly Jane, like her eldest sister, preferred a quiet life,
and at thirty had outgrown any taste for the noise and rush
of fashionable existence. She was at this very time carefully
avoiding an invitation to stay with Sheridan at Polesden,
while Sheridan was taking a good deal of trouble to invite
her. He, I think, had a genuine regard and affection for
Jane, and stood her friend very effectually a couple of years
later; but Jane really did not like Sheridan. Having lived
long in his house she must have known the essential kindness
and cordiality of his nature; but evidently his " ways " were
uncomfortable to her, and she was not susceptible to his
charm. Moreover she had certainly imbibed a belief that he
was not dealing fairly with her own family in money matters.
To stay under his roof was by no means a pleasure to her.

Not all the brilliance of his talents would be a compensation for the irregularity and racket of the life he leads—
besides Charles I could not be an indifferent Witness to his
unpardonable extravagance to say no worse of the style in

which he lives; every article of luxery I should see introduced
upon his table would excite painful sensations. Do you think
I could be happy to join in pleasures I knew to be purchased
at the expence of others! I say this in confidence my dear
Charles, there are People enough in the World ready to
abuse poor Sheridan, & however indignant I may sometimes
feel at his conduct, I am far from wishing to publish my
sentiments.

It is a curious reflection that if she had gone to Polesden
at this time, and had talked over with Sheridan—as she
probably would have found herself doing—the position of
her love-affair, she would most likely have expedited her
marriage by a couple of years.

In the early part of September, Mr Lewin returned home
and the card-table gave place to music, a welcome change
for Jane. Poor Mrs Lewin, afflicted with earache, had tied
up her face,

just in the same Lady Macbeth fashion *I* did when I had
such an interesting swelled face.

—a reminiscence not without charm for Charles.

So you remember the Lady Macbeth fashion[1] & perhaps
the resemblance in mouth and chin to Mrs Siddons, who
discovered that? who? but one who discovers fresh beauties
in you every hour.

Another diversion was by and by provided at Eltham by the
visit of " a groupe of gypsies " to the gate.

By way of a frolick we had our fortunes told—it is odd
enough that those People do stumble sometimes upon *the
truth*. I was told that I had been disappointed in my first
attachment and that the Gentleman whose name began with

[1] A portrait of Mrs Siddons as Lady Macbeth which shows the
sort of bandage in question may be found at p. 144 of Mrs Clement
Parsons' " The Incomparable Siddons."

a G, was at a *great distance*, but that I should soon marry *entirely* for *love*.

—a piece of *clairvoyance* so remarkable that suspicion can hardly do otherwise than point to Miss Mary Lewin as the medium. The gypsy spoiled the credit of her divination by carrying it forward into the future and prophesying for Jane a very long life, three husbands and eight children.

Towards the close of August William figures pretty often in the letters. Mrs Linley in writing to her daughter had mentioned that she had not once heard from her son.

Indeed, it is unpardonable of him to be so neglectful. I wonder how he employs his time, for even if he were in love, according to his notions, he would not wish to have an interview with the object of his Adoration above once a Week.

I am glad however you have an intention of writing to him & pray remember me very affectionately, for he is a good Fellow, in spite of his oddities. . . . Who is "the beauteous Eleanor Barwell"? I never heard of her before. Oh my dear dear Charles you say true; he never can have experienced so permanent an Attachment as ours is, & when he does may it be returned with as much sincerity. I can wish him no greater happiness. What do you think of his returning to India? alas, there is no prospect of his getting the wished for establishment here. Tell me if in his letter to you he mentions the subject & which way he seems inclined.

I think you seem to have changed your opinion respecting this abominable India business, for there was just as little chance of his having an independence here (when you gave such good reasons for his relinquishing his situation in the service, the day you called & spent with us, on which you were introduced to Ozias) as there is now. I remember Ozi was delighted with your reasoning because it coincided with his own Ideas, & I was not less so as I had not only reason but Sisterly affection on my side.

207

This is his [Mr Lewin's] waiting week, & we have got into fashionable Hours in consequence. Not a morsel of Dinner did we get yesterday till near six, & it will be the same to-day. I'm afraid the Lewins are shocked at my voraciousness & think I shall breed a famine in Eltham. The Ear-ache is still troublesome, & Lady Macbeth's Nightcap not yet discarded. This is the only intelligence Lewin House affords at present, excepting that I am & ever shall be " thine ever."   J. N. L.

A little before the middle of September the proposed return of Mrs Linley takes its place as an important theme in the correspondence, and Charles forecasts his evenings in Southampton Street.

Think of me with all the duty of an intending son-in-law set down, nailed, with your Mother, Mrs French & Mrs Lonsdale; knights in former times proved their love for their Mistresses by combats with Giants & Magicians, I go thro' nearly the same fatigue as Alley Croaker, and I think it the hardest of the two.

It was proposed that Jane should remain at Eltham, and that Mrs Linley should make a short visit there and take her daughter home with her.

I might as well play Whist in Southampton Street as in Eltham—*as* well? hadn't I better? You know, dearest Charles, I have ever given you great credit for your patience & perseverance at the card table especially when the all powerful Londsdale is of the party. I must say I think Mrs French with her long freezing Countenance is more *bearable*, she plays much more genteely as the phrase is, or much more *genteeler* as Mrs Londsdale would say.

The gaiety of this letter confirms her good account of her health. She " chaffs " Charles about his declaration that he had taken leave of ambition, tells him about her reading—

she had "begun a very voluminous work which I despair of ever getting to the end of till (I am) in a comfortable house and cosy Library of my own, it is no less a one than Gibbon's decline & fall of the Roman Empire"—and after deploring first her own want of memory and then thanking Heaven that she did not live in the days that Gibbon describes she proceeds

now Charles I am going to take a *great leap* [he had lately criticised her sudden transitions of subject] *turn over* & you will see who has taken my Pen from me.

On the top of the outside page, in the portion to be folded in, is written in that long looped characteristic "lady's hand" of the period, wherein each word is extended to cover twice its proper proportion of line:

Miss Lewin desires her Compliments to Mr Ward.

On the lower fold Jane has continued in her clear unaffected legible writing:

The young Lady would not *trust me* this time so you have it written down with her own fair fingers.   Heaven bless Thee ever!   J. N. L.   I suppose *this Letter* will be laid by with peculiar care.

The next time she wrote she returned to more anxious questions.   William had written to her a letter containing the following sentences:

Do you or do you not continue to correspond with C. W. If you say Yes! I shall expect you to follow up the Intelligence by informing me of the success of his copper speculations.   It is not very material to me whether you marry a rich man or not provided you marry a good one, but a long & uncertain courtship I can't bear & if my friend W. would reflect a little he would I am persuaded see the necessity there is of his keeping aloof a little or coming to the point at once. I am sorry to urge this subject a second time but I assure you it gives me very serious uneasiness.

For Heaven's sake my dear Charles, write to him & tell him the situation of *our concerns*. You know it is not in my power to do so, for whenever I have hinted an enquiry on the subject, you have appeared to me to wish to evade giving me a direct Answer & therefore I have not repeated it nor do I intend it. I have . . . perfect confidence in your honour & truth. . . . You will make my mind easy by explaining to him in what way your affairs are succeeding or I foresee I shall be harrassed to death by him & my Mother together on my return, but let *them doubt*, I *never will*.

Upon this letter of William's Charles found it difficult to look with "the eyes of a Brother." For her "delicate Forbearance" he thanked Jane, while assuring her that he always had been and always would be ready to confide to her every detail of his affairs.

You know, my sweet Jane, I told you that my concerns with the Copper Mines depended upon engagements with the Proprietors, and with commercial Men, but the War has so diminished all the Capitals concerned in trade that I have not yet been able to complete my arrangements with the latter, and without them it would diminish considerably my profits to engage with the Mining Proprietors. But tho' the War has thus retarded my commencement, yet it will from the increased demand it occasions abundantly compensate in the end.

How far this explanation elucidated matters for Jane we cannot tell; to an uninformed and dispassionate reader it will scarcely either clear away the obscurity or arouse any expectation of finding William's objections appeased.

Jane's next letter shall be quoted entire:

Wednesday, 26th September. MY DEAREST CHARLES, I am glad you have not written to William yet, since what I have confided to you has made you angry with him on my account, as, in the fullness of your heart you might have written rather sharply to him, which I should have been very sorry for—poor Fellow, tho' his sentiments on the subject are so very foreign to ours, he cannot have any other motive for writing to me as he has done, but anxiety for my happiness: but why should he not suppose *you* are equally regardful of it, or entertain the most distant Idea of your breaking your faith to me! alas there I cannot excuse him; however, of this I am certain, he has the highest opinion of your honour; what he means is, that in case of your failure it would not be possible for us to marry, & consequently, as *he supposes*, all further intercourse must be dropt, which he thinks would be very disgraceful to me! I declare now my Charles that even if such a thing were to happen, (which heaven forbid!) I should feel myself entitled to just as much respect in the World as I do now; but so long as our mutual Affection & esteem lasts such a seperation would be contrary to nature & reason. I answered William Yesterday, & told him very candidly that I had not, & that I *would not* alter my conduct towards you, that I was arrived at an age when I was capable of judgeing for myself, & at all events *he* had no right to controul my actions! I said, the more I had known of you my beloved Charles, the greater was my esteem for your character, that you possessed my entire affections, & *knew* that you possessed them, & if our union could not take place for Years, I could not understand why He or *the World* (upon whose opinion he lays a *great stress*) should interfere, or harbour a thought to the discredit of either of us: after having said much more in answer to what he had further written on the subject, I concluded by intreating him not to worry me any more about it, or encourage my Mother to do so, as it would answer *no end* but that of making my life uncomfortable to me. I informed him of my having desired

you to give him an account of your affairs, which you may
do without giving him cause to suspect that I had quoted any
part of his letter to you, & say all you can think of dearest
to make his mind easy. *He* doesn't deserve it, but you
will do it for *my sake*. Perhaps you will be able to
convince him how erroneous his opinions are, & bring him
to *reason*. I thank you my dear Charles for your Information: I trust you will succeed to your fondest wishes, & shall
be always anxious to know what progress you are making,
therefore don't think any communication on so momentous
a subject to us *both*, can ever be obtrusive, but I had rather
it should come from *yourself* unasked for, or I might be
plaguing you with questions wch you might not be able to
answer; & that would be so much precious time *wasted*
which would be better spent in writing or talking on other
matters. *You know* Charles[1] I have sent off an invitation to
my Mother this Morning; Mr Lewin will drive her here
either on Friday or Monday, & her stay cannot exceed a
Week, as the Lewin Family make their Visits Saturday
Se'en-night: oh how happy I shall be to meet my dear
Charles again! I assure you if it was not for that expectation,
I should very much regret leaving Eltham. Your society
makes amends for many unpleasant hours I pass in Southampton Street, & long before I knew of your affection for
me, your visits there, gave me more pleasure than you were
aware of. If you have heard anything from my Mother
respecting the settlement of our affairs, that will give William
any satisfaction, don't omit to inform him of it, he has desired
me to ascertain for him, whether the Annuities upon the
Proprietor's[2] shares are as Peake[3] said put into the hands
of Trustees Nightly. Of this I am ignorant, but I very
much fear it is not done, & Will: swears no power on earth
shall prevent his going out to India if on his return to Town

---

[1] She underlines " You know " because he had criticised her
frequent use of these words.

[2] She should have written " Proprietors'."

[3] Peake was the treasurer of the theatre.

he finds everything in the same unsettled state as when he quitted it. I am afraid we must lose him then after all! God ever bless & prosper you my own Charles! Yr affect^e.

J. N. LINLEY.

The answer immediately sent by Charles is very pretty and rather touching.

MY DEAR JANE, I will honestly confess, well as I knew I loved you, I did not think you had so much influence over my *mind* as your letter convinces me you possess; over my heart I knew you had the greatest. I will acknowledge the extract from your Brother's letter gave me—come, I'll say, uneasiness; subsequent reflection did not diminish it in the least; I was willing to believe I saw clearer into the tendency of expressions than your Brother; or ascribe it to the looseness and inaccuracy of his pen, rather than admit the very unpleasant imputations his language certainly conveyed. I anticipated your answer to my letter. " I know I said, my Jane will write full of Love & confidence, she will exculpate William from the intention, by ascribing it to his care for her happiness, she will lay it all upon his fear of the opinion of the world, but I shall see it just the same!" Your letter is come & I see it with the eyes you wish me to have.

On the 28th of September Jane had a surprise for her lover.

Did you go to see Biggs? Now Charles, how will you be surprized when I tell you *I was at the Play!* If it had been possible for me to have apprized you of my going you may be assured I would have done so, but there was no time, the party was made so *suddenly* & *unexpectedly*. Oh you blind creature not to see your Jane! perhaps you were not there for I looked in vain for you? I am delighted with Biggs, & was excessively entertained altogether, & so were the Lewins for they *all went*. I assure you it was a great indulgence from Mr Lewin for he had been complaining of a sore throat & objected to it at first from the fear of increasing his cold as the Weather was so unfavourable.

213

All this carefully worded narrative was a hoax, in revenge for some ostentatious mystery about nothing that had been kept up by Charles in conjunction with Jane Ireland.

Come, don't look grave and think I have been telling an Untruth. No! that I never do even in joke. (I have seen Biggs in Bath) the party really was proposed by me—I thought we might eat our bread & cheese afterwards with my Mother, sleep in Southampton Street and bring her here the next day, but that cross patch (her host) would not hear of it. The next day we were informed that the *Eltham Theatre* would open as last Night, with the Comedy of the Jew, and the *musical* Entertainment of the Purse or benevolent Tar, & by way of making amends for our disappointment of going to Town, we all *honoured* the Eltham Theatre. There was a brilliant & overflowing Stable on the occasion, & the Cocks & Hens in the Yard formed an admirable Orchestra with the trampling of Horses, which I expected would come upon the Stage & put all the paraphernalia to confusion every moment. I never laughed so heartily in my life. The Jew was not amiss, but the Gentleman who performed Frederick Bertram delighted me when he Hassured *is hever* dear Eliza of the *Hardency* of *is* affections.

Her little trick fell flat, however, owing to her correspondent's bad habit of turning first to the end.

Oh my best beloved, the very first thing I always look for in your Letters is the dear Signature & before I could unfold it my eye caught the mention of Hens, Chickens & Horses.

He on the same evening had accompanied Mrs Linley and Mrs Lonsdale to the theatre.

Think of your Charles in the Box Lobby, with your Mother on one side with her gown over her head & Mrs Lonsdale on the other with a red, deep red pocket Handkerchief over her's to save a new bonnet.

214

Mrs Linley was to come down on the 1st of October with Mr Lewin in the famous buggy.

I hope she will not object to being of our party to-morrow for you must know Sir we have *commanded a Play* & all the Noblesse of Eltham are to be present. Jane Shore & the agreeable surprize are to be the performances and part of the Gallery is to be laid with the Pit on the occasion.

" By this time," wrote Charles on the evening of Monday October 1st,

in all human probability your Mother has said " who is that from Jane? " by this time Miss Lewin has looked with an eye of intelligence & by this time you have had time to recover your countenance.

But this prophecy was not fulfilled, because, though Mrs Linley came at the proper time, Charles's letter was delayed. Mrs Linley was

in a sad croaking humour . . . but I am so accustomed to it & see so little prospect of the *cause* for it ceasing that I think the wisest way is to make up my mind for the worst & *hope* for the best! but I am so happy in your *disinterested* affection my Charles that it makes me insensible to what might otherwise give me concern. £30,000[1] would not compensate to me for the loss of that blessing. Oh, but a sixth part of that sum would facilitate a *still greater one* & when I think that nearly such a sum ought in justice to be *mine* I cannot but lament the loss of it.

On the 8th she announced that in all probability her mother and she would return home that day; and with this announcement the first series of letters closes.

---

[1] The figure of a young lady's fortune whom—or rather which—Charles Ward had recently been invited to woo.

CHAPTER 10. THE SANGUINE LOVER

FROM October 1798 to January 1799 there are no letters. During the intervening months the lovers were presumably both in London; and we may imagine for ourselves evenings in Southampton Street such as Charles had foreshadowed— she seated at work, while he made a fourth at the whist-table with those assiduous players, Mrs French, of the "long freezing countenance," Mrs Lonsdale whose game was so little "genteel" and Mrs Linley. Doubtless, also, the pair saw each other at the theatre as well as at the friendly houses of the Irelands, the Barnards and the Cockers. When the New Year began, William was still at home, and still talking of a return to India; Sheridan had still "settled" nothing; Charles Ward was still "morally certain" of an "independence"; and Mrs Linley still unfavourable to the engagement.

The first letter of the second packet comes from Charles, and is headed "Southampton." It bears the post-mark of that town, and the date stamp of 11th January 1799. The purpose of it is to inform Jane that he had met his brother Edward

here, to-day, but his Ship being under sailing orders, he is unable to proceed to Lymington with me, I therefore stay with him to-day & go to-morrow to Lymington, to which place I shall arrive too late to communicate my engagement with you to my Mother & send you word by the Post of her reception of it—& unfortunately there is no Post on Saturday.

216

From this it would appear that, until the beginning of 1799, Charles had not informed his family of his engagement, although " my brother Edward " had observed for himself the state of Charles's affections.

On this same day Jane was writing that she pictured to herself

the family party seated round the fire listening with attentive curiosity to your account of the *staid, domestic & religious* Lady you are about to introduce into it; Brother Edward perhaps edging in a word of concurrence now & then; tho' the pleasing image I drew was frequently in danger of being totally effaced by that which was *really* present to me namely Mrs Londsdale in full tongue!

She had received in the course of the day a visit from a Miss Smith, who either was, or was on the eve of becoming engaged to Charles's brother William (it is a complicating circumstance that these brothers were named respectively Charles William and William Charles).

I don't know *how it was* but, insensibly we fell to talking of nothing but *Wards* !

From Lymington all sorts of kind messages were sent by Mrs Ward and her two daughters, together with a warm invitation for Jane to pay them a visit as soon as possible. Mrs Linley and her son had, it appears, sent compliments to Charles's family, so that the engagement was now acknowledged on both sides.

From a letter dated " Monday Morning, March 4th," it is seen that Charles had again gone to Southampton and to Lymington, but Jane had not accompanied him. Indeed, it seems fairly certain that she did not become personally acquainted with his mother and sisters before her marriage.

The business of Charles in Lymington was that of

" persuading my sisters to resign their respective inamorato's,"
and the somewhat ironical contrast between his attitude as
a lover and his attitude as a brother does not seem to have
struck him. The suitors of both ladies, it appears, were
Frenchmen—" those abominable Frenchmen," Jane rather
gratuitously calls them—and may possibly have been
prisoners of war. A peace between the two countries must
at this time have seemed very far off, and marriage with a
French officer would inevitably have involved an English-
woman in painful divisions of feeling. The efforts of the
brother from London were entirely successful with the
younger sister.

The connection is broken off for ever, & happily for me
the vexation of the Gentleman has broken into a warmth so
offensive to my Sister that she allows she has had a complete
escape.

With the elder sister he did not succeed so fully, " but
I have in great measure checked the too great intimacy."
Busied with these family cares, Charles, for the first and
last time, neglected during nearly a fortnight to write to
Jane, a neglect which filled her with anxiety, and himself,
when he heard from his brother of her uneasiness, with
well-deserved self-reproach for his " vile procrastinating
habit." She meanwhile had gone once more to Eltham,
whence she wrote declaring her resentment over.

My confidence and my *reliance* on you were not weakened
by your unaccountable silence & yet I have been very
wretched. Oh Charles, I should have doubted my affection
for you & you would have doubted it too, could I have been
indifferent. . . . You have no idea how delightful Eltham
appears to me now! but *Saturday & Sunday* every object
gave my heart a *sinking feel* that cannot be described; even

218

in my Room (tho' you were never in it Charles) but there is a certain Drawer in which were deposited your Letters! The sight of that Drawer occasioned *such a sigh !*

The modest gaieties of Eltham were being resumed; William, apparently still in Southampton Street, was "fagging away" at *The Pavilion,* his musical play, of which he was both author and composer; and Charles had continued his journey to Bath. In that city Betty Tickell was at school under the care of the Misses Lee, at Belvedere House, now the Eye Infirmary. Sophia, Harriet and Anne Lee were daughters of John Lee, the actor, the eldest of whom was generally spoken of as "Mrs Lee."

Charles Ward called at the school, toiling doubtless up the steep Belmont slope, and beaten by the healthy March winds of that breezy district.

I was shown into a room where I found a young Lady alone, I took her by the hand & said "I am sure I am speaking to Miss Tickell." So it proved; had her mother walked out of the Picture frame in your Drawing room the likeness could not have been stronger. I had introduce(d) myself and a smile upon the mention of my name made me sensible I was well known. Mrs and Miss Lee joined us afterwards & a couple of hours rolled away without my perceiving it, can you guess the subjects? the number of enquiries & my answers. I made Betsy play, I made her sing. "Well then how do you like her?" I'll tell you I shall be very proud & fond of my *Niece.* Is not that exactly as you wish me to feel for her? I assure you I think her a very agreeable Girl, by no means a Beauty, her eyes are too light, the contrast between her hair and her complexion is not good, the form of her full countenance is not handsome, it is not sufficiently oval, and her neck is not well shaped, to which may be added that in her countenance there is a want of the delicacy & sensibility which so

eminently distinguishes above all countenances I ever saw
in my life, that of—Ah vain creature need I say more?
don't you already know who I mean? No, dearest Jane,
I don't think you handsome, had you been so I perhaps
should have admired without loving you, but I think you
more, I think you beautiful; by that I mean a Heart &
Mind warm & pure visible in your face, yes in yours there
is sense and feeling governed by Delicacy & these, which
would make every face good, beam in features and complexion which would be admired without them; what
must the conjunction produce? *Love*, such as your Charles's.
But how you run away with my Pen? here have I left poor
Betsy with all her faults upon her head to praise you. The
little faults I have enumerated are nothing, the whole is
agreeable & attractive & when she drops the *sliding looks*
taught her by Miss Ann Lee, which gives an *affected softness*
but *real slyness* to her countenance for the *delicate openness*
which her Aunt will teach her—she will be doubly attractive.
She appears sensible, good tempered, affectionate and well
educated, I like her musical talents, but I think her Aunt's
Example will induce her to drop a few misplaced graces;
hers indeed are very sparing & perhaps I should not discover
them but in songs I have heard sung by her Aunt.

At the end of this letter, which itself throws so much
light both upon the aunt and upon the niece, comes a report
of Edward Ward's replies to the inquiries of his sisters
about Jane.

Miss Linley, said he, from the little I saw of her seems to
have retained the polish of high life without its tinsel, she
is possessed of sensibility, good humour & good sense, and
moreover all is extremely pretty.

The good opinion thus expressed was the first stage of
a steady regard and kindness extended invariably not only
to Jane herself and to her children, but to her niece and her

grand-niece. No brother by blood could have been more truly a brother than Edward Ward became to his sister-in-law, and the assurance that her infant children could count upon his wise and benevolent guardianship must have been the greatest possible comfort to her when she lay dying.

Jane could not at all agree with Charles's very moderate estimate of her niece's charms. Most people, she maintained, would certainly consider Betsy a "very pretty girl." As to those "sliding looks" Miss Ann Lee was not to be blamed. "I remember her having them from a child & both her Aunt Sheridan & I have in vain attempted to cure her of them." The family attachment which was so strong in the Linleys led Jane to hope that "Betsy's" home might be with herself and her husband. She mentioned the hope to her mother, who remarked that she did not think Charles Ward would like the plan; Jane immediately replied: "Oh, indeed he will consent to anything that will contribute to *my* happiness," and in so replying she did less than justice to her lover, since he had not waited for her suggestion to frame that very project.

I had intended as a marriage present for you to have wrote to her, that with a *new Uncle* she had got a *new home*.

Even if Betsy had not "answered his expectations" and proved to be agreeable, he should have done this for Jane's sake;

Besides, my dear Jane, you are not only bound to protect her by the common tyes of blood called Duty, but you are by the obligations you have received from her Mother. I assure you they stand first in my mind & the gratitude I *feel* for Mrs Sheridan & Mrs Tickell making my dearest Love what she is will manifest itself in my regard for her Children.

Jane was now about to leave the kind Lewins and return home.

I have a particular Engagement on Thursday, which I have promised faithfully to perform. You say you do not care where I go so I need not fill up a line in my Letter to inform you what that Engagement is.

Her mocking reference is to a declaration at the close of one of his letters a few days earlier: " I *care not* where you go, but I *care* what you think & feel." The mysterious engagement is by-and-by explained as being, " to the altar at St Martin's to receive a spiritual blessing from the Bishop of London "; in fact she was going to be confirmed, having promised Ozias that she would take advantage of the next opportunity.

The great interest of the Southampton Street household at this time was William's operetta or " musical entertainment," *The Pavilion*. The first night was now eagerly anticipated, and Jane was sorry to find her brother so sanguine. " The Performers praise his Piece and tell him it is sure to succeed, but are they *sincere* ? " A little instance of that tiresome tendency constantly to change her determinations which seems to have become characteristic of Mrs Linley in her later years now occurred. Charles Ward had, it would appear, been entrusted with the duty of collecting, while in Bath, certain sums due to William and Jane—very probably under their grandfather's will. Now Mrs Linley desired " to wait till she goes to Bath, that she may receive it for us, but that won't do, my dear Mamma ! "

Early in April the traveller crossed from Bristol to Swansea, encountered " a complete gale of Wind " and " suffered all the horrors of Sea Sickness." As he was going into comparatively wild parts of Wales he proposed to purchase a " Poney," a plan of which Mrs Linley greatly approved as showing some tincture of " œconomy." To her Charles endeavoured to explain certain points in regard to income-tax—which the good lady, as indeed might be expected of her, was extremely anxious to avoid paying. So complicated was the case that both spelling and grammar were cast to the winds in the effort to expound it.

Tell your Mother (to whom give my Love) that Mr Pit was aware that a number of people would make the same divisions of property as she has done to avoid the Tax & therefore fixed a day before the Tax commenced for all these arrangements to be made on or before & that hers was afterwards.

Charles's journey from Swansea to some spot with an illegible name, halfway to Caermathen was after all performed either on foot or by means of a hired mount, Swansea proving to be " not at all well provided with Poneys for Sale." His brother (William) on hearing this advised the purchase of a goat, " to make your peregrinations upon "; as for Jane, she cared nothing how he was mounted " so you are safely conveyed back to me with all our hopes realized & a nice little white Cottage bought." On another point she was not so indifferent. The ring which she had given him, and which had once before been broken, was now lost, having, he thought, probably slipped off when he washed his hands at the Neath copper works. Its absence perturbed Jane considerably.

If my Mother should ever enquire for it I don't know how I shall bring myself off tho'; she values the ring as it was a token of affection from her husband & I suppose would be highly offended with me if I were to inform her in what way I have disposed of it, but when I gave it you I thought

223

it as safe as if it had been on my own finger. If you should get it again, my Charles, oblige me by laying it by, & I will give you something else in lieu of it when we meet.

She was busy when she wrote this with preparations for a dinner-party. Mrs Lee and Betty Tickell were now staying in Southampton Street, and the party was probably in honour of the former. The Jacksons, Porchers and Cockers were expected, and in the evening, some " Beaux " " to our Concert." She heard " Betsey's little pipe " at the moment.

The production of *The Pavilion* was for the second time delayed and Jane evidently suspected some hidden animosity at the theatre—apparently with justice. She was glad that William's name had been mentioned in the newspapers only as that of the composer, " but it is a hard thing that there should be a possibility of so unoffending a creature as he is, having Enemies."

At Caermathen, where he was now arrived, Charles called upon Charles Sheridan, who to the surprise and mortification of his visitor remembered little or nothing of Jane, of whom he recalled only that she was a pretty little girl. Considering that, when Charles Sheridan left England for Sweden, Jane was not yet four and a half years old and that he had in all probability never seen her since, he might easily have remembered even less. Charles Ward found him " a man of great abilities indeed, but a consciousness of his powers, the constant current of his eloquence makes him rather discourse than converse." Mrs Charles Sheridan was beautiful and agreeable, but the charms of her conversation were, to her visitor's taste, diminished by an Irish accent. In speaking to each other the pair were more effusive than he considered seemly, the husband using terms of fondness and the wife her consort's Christian name. It would be interesting to know at what date it ceased to be an impropriety for a woman to address her husband as " Charles " in their own house and in the presence of a third person.

At about the same time Richard Sheridan had been calling in Southampton Street, where he had repeated " some beautiful words that are to be set for Mrs Jordan " in Kotzebue's play (i.e. *Pizarro*) " & William is to be the composer." Sheridan added, that in respect to *The Pavilion*

the performers were a set of Hypocrites . . . for that they told *him* he [? they] did not think it would do! and added that nothing would give him more severe Mortification than its failure, that he knew there were a set of envious Rascals in the House who would endeavour to keep him back & would never suffer him, if they could prevent it, to be in any musical department there.

All of which William heard " with the greatest sangfroid, either from Incredulity or a confidence in his own Abilities." Next day Mrs Linley is reported as " *niggling* " William to go to Hertford Street, about this song " but his proud Spirit will do it with a very ill grace."

Mrs Linley, with her usual eye to the main chance, had now " engaged a Gentleman Lodger who takes possession of his Apartments when she goes to Bath." This lodger was a young man called Morris, who often appears in the correspondence under the nickname of " Signor Morici." He seems to have held some small Government appointment, to have been an author in a small way and a quiet and meek person. The plan was that he and William should live together in Southampton Street during the absence of the two ladies, but should not board there, " which they will certainly find much pleasanter." At this stage, Jane approved well enough of the arrangement, which was adopted apparently as an alternative to the removal of the family.

I believe it would fret my Mother to death either to leave the House or to lose William. Indeed, as the India situation is not relinquished, I think he might manage to Weather out another year in Southampton Street.

Charles, now at Bangor, and in the eighth week of his absence, wrote most hopefully that he had made an expedition to Anglesea, and that his object was now nearer to success than he had expected. His enlargements of this statement do not however indicate anything more decisive than his observation in action of some process which he had hitherto known only in theory, and his finding certain difficulties smaller than he expected. This degree of encouragement was enough for his ever sanguine temper, and from the tone of his letter one might suppose that he reckoned upon returning to marry in the course of the summer. To what degree Jane had already fathomed the Micawber-like disposition of her lover remains uncertain; but her observations show that she did not count as he did upon his eventually succeeding. She is not, she says, of so sanguine a nature as he, and although she loves to encourage hope of success is yet perfectly sensible of the uncertainty of it. She was, as Elizabeth and Mary had each been, a woman who faced facts; the sincerity characteristic of her was, as it so often is, an intellectual as well as a moral quality; if she did not deceive others it was because she first did not deceive herself.

The presence in town of Betsy and of her friend Miss Lee added to the gaieties of the Southampton Street household. " Engagements," Jane reported, " come upon us thick & threefold," and presently aunt and niece were " very busy making preparations for a masquerade " and the ward-

robe of the theatre was being ransacked to provide gypsies'
dresses for them. On the morning after this entertainment
Jane thus summed up her experiences and conclusions:

Well I think a Masquerade in *itself* an Insipid Amusement.
After all an hour is sufficient to show you the different
characters, & the eye being gratified you listen in vain for
any other entertainment. This was my case last night, who
(to do myself justice) was as dull a person as the rest of the
groupe; the party consisted of Mrs Boscawen, as one of the
Turks (no bad Mask) myself and Betsey as Gypsies & Miss
Siddons[1] in a fancy dress, who was as fatigued as myself
with five hours of empty noise—indeed she did not enter
into the spirit of the thing so much as I did, for when I saw
our Neice tripping on the light fantastic toe with a smart
Domino I joined in the dance by way of being a Chaprone,
tho' they held out so much longer than I could do that I was
obliged to leave her at last to the care of herself. I assure
you the young Lady likes a little flirtation as well as the
rest of us, and as she has no mean opinion of her beauty she
was quite eager to unmask her pretty face when she saw
two or three more do it towards the conclusion of the
Evening, or rather the beginning of to-day, as we did not
get home till near three this morning, Betsey enchanted with
everything she had seen & heard, & I still more delighted to
find myself in Southampton Street again. See the difference
between seventeen and——

Charles having sent a message to Betsy in which he
desired her to

take up your pen & describe with the utmost exactitude your
Aunt's Appearance and Spirits,

Jane's next letter contained her reply.

[1] Miss " Sally " Siddons, whose tragic love story came to its crisis
in the preceding year, when her dying sister, Maria, extorted from
her a promise never to marry Sir Thomas Lawrence, whom both loved.

Sir in pursuance of your directions, I proceed to inform you, that my Aunt I believe has had a disorder called the dumps on account of your absence, for I can't prevail on her to dance at a Masquerade or to like what is becoming in dress, pray Sir, reply whether this be a desire to see you or a total *lassitude des Esprits*. But to be brief, she is I take it no taller than when you left her certainly no fatter (for raking does not improve people in that) as pretty as ever & always at her writing Desk which my G. Mother calls Fiddle faddling. Having now fulfilled my *duty* Sir, it remains for me to assure (you) that I shall gratefully remember the faults you speak of & am your devoted humble, most obedient &c. &c. &c. &c.

The writing of this lively little note is of the Linley type, but larger, less regular, compact and well-finished than Jane's. Some specimens of William's writing closely resemble this sample of Betsy's. Later in life—thirty-eight years later—hers had grown more angular and longer in the loops—had come in short to be the handwriting common to all the grandmothers and great-aunts who wrote letters in the decade 1830–1840; and the liveliness had faded from her style. The "raking" of which Betsy wrote was continued by a dinner at the house of Mr Woodfall—no doubt the printer of the Junius letters—who was a friend of Miss Lee, and had invited Mrs and Miss Linley to accompany her.

The Evening was spent wholly in conversation excepting that it was once interrupted by a song from my Ladyship & a Duet with Betsy. We should have had more Music, but the Instrument was not playable & we were obliged to tune our pipes without it, which I did not like at all, but as I told you, I had determined to be all over *Amiability*, I complied with all the grace imaginable; as for my Mother I was thunderstruck at her good behaviour; she yawned but twice, & did not mention cards once.

Charles had now reached Garstang, whence he wrote more hopefully than ever. The " material " that he needed —whatever it may have been—was plentiful and neglected, therefore cheap, in that locality, and from it he expected to extract, " Sulphur, Independence and Happiness." The pair had now been engaged for a year and, since the anniversary found them many miles asunder, their glad remembrance remains recorded.

" Since the last seventeenth of May, Jane," wrote Charles, " I have felt

a happiness I never knew before . . . what would be my sensations, my hopes, my expectations if you were not. Oh, a blank in which Misfortunes & Ills would write their character, but in which there would be no trace of Joy or Comfort.

He had at this time seen a prosperous cousin and felt sure that Northumberland would be the place in which he would establish himself. He looked forward to coming to town in some three weeks' time in order to make a contract with Sir M. Ridley, and to live happy ever after as Jane's husband. Jane on her part was about to lose the pleasant companionship of her niece, for whom it had been settled that she should return to Miss Lee's until she was eighteen. After that period,

Mrs Boscawen has it in contemplation to procure her a situation with one of the Princesses which may certainly be of advantage to her & therefore I could not speak against it especially as she likes it herself, & Miss Lee & her Grandmother are desirous of it.

Evidently Jane's taste would not have lain in the same direction, but she reflected that the post might be resigned whenever a home was ready for Betsy with Charles and herself, and that meanwhile anything was better for the girl than a home in Southampton Street.

Your Favourite, Ozias is with us, & the same odd creature as ever. He frightened his Mother to death yesterday by declaring he should have a *red hot fever* in consequence of having eat too much Dinner the day before at Mr Palmer's,

—a prognostication happily not fulfilled. A visit had been received from Charles Sheridan who had remarked upon the likeness of Jane's eyes to those of her eldest sister, and had seemed moved by the family's music, which he said, "put him very much in mind of old times." She mentions that the Sheridan brothers had not met, although they had not seen each other for seventeen years. Charles did not "chuse to go to the great Gentleman's house," and Richard had been "too much engaged to wait upon his elder brother, & there the matter rests!"

The hopes of which Charles had recently written almost as though they had been certainties were proving altogether illusory.

I am sorry dear Love to tell you, that the result of my enquiries here have not been so satisfactory, Sir M. Ridley's Works are under Contract for a term of years & so much of the mineral I am in search of is engaged in the same way, that I apprehend I shall not be able to make myself certain of a sufficient annual quantity.

Northumberland therefore was no longer the Eden destined to contain their cottage: and from Newcastle Charles was proceeding into Derbyshire in order to visit certain mines belonging to the Duke of Devonshire. This change he urged her not to consider as a disappointment or as very important.

. . . it is only my sanguine disposition, my Castle building imagination which gives it that complexion—& already I hope I may fix in Derbyshire—& then Oh Jane, while I am carrying my plans into effect at Cheadle, if you were to pay a visit to your friends at Ashbourne. My Heavens, what happiness! How much better than my fixing here!

And he begins to inquire whether he cannot possibly be introduced to and call upon her friend Mrs Lee (whom he ought to have spelled " Leigh ") at Ashbourne. This lady I suppose to have been the friend and probably relative of Mrs Stratford Canning, whose husband read the service at Mrs Sheridan's funeral. The letter of introduction Jane was ready to give him, but could hold out no hopes of a visit to Ashbourne from herself. It was several months since she had heard from Mrs Leigh, and although Mr Leigh had been in town he had not called at Southampton Street. Ozias was still at his mother's and sent his compliments.

I believe he guesses I am writing to you by his sly saucy looks. He said the other day, " Jane! how go on flames & darts! When is the happy knot to be tied ? " I asked him if *he* would tie the happy knot? But he declined it from a superstitious Idea of the marriage not proving happy, or one of the parties might die & *He* of course would feel uncomfortably in case of such events following.

Mrs Freeman, a lady whom in spite of her friendliness Charles found it impossible to like, had had an odd vision; she had seen him walking in Marylebone Street with a smart young lady to whom he was talking very seriously and of whose arm he had hold in precisely the same manner as that which he used with Jane. So strong was the likeness that Mrs Freeman was rooted to the spot with astonishment. Here was a fine opportunity for jealousy if Jane's temper had inclined in that direction, but she, with her accustomed reasonableness, accepted at once the likely solution proffered by her lover—namely, that Mrs Freeman had seen his brother William walking with Miss Smith. The day on which she wrote, 24th May 1799, was to see the first performance of *Pizarro*, that highly bombastic melodrama, which, incredible as it seems, Sheridan pronounced to be " the best thing he ever wrote."

In Derbyshire Charles recovered all his hopes. Here no hindering contracts were in force, and once more he declares that never was he more sanguine in his views and never believed them nearer completion.

Jane's last letter of the series contains one of many references to Mrs Linley's custom of letting her box at Drury Lane Theatre—much to her daughter's displeasure. How far Mrs Linley was transgressing an actual rule, or how far Jane's objection rested upon a ground not so much of probity as of dignity, it seems impossible at this distance of time to be quite sure. On this particular occasion, Sheridan had called to borrow the box for the Speaker, " and it was fortunately *disengaged !* " He further

invited us to dine with him in the Prince's Room at ½ past four: my Mother *would* go, tho' I would *very* much rather have declined it, & Ozias very wisely preferred going to the Howards': at the appointed hour we went, & after groping about behind the scenes in the dark half an hour, we found the apartment, but no one in it, or any preparations making for Dinner! We heard that Mr Sheridan was gone to the House of Commons & desired we might keep some hot for him; you may conceive my Mother all this time fretting & abusing by turns, and at last *I* was obliged to send to the Shakespeare to know if there really was any Dinner coming or not! to conclude this agreeable adventure, a fine boil'd fowl & Asparagus made its appearance at last & restored us both to good humour, but we were tete a tete, & I left my Mother sitting over a bottle of port at six o'clock, to join the Irelands and Mrs Marsh at the Play. Charles Sheridan was here this morning. He and his Brother have met at last and Sheridan wants him to be of his fishing party, but he had other *fish* to fry! (I hope you don't think now y^t his superior mind stooped to this pun; no, I was struck with the *Novelty* of the Idea & have therefore treated you with it.)

Her lover's reply is still dated from Derbyshire, but bids her direct the next to Birmingham. To that place travelled on June 10th one of her most characteristic letters.

. . . He (William Ward) called here upon a most gratifying occasion to me, & as I know you are free from jealousy I will inform you that he brought me a present from a young Man for whom I have conceived a sincere regard, & so kind a letter that I could not deny myself the pleasure of answering it immediately who think you can be this new Correspondent? Who, my Charles but our worthy brother Edward! . . . his present is a book Charles very handsomely bound which I mean shall have a conspicuous place in our Library! it shall be placed next to the Family Bible & Prayer Book; I will have no treatis's on Chymistry, no speculative thoughts upon the respective virtues of copper or leaden Ore within a Shelf of it.

The book was "Wilberforce on Christianity." After a little talk of summer plans, disconcerted by a resolve on the part of Mrs Symmons to move to a new house, she falls to reminiscences.

Yesterday was the ninth of June; do you remember the last ninth of June? No! Have you forgotten when, as our dearly beloved *Cousin* you were introduced to the hospitable couple in Palace Yard? The poor old Halls commemorated their nine and thirtieth anniversary with the same glee and merriment as last year . . . all the old Souls enquired very kindly after you & the good Dame Kemble observed you were a very well-behaved agreeable young Man!

Pizarro has "set the Town a madding," she begins to think it will run as long as *The School for Scandal.* On Friday *The Rivals* is to be acted at "The Lodge."[1]

William plays Falkland: my Mother & I go with your Brother W. Welbanke & Lawrence[2] & poor Jane (Ireland) is excluded tho' I begged hard for her, & indeed had the pleasure of a *Set to* on the occasion, well,—I will make her amends when I am my own *Mistress.*

On Saturday she is to sit to Lawrence, but does not know whether he means to begin another picture or to finish the old one. In all probability the portrait for which she sat at this time was that still preserved by the Ward family and reproduced in this book. The very large, pale pink hat, though picturesque, is a little overwhelming, especially for so diminutive a person as Jane seems to have been. If it was her usual wear and not merely an "artists' property" it shows—what indeed I should be inclined to think—that the youngest Miss Linley by no means disdained to dress in the height of the fashion.

After this letter comes an interval of two months without any record. Charles must have fulfilled his intention of hurrying back from Birmingham, leaving some of his business there to be completed on a later visit. Certain it is that he was in London when she left on August the 7th or 8th for Rugby. He escorted her to the coach and recommended her to the care of a lady who was to be her fellow-traveller.

[1] See p. 194.
[2] Probably Sir Thomas Lawrence, not however yet knighted.

234

CHAPTER 11. JANE'S FORTUNE

ON the 9th of August 1799, Jane wrote to announce her safe arrival at Rugby, to which place she had driven from Dunchurch, after dark, in the pouring rain and in an uncovered carriage, without any extra wrap to protect her:

But, Charles, I certainly must have a most *robust* constitution, after all, for owing to the immediate remedies I had recourse to on my arrival & the kind attention of Mrs Ingles & her Servant, I have had a very good Night, & am risen perfectly refreshed and well.

Judging from the well-known customs of our forefathers, we may surmise that these remedies took the form internally of hot spirituous drinks and externally of a bed thoroughly heated with a warming-pan. The lady with whom she travelled had proved to be a very agreeable companion.

From her manner & conversation, I judged her to be a Woman of a superior education, &, with that, her countenance expressed such gentleness, & benevolence that had I been a young Heroine in distress she would have instantly won my confidence.

This amiable lady turned out to be " an old acquaintance " of the friends to whom Jane was going; she was " Mrs Emelia Coxe, the female Mentor, who has written several things, & Sister to the Coxe who wrote the travels." The " Coxe who wrote the travels " was Archdeacon of Salisbury; another brother, also in holy orders, met his sister at Stony Stratford, and yet a third, who " was not a clergyman " had seen her off; possibly this was the Peter Coxe who, several

years earlier, at Mrs Thrale's Brighton house, repeated some
of " his own compositions in verse," in such melting strains
that Miss Burney thought he would have wept over them.
In short the Coxe family were literary, but not, it may be
suspected, lively.   A few words about the " almost impassable
roads," the difficulty of the " poor, miserable horses " in
advancing and the manner in which they were " most
unmercifully beaten by the Brute of a Coachman " remind
us of evils that this generation has outgrown and forgotten.

Jane's host, Dr Inglis, of whom she writes, according
to the pronunciation, as " Ingles," seems to have been a
master at the school.

The society of Rugby was better than that of Eltham;
" the Masters must necessarily be men of Education, but I
assure you, Sir the females of Rugby form no despicable part
of it." Mrs Bloxam—or " Bloxham," as Jane spells it—the
sister of Sir Thomas Lawrence, was one of these agreeable
ladies.

Her gay letter was still on its journey when a packet was
despatched to her calculated to render insipid all the attrac-
tions of Rugby.   William Linley, now in Bath with his
mother, had written thence to Charles a proposal that he
should marry Jane immediately and take the place of Mr
Morris as his mother's lodger in Southampton Street.   Such
a proposal could obviously not be declined by the bridegroom,
nor, indeed, was Charles at all disposed to decline it.   His
hopeful temper perceived in the scheme a prospect of instant
happiness, and although he leaves the decision entirely in
Jane's hands, it is easy to see the direction of his own wishes.
By the malice of Fate, the packet was delayed; poor Charles
waited in vain for her reply, and was obliged to write repeating
the information.   Jane answered at once; her lucid intelli-

gence saw both the motives at the bottom of her mother's mind and the many drawbacks of the scheme. For herself it would be in the main advantageous—the change would make Southampton Street a paradise—but how would he bear to be living under the same roof with her mother? She acquiesced, however; evidently her hopes prevailed over her fears; and apparently Charles's answer to William included an expression of consent from her. William on receiving it wrote a most kind and affectionate letter, but, before he had posted it, had a further talk with his mother, and lo, that most provoking woman had taken a new turn. She had calculated that the pair would not require all her spare rooms, and was now resolved that Morris also should remain.

Well, dear Girl, observe the sequel, William flys in his usual passion & makes a solemn vow that he will only remain in England & stay in her house upon condition that her Daughter & Son in Law shall be the only inmates.

William, whose " usual passion " under what appears to have been a usual provocation, can hardly be much blamed, in reporting this change of front besought Charles to write and dissuade Mrs Linley from her new plan, and to write also in the same sense to Mr Morris. Next morning came yet another letter. Mrs Linley was now ready to assure her family that Mr Morris should stay only until Christmas, and that the marriage should take place then. But how could any of them rely upon the word of such a woman? Even the ever sanguine Charles could not suppose that Morris would really be allowed to depart at Christmas; and the prospect of a marriage before or at that season must have begun to appear extremely remote.

His outspoken denunciation of Mrs Linley's " deceit & parsimony " arouse a certain sympathetic satisfaction.

237

Early in October Jane went with Miss Sarah Bird to Birmingham, where Charles intended also to be later. On or about the 25th of the month Jane received a letter from her brother, written, as he told her, by the express command of his mother, and representing not his feelings but hers. William, to do him justice, appears to have been consistently anxious for his sister's marriage to take place without delay, so that he might return to India, leaving her under that " protection " which every man of the eighteenth century conceived so essential for the " females " of his family. Certain passages of the letter Jane quotes, and her inverted commas, though they enclose a sample of very odd, oblique narrative, and a curious confusion of pronouns, do not at all obscure Mrs Linley's intention. Jane was required

to get the better of my attachment to a Man, who in every other respect has my Mother's fullest approbation, but whose total want of fortune to support you creditably in life would render your marriage with him a source of wretchedness to yourself & your Family, that if notwithstanding, you are determined to persevere in your attachment she at least hopes you will see the necessity of Mr Ward's discontinuing his visits till the period arrives at which he can come forward with his proposals & is able to receive & support you as you deserve.

. . . I shall answer my Brother's Letter in a few days, & shall inform my Mother of *my determination* still to consider you as my future Husband. Yes, if you were reduced to absolute Beggary! that if she will not allow me the happiness of seeing you sometimes in *her* House, I shall certainly think it my duty to obey her in that article, but I will promise no further—we will proceed openly Charles, I will have nothing done clandestinely altho' I fear it will cost me dear, for my Mother's violence is sometimes too much for me. I shall therefore caution her not to be too severe upon the only

Daughter she has left. Agitation of Mind is injurious to my health. I feel that it is.

On his own account, William begged her to come home as soon as she could, that he might enjoy as much as possible of her company before they parted, his passage being now actually taken for February. The appeal melted all her anger. She felt that she might never see him again—as I think she never did.

Not content with banishing the unwelcome suitor from her own doors, Mrs Linley tried to close against him those of Mr Ireland.

She accuses me of deception & says " you'll soon overcome this attachment; that you are not possessed of much feeling."

Charles himself suspects that the improved income of Mr Morris had some share in Mrs Linley's determined opposition.

She already thinks Morris was & might be again attached to you & after the lapse of a little time, how could you hesitate between C W Ward absent & poor & Morris present with a place of £800 per annum.

On Sunday, 4th of November, Jane was eagerly expecting the arrival of Charles in Birmingham, where he wished to see Mr Boulton. The sermon seemed long to her, and as she returned from church she fancied every figure descried at a distance by her " purblind eyes " to be his. But his coming was postponed; some " Drawings of Machinery " had to be finished; her hopes were delayed until Wednesday. For once she breaks into a denunciation of the world around her:

It provokes me to see so many wooden headed brainless Beings, rolling in riches that they have not hearts to spend, whilst You & the very few who resemble you, possess dispositions to do good without being blessed with the means.

Both were now agreed that to live with Mrs Linley would have been, as Jane temperately puts it, "a comfortless plan" or, in the words of the more emphatic Charles, "a state of inquietude & torment." Probably they were right; but the prospect actually before them was not very smiling either. For the last three months Mrs Linley had succeeded in thoroughly harassing her daughter, her daughter's lover, her son, and even, perhaps, herself; and there appeared every probability that the next three months would be passed in a very similar manner. Let us at least hope that the fortnight spent together by Jane and Charles in Birmingham was peaceful and happy. During that interval there were of course no letters, and the next packet opens with a letter from Jane, in Southampton Street, to Charles, still in Birmingham, but about to return shortly.

Southampton Street, with Charles Ward now definitely excluded, and with Mr Morris still an inmate, can have been no very happy home for Jane. Mrs Linley, we may be sure, did not preserve silence upon the burning topic of her daughter's engagement; and although the lovers still met, walked and talked together, their conversations must have been saddened by the position of their affairs.

There were compensations, however, for the jars of Southampton Street, since Charles was now in London, and Mrs Linley's passion for whist disposed her to stay at home of an evening without requiring her daughter's company. One of the letters, written on a Saturday, concludes with a suggestion that she may be able "to go again to-night" to the theatre, where they may meet as they did last night.

By Monday evening she had to report "another altercation with my Mother," and this time Charles was its subject. Both Mrs Linley and William found his answers to the inquiries of the latter unsatisfactory, nor, considering such samples of business explanation as remain from the pen of Charles, is it possible to be surprised at their attitude.

His [William's] idea now is that you have nothing at all in view. Convince him that you have & he says he shall be satisfied. . . . My dear Charles, will you, for *my sake* will you write to William again and tell him all the particulars you acquainted *me* with, relative to the scheme you have lately submitted to the opinion of Mr Watt.

On Tuesday she will probably be at the play, with Jane Ireland, and her mother probably will not, a hint by which he is intended to profit. His answer came by return of post; he had promised his " two Bones " to Woodfall for Tuesday, and moreover had promised " one of yours to my brother." A " bone " being a permanent ticket, it would appear that even at this time Charles Ward possessed a free pass not only for himself, but also for a companion. How these came to be given to him, I cannot conjecture. He had, indeed, written a play—Jane's comments upon it exist in the correspondence—but the play had certainly not been produced, and it does not seem to have had any predecessor. Clearly he had not at this period any post at the theatre, nor can I find—although I should not be surprised to do so—any evidence that he was acting as dramatic critic for any newspaper. By some means he proposed, notwithstanding this reckless distribution of bones, to be at the theatre, and also apparently to meet Jane, if possible, in the afternoon. The weather, however, as is apt to be the case in London, towards the end of November, looked unpromising, and he therefore elaborated a scheme to meet every contingency, which indicates to what shifts their intercourse was now driven.

Let the weather be good or bad I will be in the rendez-
vous at 2, if it is so fair as to allow you to *pretend* to try if
you can walk I will there wait for you, if it should preclude
the possibility of your walking, I will pass your window &
will interpret a Nod of the head for your sending for a Coach
at ½ past 2, & a shake of your *wise* head for 3. Now mind
you are correct & don't nod to me (which as a mark of notice
& affection my heart whispers you will be inclined to do
without reflection, when you ought to shake it).

A brief, undated note, marked Wednesday, seems to follow
this, and then comes an interval; that letters passed I am,
to borrow Charles's phrase, "morally certain," but very
possibly they were but mere scraps.

The uncertainty of his own plans and hopes sometimes
weighed heavily on Charles, and when the English climate
was so malicious as to prevent him from meeting Jane, his
complaints of this "vile weather" broke out quite indignantly; he had no occupation but to wait for a reply from
Lord Stanhope, to whom he had submitted a scheme, and
from whom, it is to be supposed, he was hoping to get
capital; the uncertainty and suspense of his existence, he
wrote, were almost intolerable; and although in their letters
they asserted their unalterable attachment by calling each
other husband and wife, they can scarcely have found very
much solid comfort in the custom. Jane, indeed, saw another
side to the situation, and urged him not to regard their
separation as altogether an evil:

I declare to you that I prefer infinitely this intercourse
of *Souls* to your coming here to be insulted by rudeness, and
to see me cobbleing at table cloths, whilst your conversation
would necessarily be confined to the common occurrences
of the day, as being not wholly addressed to me,

—the joys of the family sitting-room, in fact. With this

opinion Charles could not at all agree; the delights of presence, even under any conceivable conditions of discomfort, outweighed in his estimation those of the happiest possible correspondence. Some observations of his upon literary style in general, and the style of her letters in particular, led her to a few answering remarks about herself:

You commend me for writing good grammar & upon my word I am quite ignorant of its rules; the accuracy which you praise me for is owing to the goodness of my ear: I never learnt french grammatically & yet I think I could construe it pretty correctly without being able to decline one verb in it; another proof of my ignorance! & yet Sir I have had the presumption to translate two Plays & am translating a third.

One would like to know more about these translations. Did she make them, as her sister used to make translations and adaptations of songs, for the current use of the theatre, or were they mere private exercises?

By the 22nd of December Charles was in a mood of greatly diminished hopefulness, and driven to contemplate the possibility that his own projects might never come to anything after all.

Dear & only beloved of my Soul, I here declare that should I be ruined, and completely undone, I will be yours, whenever your fortune affords us means upon which we can live. We well know that after affection is given upon both sides, there can be neither obligation nor gratitude. . . . Most probably before we meet again my fate will be decided (our fate, I mean) & then, dear Love, we must come to some resolution relative to our future.

Jane's reply is characteristic. She grieves not at poverty but only at separation; if they had been already married, as

243

her mother and brother had proposed, and if now poverty
were driving him from her mother's house,

with what joy would I have accompanied you to the poorest
Hovel, & have assisted in the most menial offices had it been
necessary to our support. Do not suppose dear Husband
that the Asylum for which you stipulated with my Mother
would have afforded me comfort deprived of your society.
No I never could have borne your absence, and as your
wedded Wife, I could freely have done what the World
would now condemn as criminal for it would not believe
that esteem and respect for each other's character would
be our safeguards & that we should be above degrading
ourselves to that class of Lovers who are blinded by passion
& infatuation. . . . You know Charles, *I* have never been
sanguine with respect to your affairs, I therefore read that
part of your letter where you *hint* at the possibility of your
ruin with the less concern; not a tear, not a sigh escaped me,
dear Husband; oh how different would my sensations have
been had I thought there had been the least degree of coldness
in your Letter; but that was impossible & the blessed
conviction of your being *mine for ever* made me insensible
to every other consideration. I have very little hope of
Mr Sheridan's assistance altho' I have not the slightest
doubt of his inclination to serve us & that is something in our
favour. . . . With regard to our future line of conduct
I here declare most positively I will make no further sacri-
fices—with the certainty of your utter *irretrievable ruin* I am
yours for ever and would not relinquish the Intercourse I
now enjoy were I to hazard by it all the gross imputations
on my character I have been so delicately informed will be
the consequence of it.

With these words the page ends, and no more appears of
this letter. Perhaps there was no more; the creases show it
to have been folded into the small dimensions of a note to

be given, rather than into the squarer shape of one for the post, and there are no marks of seal or wafer.

On poor paper, in the palest of ink and with a worn pen, Charles wrote from Sevenoaks at " 9 of clock " on New Year's Eve. She, no doubt, he reflected, was delighting every eye and ear, but he was assured that his image was present to her heart and that she had already whispered with a sigh to " our friend "—no doubt, Jane Ireland—

" Ah last year, my Charles was with us, but now perhaps he is alone, melancholy at an Inn." Exactly so, dear Jane, Lord Stanhope dined out & was gone before I reached his house.

Moreover no conveyance went from Sevenoaks in the mornings to London, so that they may not be able to meet so soon as he hoped.

Ah, my beloved! why cannot we command & direct our thoughts? To-day while in exercise, my spirits all alive & sanguine there was no obstacle which could long oppose our union, every thought was joyful & ardent expectation, I *was happy*, but now, both body & spirits weary, compelled as Johnson truly expresses, to suffer the tyranny of solitude, my thoughts conjure up nothing but apprehensions of long continuance & uncertain termination.

Four days later he and Jane had already met, and she had learnt from him that hope of profit from his scheme was at an end and that the total failure which he had been foreboding was now an actual fact. A letter written in 1809 by his sister, Mrs Snook, alludes to his having, at some earlier date, failed in business and involved his family—that is to say, his mother, his brother William, and probably also his brother Edward—in his losses. In all likelihood that letter refers to the troubles of January 1800.

On Tuesday the 7th, Jane wrote:

I hoped nothing from your interview with Lord Stanhope, & I am not disappointed; my mind is quite reconciled, no, *not* reconciled but resigned to your present ill fortune & never *never* have I felt more bound to you than I do at this moment . . . the first moment *I* can command an Independence adequate to the necessaries and comforts *I* require, I will claim the promise my dear Husband has made me of living with me, and then whatever distresses may befall me, He will never have to reproach himself for the Inconveniences that I may have to struggle with, for (contrary to the usual Modes and etiquettes of the world) I shall court him to a participation of *my* fortune, instead of his inviting me to be a sharer of his.

Charles replied in the same spirit; the two had made up their minds that their interests were one and that there could be no real happiness for either but in their marriage, and there were no ridiculous flights about waiting until money enough had been collected in his hands instead of hers. He tells her that she realised Prior's romance of the Nut Brown Maid. "How am I to repay you? perhaps owe everything to you after all. Well, Love is the great equalizer."

They must have determined that Jane should now separate her interests in the theatre from those of her mother and brother; whether she proposed to sell out entirely is not absolutely clear; but it is plain that she, desired so to arrange her affairs as to receive a fixed annual income, and that the next step was to approach Sheridan and obtain his consent to her scheme. They seem however still to have paused a little before approaching him. Perhaps they were waiting until William should be gone, so as to avoid involving him in any dissensions that might arise. William's passage, we know from earlier letters, had been taken for February, and although there is no precise statement to that effect he seems to have left home by the end of the preceding month. Perhaps his departure may have had a bad effect upon the temper of his mother, who, about that period, began to make herself exceedingly disagreeable. She was displeased about a proposed dance, and made a scene, the consequence of which was that Jane Ireland feared she would be unable to go. Next Mrs Linley opposed the going of Betty Tickell, who was apparently now staying in Southampton Street, and who

is sadly disappointed and [   ] tends to acquaint Mrs Lee with it [   ] may perhaps still bring it about. At all events *I* shall go, so you must settle with Mrs Smith about calling for me. My Mother *pretends* to object to our going to a *Tavern*

(I suspect that it was a Freemasons' ball)

as thinking it a great impropriety; but we know what her real objection proceeds from

—the real objection being of course the presence of Charles. Whether poor little Betty got her evening's pleasure does not appear, but no doubt Mrs Smith duly called for Jane, and the latter was ready, as Charles bade her be, " to leap into the Coach as soon as the knocker is heard." The rising storm indicated in these communications burst on the 1st or 2nd of February, and the outbreak must have been serious. On Monday the 3rd, Jane wrote:

I have the pleasure of informing you that all is well again; and excepting the one day's further sacrifice I am *determined* to make, I trust we shall continue to meet as usual; for my Mother, upon seeing how very wretched I was yesterday began to soften, & of herself offered me the kiss of peace before I parted from her for the Night; at the same time she told me that since she found I could not, as she had hoped, conquer my unfortunate attachment, she would never

247

mention the subject again, but leave me to my own discretion: I have said my dearest Charles that kind treatment instantly disarms me of resentment, however justly excited & when I quitted my Mother last Night who blessed me & really appeared to feel for the misery she had occasioned my heart was full and I reproached myself for having spoken so bitterly against her as I had done.

She was at a loss to know, she added, how her mother had learnt of her having so frequently seen Charles, but as Mrs Linley particularly dwelt upon their having met in the streets, she surmised that some neighbours had been chattering, especially as they had more time for observation on Sundays; she resolves to avoid henceforth any meetings after church,

for altho' my Mother has imposed silence upon herself in future; Yet she would be inwardly vexed, & perhaps might in an unguarded moment break it, and then would follow another scene of violence & unhappiness. . . . I would still have you go to Sheridan, but don't tell [   ] the *particulars* of Yesterday.

Charles had already, before receiving this letter, called upon Sheridan, and had seen his son Tom, from whom he had learnt that Sheridan was too busy preparing for the day's Debate to see anybody. Tom promised to see his father, and it was agreed that Charles should call early the next afternoon. But Sheridan, as everybody knows, was a man not easily to be pinned down to an engagement, and more than a week later Jane was writing to Charles that she had just seen Sheridan, who will expect him the next day, punctually at twelve, and has promised to call upon her at three, after their interview. It seems doubtful, however, whether any such interview ever took place; if so, it must have been of a purely preliminary character, since, on the third or fourth Sunday in March, he announced to Jane that, upon further consideration he thought he had better write to Sheridan instead of seeing him.

> However well I may think of myself, I doubt my being a match for him in Conversation! especially, too, with all the ill impressions he has imbibed from the representations of your FRIENDS.

He was resolved, therefore, to write. Apparently he did so, with favourable results, for on the 26th he was able to write an account of a satisfactory meeting between them. Sheridan said that Charles had done right

> in putting my sentiments upon paper relative to your theatrical property, that he had followed my example & done the same for my examination & that then he would propose a meeting of *Mr Lewin* or any other friend of the Family I *might approve of, me & himself,* who should finally agree upon the ballance of both statements—I replied that was more than I wished, that being confided in by you I found myself bound by every tye to be explicit in my statement, he approved of my conduct and said " But when are you to be married? " Oh Sir that depends upon means; but I have another subject of most serious import to mention—it does not regard fortune, it does not regard Marriage, Mrs Linley in her animosity to me is doing everything to shake the constancy of her Daughter's attachment to me. " True "[1] said he, " I know it, but that's of no avail." I know that Sir, but in the trial Miss Linley's Health & spirits sink under her Mother's oppression & I appeal to you to interpose. He replied if it was once done she would become quiet. " Let Jane go down to Polesden[2] & write her Mother word of her determination & I would then interfere & I warrant we will settle it—but do you come & breakfast with me to-morrow at 10, if I am in bed, send up to me. I will examine

---

[1] Or possibly " Sure "; the writing of Charles is seldom very clear.
[2] The estate which Sheridan had bought and settled upon his second wife.

my proposals with you & settle everything. I am now obliged to go with Tom to the Prince of Wales to get his interest for Tom to succeed Col. Rawdon at Lincoln." So ended our conversation.

Warned perhaps by his own " vile procrastinating temper," Charles did not yet feel a perfect assurance that Sheridan would prove sufficiently in earnest to produce any statement; but, as he sagely remarked, " we have not to choose "; Sheridan's terms must be accepted, be they what they would.

All through April matters seem to have hung uncertain. But the cheerful tone of Jane's letters shows that she, whose judgment was generally to be trusted, was now hopeful. On the 29th she wrote putting off an engagement to meet her lover on the 1st of May. Mrs Linley had borrowed General Paoli's carriage

to take us to Mrs Montague's . . . to see the Chimney sweepers eat roast beef. I *must* go, or I should be thought wanting in curiosity & I cannot plead an Engagement to walk with the Person dearest to me in all the World![1]

Both lovers had been at the theatre the evening before and had seen Joanna Baillie's *De Montfort*.

If I rightly understood Your action at the conclusion of the Play my Charles, it signified Your approval of it, & did You see *me* second the Applause You gave it? indeed I liked the representation of it better than I thought I should, for Kemble & Mrs Siddons conceived their characters very finely but still Charles, you must allow the subject to be a very unpleasing one, & therefore I don't think it will ever become a popular Play altho' the language is infinitely superior to any which has been produced for some time; I felt much disappointed at Kemble's substituting one of his long *o—h's* for the few words which De Montfort says upon

[1] It is perhaps necessary to remind younger readers that chimneys were at this period swept by boys, who were made to crawl up them.

finding his suspicions respecting his Sister & Rezenvelt unfounded; I recollect your pointing them out to me as composing one of the finest parts of the Tragedy, & I listened for it with a degree of impatience & curiosity to know what effect Kemble would give it; I cannot at all account for its omission, for what Demontfort says comprehends so much, & the Audience would more clearly have understood the state of his mind upon his being undeceived. . . . I am glad Charles Kemble did not play Rezenfelt for his countenance is too prepossessing to make it conceivable that any one should take such a mortal Antipathy to him; poor Talbot *looks* the character much better, & he had a pertness & Insolence of manner which young Kemble could not have assumed so well; what do you think? My Mother did not like the Play at all which I don't wonder at; *she* cannot enter into all the finer feelings, as *we* know but too well!

After this letter the passage of several weeks is marked only by brief notes of appointments made or unmade, meetings hoped for or missed. On the 25th of June Sheridan was called away from an interview by the important news which had just arrived of " the complete success of Bonaparte "; " but he pr[   ] to meet me to-morrow at Cocker's." As Mr Cocker was the solicitor by whom the necessary documents were to be drawn up this meeting-place seems to indicate that some advance had really been made by this time in the negotiations. A week later poor Charles was still running after Sheridan, had missed him by two or three minutes, and lamented that he would be obliged to " follow that *ignis fatuus* " again the next day.

Jane had opened his letter with

the most delightful sensation, for I thought nothing would induce you to write but your meeting with a successful Interview with Sheridan. . . . If he really has any *heart* he will not be so cruel as to desert us now, & leave us to

251

suffer Months of suspense & anxiety before another opportunity will offer for him to complete our happiness.

She had received a "melancholly letter," which made her "very low," from the second Miss Lewin. Poor Mary Lewin, whom we have seen so gay and full of hope, was apparently dying "snatched away from her approaching happiness." The incompleteness that marks a series of real, as distinguished from a series of fictitious letters, leaves us without further information as to the poor girl's fate.

The anticipated "important meeting" with Sheridan must have occurred very soon, for, by the 25th of July, matters were well advanced. Charles was to meet Mr Cocker on the 27th, and

if I don't start any material objection to the manner in which the separate trusts are conveyed I shall carry them to Richardson for the aid of his opinion & then nothing remains to be done but the ingrossing.

The usual summer exodus from Southampton Street had now taken place; Mrs Linley had gone to Bath, and Jane was staying with the Angelos at Eton, whence she renewed

our long neglected Correspondence with the most delightful Hope which has hitherto cheered us during our frequent separations—we have the prospect not only of meeting again *soon*, but of meeting to become *inseparable* for Life.

She could not feel perfectly easy, however,

until I have written to my Mother & received her answer. You know the effect her parting from me had upon my mind; the impression her unusual manner then made upon it was renewed Yesterday by a Letter I received from her written in the kindest & most affectionate terms; she has not mentioned a word about you, but speaks of the pleasure she shall receive from my joining her at Bath, says she intended to have made me a little present to have assisted me in bearing my expenses thither, but Mr Morris prevented her by disappointing her &c.   My Beloved I do not feel deserving of such a Letter from her whilst my conscience tells me I am deceiving her, but I am somewhat reconciled to it from the consideration yᵗ I have preserved the tranquility of her mind by it & I hope that she will accept of that excuse for the ignorance I have kept her in.

In another week she would, she hoped, be able to send Mrs Linley the news that instead of coming as an obedient spinster to Bath, her daughter proposed to establish herself immediately with a husband and a house of her own.   When once all was settled, Jane trusted that resentment would soon be over.   " I believe she loves me too well to embitter the happiness I shall enjoy with *the Beloved* of *my Soul*."

Her chief news is that she has narrowly escaped having " a *black eye* instead of a grey one, Yesterday Evening (& I shd have been much vexed, because you have told me you don't admire black eyes)."   She had been strolling with some other ladies in the " Playfield," where the boys were at cricket " at some distance," and a stray ball struck her on the hip and " my Cloaths which [   ] *unfashionable* thickness saved me "—it was the era of pseudo-classic muslin draperies.   This, her first letter from Eton, was delayed, as afterwards appeared by the advent to Staple Inn of a postman who regarded the delivery of letters as a purely personal transaction, and who had to be taught that the slit in Charles Ward's door was intended for their passage.   Charles, though a little anxious, comforted himself with her standing promise always to let him know if she were ill.   He had seen Cocker, the deeds were all settled, by Tuesday morning they would all be " copied."

Cocker dedicates Wednesday to a general inspection to

correct errors or mistakes & on Thursday I am to have them for Richardson's perusal & if he does not object to any part they will be immediately engrossed.

Mrs Boscawen, with whom he had dined, and in whose house I think Betty was staying, had inquired into their plans (which were, of course, to be married directly the deeds were completed and before the home-coming of Mrs Linley) and had expressed a hope that if it were possible to fix the wedding before the date at which she was compelled to leave London, Jane would be married from her house. At this point, Charles thought, their designs might safely be revealed to Mrs Linley, and her consent requested.

Jane, who was most desirous to have no concealment of her doings from her mother, wrote at once, both to Mrs Linley and to Mrs Symmons, with whom Mrs Linley seems to have been staying. The house of the gentleman described in Robbins' Bath Directory for 1800 as "John Symonds, Surgeon," was No. 22 Camden Place, so that Mrs Linley was sojourning upon a breezy height well above that heated oven to which a July sun can transform the lower parts of Bath. Miss Lee's school was on the same slope, within a few minutes' walk, and Miss Lee was at this time at home. Betty Tickell, however, had now quitted that establishment, and was a grown-up young lady, about whom her aunt made inquiries by the name of "*Eliza*." The new title thus underlined seems to suggest that its owner chose to adopt what was considered the more elegant abbreviation, and apparently it was by this form that she continued to call herself, for a letter of hers, now in my hands, written thirty-seven years after this time, is signed "Eliza Anne Tickell."

Jane, like other visitors, was taken, on a fine Sunday, to attend what Miss Burney calls "the Terracing," the parade, that is, of the royal family on the Terrace of Windsor Castle. She saw " all the Royalties," and found the Terrace

more crouded than I had any conception of. What a life for the *poor* Princesses to lead! how much happier we shall be in our own little Cottage & Garden where we shall live for ourselves & forget the World & all its forms.

The letter of Jane to her mother was to be reinforced by one from Sheridan to the same lady, and although there is no evidence that he did actually write, as he had declared that he would, it is difficult to believe that even his habitual procrastination would resist the dramatic piquancy of his intervention with Mrs Linley upon such a topic. The whole situation must have recalled acutely his own experiences of twenty-eight years earlier, when *he* was the suitor esteemed neither rich enough nor settled enough in life to become the husband of a Linley. Now, he was the great man of their connections, his advice and approval carrying weight, his very intercession something of a compliment. Moreover that pleasant human kindliness which all through his life was one of Sheridan's leading characteristics was strongly engaged on behalf of these lovers. He liked Charles Ward, whom he by-and-by established in the closest relations with himself and his own business; and he had a real affection for Jane, who was intertwined with some of his most poignant memories, who must often have seemed to him the one close link remaining with his dead wife, and for whose character he must have entertained a respect. I believe therefore that he did write, and I wish that Mrs Linley had preserved the letter.

Very anxious was poor Jane, now that her communication to her mother had really gone.

My mind is so restless & uncomfortable from the suspense

255

I suffer, that I am really glad if I can divert it from dwelling too long upon the various conjectures which are constantly arising in it, & even *Pam loo* is a little relief to me, or if I can engage it sufficiently by reading or music the time then *goes* on—but otherwise when you my Beloved employ my thoughts, every minute is an hour.

On the whole it may be surmised that the Angelo family entertained in August 1800 a visitor who was somewhat silent, self-absorbed and even uncompliant—for singing was a difficult task to a person so much perturbed by private anxiety; and the relief of communication was not possible. Mrs Angelo, indeed, knew something of what was going on, but she did not approve; she told her daughter that she thought Jane was taking an imprudent step and that it was a pity, as she certainly might do much better. "Is it not a hard thing," remarks Jane, in repeating her hostess's opinion, "that this—World will not let one chuse one's happiness one's own way!"

Charles meanwhile was growing impatient of the law's delays.

I write to you my beloved to vent my spleen against that " little puckering fellow Cocker "

—who had put him off with an assurance that

everything is copying out as fast as possible . . . we are now waiting upon the pens of his Clerks. Well, perhaps I am too impatient, & think of two or three deeds without counting the number of words in each & Cocker is famous for amplification, (he charges by the length).

When this copying was over, and when Richardson had looked through the documents,

I shall have to carry them to Sheridan for his examination, *there's the danger.* But I trust I shall be able to influence

256

him to a speedy approval, he will of course trust to Richardson & me for our side of the question & he most likely will trust to Cocker for his side, so after keeping them a few days, under pretence of examining them, he will sign them without examining them at all

—a forecast of which the extreme probability cannot be denied.

The only serious point of anxiety now was the nature of Mrs Linley's reply, but a minor distress lay in the apprehension that Sheridan's kindness would take the unwelcome form of wanting them to go to Polesden for their marriage and honeymoon. Clearly they could not, after all that he had been doing to help them, refuse any such invitation, but both of them were desirous of evading it; a cottage had always been their dream, and Charles was employing his leisure in seeking for one that should be at once sufficiently retired and sufficiently convenient. Sheridan probably was quick enough both to see and understand their preference; his goodwill merely took the form of a few words of counsel.

Œconomy must be the Word, he said. You may depend upon us both, I answered.

Still the letter from Bath delayed, and Charles tried to plead that delay was an auspicious sign; but his own anxiety revealed itself in the entreaty that he might not be kept one unnecessary moment in suspense. " Never mind the expense of Postage now, we will save it in future by never separating."

Meanwhile another of her letters had failed to reach him on the expected day, or for two or three days after; it had been entrusted to a faithless youth called Gandy, who should have posted it in London. " As for that Mr Gandy," cried Jane when she learnt his sin of omission,

I wish he may fall in love with a Coquette who may promise & disappoint him fifty times a day! it was to him I entrusted a few lines merely to inform you I was well: he left Eton last Thursday at 12 o'clock & I gave him a letter at the same time to leave at Hounslow for Mary Pratten; perhaps they are both on the Road to Devonshire by this time for He was to set off in the Mail for London the next Evening—the Letter to you was not of any consequence or I would not have hazarded such a conveyance you may be assured & when the Man finds out the negligence he has been guilty of, I daresay he will be in a fine fantigue & will put the Letters into the first Post Office he comes to.

Some such course Mr Gandy seems indeed to have pursued, for the missing letter—written on the last day of July—lies here with a post-mark upon it of the 4th of August; and it is to be hoped that his perturbation upon discovering the belated document was fully equal to Jane's expectation.

At last, on the 5th of August Jane was able to send news from her mother; she transcribed in full a letter which she justly characterised as " very unsatisfactory."

MY DEAR JANE—I have too much to say to you on the subject of your Letter to explain in writing what I wish to advise, come to Bath as soon as you can. Mrs Symmons will be happy to receive you. I have consulted my friend Miss Lee on this unfortunate business & we have fixed on a plan which if you will consent to it, that will answer without your disposing of your share in the patent of the Theatre—if you do that you will repent it as long as you live. I have but one objection to your union with Mr Ward you know what I mean if he has any Income of his own. I have now his Letter by me wherein he says he has no opinion or reliance on Mr Sheridan and that he had it in his power to offer you an Independance. If this is made clear to me I will give my consent to your Union. I speak so far on Mr Ward's account for I think it will be disgraceful in him to be maintained by his Wife. I shall not say any more on the subject at present but whatever you do dont sign anything till you see me—You affect^e Mother

M. LINLEY.

On receipt of this epistle—entirely worthy of its shifty and provoking author—poor Jane was " more upon the rack . . . than ever." She could not conceive what plan could possibly have been devised between Miss Lee and Mrs Linley; and she felt that she could not write again until she did so as a married woman.

As for Charles, he knew not " when I have felt more indignant than in reading your Mother's letter." He declared—very truly—that it was full of duplicity;

her design is this, to get you to Bath, then she will renew the stale idea of my coming forward with an Independance & our all living together, this she well knows I cannot execute, well then, what are you to do? I cannot come & marry you under her eye, in her express disapprobation, nor can you, upon disapproving of her plan, step into a Coach & return to Town.

The whole attempt he pronounced to be " an ungenerous trick." He suspected that neither Mrs Symmons nor Miss Lee had really been consulted, and enclosed a letter for Jane to forward to the former. Both he and she thought it but too probable that her mother would write again and urge her going to Bath; " when she has a design in her head, you know, she never lets its sleep."

Firm as she was in her determination not to be " decoyed " to Bath, Jane could not be quite easy in actually disobeying her mother until she had learnt what Mrs Linley's plan was. In any case she had no doubt that she would incur the condemnation of Ozias,

259

for his notions on the subject are so mighty strict, as you know, that I believe he would almost commit *a Sin* upon a principle of Duty to his Mother.

Mrs Boscawen having been now obliged to go out of town, and the Polesden scheme having happily come to nothing, it became necessary to decide where Jane should dwell in the interval before her marriage. Mrs Freeman had offered her house, and from it there is evidence that Jane was eventually married, but this arrangement did not quite please either Charles or Sheridan, neither of whom could succeed in liking that lady in spite of " all her kindness & regard." " On the contrary," added Charles, " I find my dislike increasing with every conversation."

Mrs Symmons and Miss Lee both answered promptly and plainly, and from them Jane learned what her mother's mysterious project really was. Mrs Symmons wrote:

I do not at all understand that any *plan* has been proposed much less agreed on; only Miss Lee had hinted to your Mother that if you chose to exert your musical talents with a view to the increase of your present independencies she thought it might be done here with a certainty of considerable advantage.

Miss Lee said:

What your Mother calls *the plan* I meant only as a last resource shd. Mr S. fail in his part of the compact, & not to prevent your disposing of your share in any way that may add to your comfort. I am led to suppose your [   ] wishes to get you down to Bath while you are [   ] loss to discover what she means; let Mr Ward know he was in the right to be incredulous.

In fact Mrs Linley, who had once before spoken with some resentment of Jane's having been " bred a lady," was

260

tempted by the idea that, if her daughter would only settle down to teach singing, she might, like her father, make a good income. Jane "entirely disapproved" of any such scheme, and being now aware of the nature of her mother's dangled bait, was prepared to go on without one backward glance of hesitation. The letter which enclosed these extracts was written at midnight; she had been out from ten in the morning until ten at night, and had dined at "Clifden Spring." Of course the post had gone already; but fortunately George Angelo would be going to town early next morning, so that her letter would scarcely be delayed. When next morning came, however, the young gentleman proved unwilling to depart, and instead of being off at six, hung about until eleven.

Poor Charles, whose nerves were evidently suffering from the prolonged strain of the last month, was uneasy when his expected letter failed to appear on Wednesday morning, became almost distracted when Thursday also was blank, and wrote much such a letter as Sheridan's "Falkland" might have written to his "Julia":

No letter yet—what can possibly have happened. Your Water excursion cannot have been of two days' continuance. My Mind misgives me, just upon the eve of every thing being happily settled, everything going on well—Richardson having approved of the deeds and Sheridan too—Am I forever to be doomed to misfortune? . . . Were you careless or thoughtless, but you who are so considerate of others, no, it can't be the omission of Negligence, were it possible for you to change in your attachment, your Candour would at once have told me. Was your mind poisoned by reports against me your regard for truth & promise would have directly appealed to me for denial or admission, a slight illness would not prevent your writing & after what has passed you would never again entrust my happiness to the cursed precariousness of a private hand. . . . I am certain as I am of my own existence that if you could have wrote you would, & what could prevent you but what I dread to think of . . . perhaps at this moment I stand alone in the World, fye, fye, I ought not to give way thus, but Jane my only hope my Heart knows not reason. The Newspaper gives no account of an accident. Jane, my heart sickens with apprehension!

Jane herself had thought the water party in some danger on their return,

but you know I am a great Coward on the Water. It was so dark that the Steersman declared he could not see ten yards before him, & we were within an ace of running foul of an immense barge which the Man said would certainly have overset us. There were sixteen of us in the boat & the Men were continually moving about to my great annoyance; Mrs Angelo remonstrated with me in no very civil terms & said all their lives were as precious as mine, but I knew of one dear Object who valued it more than those of the whole party besides, & who had charged me with the care of it, & therefore I was the more anxious for its preservation.

Mrs Leigh had written congratulations from Ashbourne —there seems to have been no further concealment of their intentions from anybody—and among other messages had desired that Mr Ward might hear that she was getting her little girls on in their music and that he would say they were much improved. "You conceited Creature you! I'll warrant me you have been making them all believe you are quite *au fait* as the french say at the business."

The income upon which the pair were marrying seems to have been £300 a year; but Jane's total fortune must have amounted to more. The only direct information comes from a letter written by Charles after the conclusion of the various transactions;

Your Annuity commences the 24th of June, so on the 24 of September, there will be one quarter due or £75 which with the £300 advance & your Legacy of £100 makes our Stock to commence with. Why it is absolute Opulence, talk of Percy Street! pray would you rather have your residence in Grosvenor Square or Portland Place?

On Tuesday 19th of August Charles wrote his last letter to Jane as "Miss Linley." He had borrowed "Wills's Gig" and was going to hire a horse; the moment he had secured one he proposed to set out very early in the morning for Eton, so as to return with Jane the same day, and save a second day's hire of the horse. She is requested therefore to have her baggage in readiness for Thursday or Friday.

She returned "a line" entreating him to be very particular in his selection of a horse, "those light Carriages" being rather dangerous. The caution, she assured him, was all for his sake. "I am not afraid for my own little bones."

On the Wednesday the Angelos were having a large party to tea and supper, and she was expecting to be "tiezed" to sing. "As it will be the last Evening, I shall e'en oblige them with as good a grace as I can. . . . Oh Time Time how wilt thou creep till to-morrow or Friday!"

The next document of the series is to be found not amongst these packets of letters, but at the church of St Clement Danes; and sets forth that on the 24th of September 1800 Charles William Ward, Bachelor, was married to Jane Nash Linley, Spinster, by licence, the officiating clergyman being George Lawrance, Curate, and that the witnesses were John Briggs, W. C. Ward, Jane Ireland and Mary C. Smith.

263

CHAPTER 12. THE LAST OF THE LINLEYS

THE first document that throws any light upon the married life of Jane and Charles may be found in the British Museum. It is a letter from Charles to Sheridan, and is dated "Friday 6th, 1801" "Sutton, Hounslow"—an address which suggests that the cottage so eagerly sought by the pair may at last have been found near to Hounslow.

The note, brief though it is, exemplifies amusingly Charles's curious practice in respect to commas, which, here, where he wrote with care, had full scope. Fortunately for me, he generally wrote in a hurry and did not pause to fill in all the commas in what he would have considered the proper places.

DEAR SIR I have only to request you to reflect, that the attention of half an hour to this manuscript, may determine my future fortune, to be certain, of your giving it that half-hour.—Yrs. most respectfully   C. W. WARD.

"This manuscript" is a play, called *D'Olbach*, which, I am inclined to think, must have been an adaptation of a German original *viâ* a French translation. On a slight inspection, it appears to be extremely dull, though not, perhaps, duller than some other German plays that were acted at that period with profit and applause. It does not seem ever to have been produced.

The wooden box that contained the love letters of the pair contained also a collection of odd letters and papers, one group of which, though intrinsically valueless, throws a curious light upon a bygone state of things. On old letters and small scraps of paper, some person has written in a very small hand various fragmentary snippets of miscellaneous information, collected, I should suppose, from some school book of the *Mangnall's Questions* type—possibly from that classic of wrongheadedness itself. On one such sheet, for instance, the following paragraphs, written apparently at different times—certainly with different pens—succeed one another:

Paraguay, a tract of America belonging to the Spanish Crown, where the Jesuits took up their residence in the year 1550 & in the time of Phil: 39 founded Missions called by the Europeans Paraguai or Uraguai, they were 37 in number.

Sir Hugh Willoughby attempted the discovery of a North east passage to China & Japan in 1553. He sailed to the Latitude of 75 degrees North, but was driven back by a Storm & winter'd in the river Arzena in Lapland where he & his company were frozen to death.

Lempriere made a tour through the Empire of Morrocco having been sent for thither by Muley Absulen the Emperor's favourite son who was in a bad state of health & wanted medical Assistance.

Some of the letters that have been thus employed in the service of learning are notes to " Miss Linley " asking for a theatre ticket or making an appointment; sometimes the address is to " Mrs Charles Ward " at Sutton, or at 34 Great Queen Street, or at Iver, Bucks. The small, close writing, though it resembles Jane's, is not, I think, hers. My impression is that Betty Tickell was dutifully trying to keep up or to carry on her education by extracting from some venerated volume these husks of knowledge. Jane, at her age, and conscious as she was of possessing a bad memory, would hardly have spent her time in making notes of this kind. But what a training for any human mind must that have been which set girls accumulating these dry and detached chips of fact! The hoarding of old letters to be used where now a penny exercise-book would be bought shows the vast change that has taken place in the price of paper.

The first of the letters remaining, other than those which have thus become palimpsests, is one from Edward Ward to his brother, dated 24th of September 1802, and written from the Castle Inn, Brighton. He had apparently been sent thither on some errand to the Prince of Wales, and had the pleasure, on his way down, of meeting that gentleman, " gallopping to town in order to attend a review." Edward Ward was going on to Portsmouth, and probably to sea again. His letter contains some verses, the fruit, as he pretty plainly says, of boredom, some uncomplimentary observations upon the landscape of Brighton, and some details for the benefit of Miss Smith as to the hours and pauses of the " ½ guinea coach." It concludes with: " Loving remembrances to my beloved Jane. May she sing Lady Annyee [?] for a hundred years to come." The letter is addressed to 34 Great Queen Street, so that the pair must by this time have ceased to " cottage it "[1] and have become established in London. The numbers of the houses in Great Queen Street have, I understand, been altered, and the street itself has undergone so many changes that it is impossible to say in what part of it Jane and Charles lived.

In 1803 the kind Edward, whose brotherly affection showed itself constant not only to Jane, but to her children and her niece after her, became Rector of Iver in Bucking-

[1] This expression occurs in one of Jane's letters.

hamshire; and it was probably in the same year that Charles was appointed Secretary to Drury Lane Theatre. In the latter half of that eventful year, or in the earlier half of the next, must have been born the child who received the name of Charles Thurstan.

In October of 1804 Jane was staying at Iver, whether in lodgings or in a house taken by Charles is not clear, but it is evident that she was not on this occasion at the Parsonage. On the 12th of the month her husband wrote to her:

My dear Jane if you receive a letter from Birmingham you need not send me a copy,[1] as the result of the experiment has convinced me that the discovery is not of that importance I had imagined. As I never allowed myself to build much upon it, my disappointment is proportionably small.

A scheme for the mechanical propulsion of vessels lies among these papers, and is perhaps the " discovery " referred to in this letter. The rest of it deals chiefly with a matter that does not concern any of the persons mentioned in this volume; but at its close we get a glimpse of Mrs Linley.

I shall be with you on Sunday, I believe, but not before. Your Mother has got me by the Leg & I cannot stir till I am released by getting some business done for her.

Evidently Mrs Linley had become reconciled to the son-in-law whom as a suitor she so persistently opposed. Perhaps Charles was staying with her during the absence of his wife.

The next letter (5th of November 1804) comes from Lymington.

You will be as much surprised at the place this is dated from as you must have been at my long silence. I now

[1] She would copy the substance into a letter of her own, instead of enclosing the original, because a letter containing a second sheet paid double postage.

therefore sit down as in duty bound to give an account of myself. When I reached town last Sunday I found Sheridan true to his engagement, tho' not punctual to his time, we reached Merton that Evening & the next Morning set off not for Polesden, but for this place I only intending to go part of the way, but upon reaching Guildford, where we stopped, I found that we had not time to finish our work & therefore as Sheridan said he should only be able to stop a few days & would then bring me back free of expense I determined to go on, & here I am having endured the daily disappointment of Sheridan's postponing his return. He has now been sent for by the Prince & has promised to return to-morrow. Having waited thus long, it would be ridiculous to go without him now, when he cannot possibly extend his stay beyond a day & I shall have the advantage of a tete a tete to finish our Ali Baba. . . . As my return is necessarily uncertain, suppose you indulge me with a letter, containing a particular account of everybody under cover to Sheridan in George Street Hanover Square, that it may greet me there upon my arrival. Thine. God bless my dear Love.

An undated letter seems to have been written some days later:

My dear & dearest Jane I am not gone again to Lymington but chained here by Sheridan who will not let me stir, each day of this week past have I said to William,[1] to-morrow I certainly go to Iver, and at night I have either met with Sheridan or had a message from him, which made my presence indispensable in Town. . . . Your Mother is quite well, but that letter of William's in Barnard's hands is one of her mistakes, there is no such thing. William depending upon my going daily has deferred writing as well as myself or you would by this time have known that that

[1] William had now retired for good ; and spent the rest of his days in England.

respectable gentleman is laid up with a fit of the Gout in his leg, I am serious. Wills who attends him congratulates him upon [it], he thinks his late spasms &c. owing to the disorder flying about, now that it has determined into a regular fit, that his general health will be much improved he talks of getting out in a day or two for Iver, that accounts for him. Kiss Edward in my name for Sophia.

A postscript on the outer sheet conveys important information:

I have bought your Gown, but the shop people have not sent it in time. I have not forgotten your Ribbon.

Nor did he forget it, for the next document is a somewhat crumpled sheet of paper that has been folded to contain some small packet, and that has written inside:

DEAR JANE This is exclusive of the White Ribbon for Nuptials &c. Don't be surprised at seeing me to-morrow evening & don't be disappointed at not seeing me. Thine Ever   C. W. WARD.

A hastily scrawled note without a date seems to belong here. It mentions that

Ozias is in town & it is settled that he will come down with me on Friday Morning & stay till Monday so you will take care that he has no reason to imagine his Bed to be unaired.

A few days later Jane is informed that Ozias will stay until Monday, on which day, " if the weather proves favorable his Mother will come for him otherwise he is to return to town under my Convoy "—an arrangement from which it may be concluded that Mrs Linley, now in her seventy-seventh year, was ready to drive in a chaise eleven miles out and eleven miles back in the same day, in November, provided the weather were favourable.

On " Friday 30th " Charles wrote again from London:

I am now waiting for Sheridan's appearance, we got half
thro' yesterday when a message from the Prince run away
with him, of course I can't stir till the whole is finally
determined. . . . Indeed I can well excuse him, now I see
his everyday life. At this period entre nous he is really
determining the fate of the Country. The King has quarelled
with the Prince & insists upon taking away the little
Princess from her Father & educating her himself, this the
Prince resists & the arrangement of the Contest is confided
to Sheridan, who is now fighting with his Pen both Pit & the
Chancellor & I lay a wager if you will go my halves he will
prove superior. How can he devote hours to consider Scene
shifting and artificial mules, Jane. I dined two days ago
with a Maiden Lady at her house in the City, who enquired
much after you & indeed appeared to have a warm friendship
for you her name is *land-Ire*. Do you guess who it is?

The young Roscius—*i.e.* Master Betty, who was having
a most successful engagement at Drury Lane—had produced
a very favourable impression upon Charles when he met
him in private; now, having seen the prodigy act, approval
heightens into enthusiasm, and indeed, a young gentleman
who, at thirteen, could attract, " houses of £800," could
hardly fail to seem pleasing to the Secretary of the theatre.

Marriage had not diminished Charles's old craving for
letters from his Jane.

. . . seriously let me have a line every day till I see you.
I don't care for sufficient to make a letter but a little Chit
chat; when I go to bed in the full hopes of going to you
next day & am disappointed in the morning, the receipt of a
letter is some ballance to it. . . . Kelly & I are going on
well together, he has proposed to get the music according
to the sentiment & for me to write the words. I have
consented & he goes on upon velvet, for he steals without

let or hindrance. I gave him the idea of the Chorus
beginning
                 " Join the festive dance & song,"
he forgot the words, but retaining some idea of them wrote
down
             " Let the festive *foot* prepare
               Songs of mirth & songs of Glee "
is not that excellent?

On the 13th of December the pantomime of *Ali Baba*
was ready to be put into rehearsal—none too soon!—and
Charles in his good spirits began to tease Jane about the
child whom she already had and the child whom she hoped
to have.

Talking of Boys It is our darling Child now, but in a
little time it will be " pray punish that rude boy he disturbs
the sleep of our sweet little girl—get along you little
Monkey." . . . Morris is still with your Mother and will
there remain, Mrs Lonsdale is louder than ever & Betsy
Tickell equal to Mrs Bozzy in chattering.[1]

Well might Betsy be in a chattering mood, and in high
spirits, for news had just come that her brother Dick, now
about one or two and twenty, and in the navy, had been
distinguishing himself and winning golden opinions from his
superiors. The poor boy's glories were short-lived. He
was killed in action in the next year, off the coast of Sardinia.

Before Charles was able to carry out his plan of coming
to Iver immediately, or perhaps after his week-end visit was
over, he received a letter with news very disturbing to a
parent so inexperienced. His reply shows how fully the
confidence with which Jane had inspired him before
marriage was maintained afterwards:

[1] " Mrs Bozzy " is no doubt Mrs Boscawen—" Mrs Bos," as Jane
(and Miss Burney likewise) calls her.

271

I am much obliged seriously obliged by your letter it was just what a Mother & wife ought to have written, it is expressed so fairly & faithfully that I have no Distrust that our little Darling's illness is in the least extenuated, indeed it gives me the fullest confidence that you will never disguise anything from me. From your account I do not feel any alarm, and rather incline to Edward's opinion that it is the commencement of the Measles.

There are no more letters until August 1805, when Jane was staying at Polesden. The first of the letters contains details about her health that indicate the advance of consumption; the second quotes the opinion, in the absence of Dr Bain (who, it will be remembered, attended Mrs Sheridan in her last illness) of Dr Bain's partner upon her case, who thinks the air of Polesden must be agreeing with her, or the cough would have become incessant. Probably she had been persuaded to go there for change of air on account of her health. Little Charles was with her, but there is no mention of the little girl, Mary Esther, who must have been a few months old; probably the child was at nurse. Charles's letter is full of money troubles—Sheridan's, in which his own fortunes were involved. It seems clear that Charles was the most faithful of henchmen, and also that for the next ten years his life must have been, like Sheridan's, one of incessant worries, borrowings, shifts, expedients, hopes and disappointments.

The letter with the doctor's opinion is the last letter to Jane. She died at Iver in January 1806, and her grave is in Iver churchyard. Her age is given on her tombstone as thirty-seven, but if she had lived ten days longer, until her birthday, the 18th, she would have completed her thirty-eighth year. Mrs Sheridan, too, it may be remembered, was nearly thirty-eight, when she died, and she too was the mother of an infant daughter. Jane's epitaph consists of one true and touching line:

The more known the more lamented.

Mr Sichel quotes from a letter Sheridan wrote on the 16th of January to his wife:

I have been to-day at Iver attending poor Jane's funeral with Tom. It was particularly decent and affecting. If you remember, she lived directly opposite the church of that very neat and seemingly innocent village, and like that was her burial—no hearse or coach. Her sister's was a gaudy parade and show from Bristol to Wells Cathedral, where all the mob, high and low, were in the church, surveying and surrounding the vault. The recollection of the scene and of the journey has always pained me, independently of the occasion itself, and has decided me, who am a friend without superstition to attention and attendance on these occasions, to prefer the mode I witnessed this morning—and so shall be my own passage to the grave.

But when the time came this wish was not remembered, and the passage to the grave of Sheridan was even more of a show and a spectacle than that of his wife had been.

Whether the motherless children remained at Iver from this time forth, or whether they were with their father in London I am not sure, but I believe that they remained under the immediate eye of the excellent uncle, among whose children they were certainly at a later time growing up like another brother and sister of the same group. At one period Mary lived in Iver with her unmarried aunt, Miss Charlotte Ward, upon whose death she became an inmate of the Parsonage. Betty Tickell, too, was a frequent visitor and seems to have been regarded as almost a niece of the house, while Ozias, as soon as he came to live once more within easy reach of London, was adopted as an extra uncle by the children of the Parsonage.

As for Charles himself, there seems reason to suppose that, for a time at least, he took up his abode with Mrs Linley. In February 1807, when Sheridan, as executor of Thomas Linley's will, gave a written authority, now in the British Museum, to Charles William Ward to collect money due on lands, tenements, etc., in Bath, Charles is described in the document as being " of Southampton Street." Mrs Linley of course was by that time within a few years of eighty, and it may well have been felt that one of her sons or sons-in-law ought to be in the house with her at all times. William would appear to have lived with her, but William was fond of little jaunts. Charles would, I am sure, have felt strongly that he owed a son's duty to Jane's mother. Charles's association with Sheridan and with the theatre had not, in the long run, conduced to his financial stability. A memorandum written by him in October 1805 shows that at that time Sheridan owed him £90. In February of that calamitous year the theatre had been burned down, and from that time until his death, in 1816, Sheridan's embarrassments became more and more involved, and Charles was continually entangled in them. In February 1812 he was arrested at the suit of one Scott, and the expenses of the arrest and detention amounted to £9. 4s. 6d.[1] In Sheridan's last illness, in 1816, Charles was with him daily, and was no doubt among the mourners at his grave. No more letters from him have come into my hands, but there are two letters to him, as late as 1822, from William Linley.

In 1816 Ozias, who had been incumbent first of one, then of two, and finally of three small livings in Norfolk,

[1] All these details come from the British Museum. Egerton MSS. 1975.

resigned them and became Organist Fellow of Dulwich College. His position there is pretty clearly defined by letters, written immediately after his death, to a would-be successor.

The Organist is a Fellow of the College and the late Mr Linley was a clergyman. The duties are to play the organ on Sundays and to instruct the children in music—twelve in number. The emoluments are at present about £160 a year, besides apartments, commons and wine. As the organist is completely on the same footing as the other Fellows, we wish, of course, to avoid common musicians and to have a man of education, with the manners and feelings of a gentleman.

At Dulwich, then, Ozias lived from 1816 until his death in 1831, and very much his presence there must have assisted to enliven any monotony from which the Fellows of that community may have been suffering. At Dulwich it was that the Rev. John Sinclair, who has left a record of Ozias's idiosyncrasies, learned to know him, but as their acquaintance did not begin until 1822 the account of his oddities may yield precedence to three letters belonging to the years 1819 and 1822.

The first of these, dated—not, I think, in the hand of the writer—"June 13th, 1819," was written by Mrs Linley to her granddaughter.

My dearest Mary, I am now entered into my 91st year, and yet I have the courage to take up my pen, to return you my best thanks, for your kind & dutiful letter. You tell me you are very happy with your Aunt Charlotte, wch is a comfort to me, your dear Cousin Tickell is just come to dine with me, & begs her kind love to you, I show'd her those lines wch pleas'd her very much. Your little Bird is just peep'd out of his shell and will be likely to give you a Song

in the Summer, my eyes now begin to fail me, I must therefore conclude with best and kindest regards to the Rev^d.
and all his kind familey, and thank God who has enabled me
to sign myself Your affectionate Grandmother

MARY LINLEY.

Mrs Lonsdale is a great deal better & sends her kind love
with Mrs Bevan and Betsy Shaw.

The writing of this letter, which, except in the postscript,
is by no means very shaky, bears a strong resemblance to that
of Ozias; and the contents present a pleasant picture of the
grandmother writing to one beloved granddaughter, while
the other sits by. I am glad that Mrs Linley's last appearance should be so kindly a one. She died on the 18th of
January (the day that had been Jane's birthday) of the
next year, and was buried in the churchyard of St Paul's,
Covent Garden; a tablet to her memory may still be seen
in that church, where for many years she was a regular
attendant. The inscription on it is as follows :—

Near this place are deposited the remains of Mary Linley
widow of Thomas Linley Esqre late of this parish who
departed this life on the 18th of January 1820 aged 91.
In the humble hope of a joyful resurrection through the
merits of her Blessed Redeemer. In grateful remembrance
of an ever careful and indulgent mother this tablet is erected
by her dutiful & affectionate sons Ozias Thurston and
William Linley.

The first letter of William to Charles is dated from
Midgham on the 20th of September 1822. It informs
Charles that he has accepted " your bill in favour of Mr
Robins," but that he rather wonders " you did not apprise
me first of all, of your intention to draw upon me." The
Michaelmas dividend (from the Chapel) will not, he thinks,
amount to the £50 upon which Charles was evidently

276

reckoning. Moreover a new roof had become necessary—
the chapel was just fifty years old—and was to be paid for
by a deduction of £50 from the total sum to be received at
Michaelmas, of which total sum a third part came to Charles,
as the heir, I presume, of Jane.

You must also recollect that I have a *Lawyer's* notice of
some *protection* from the Court of Chancery by which I may
be enthralled—but, as I have heard nothing further from
Mr Young on this subject, I take it for granted you have
come to some settlement of that affair, and I shall be glad
to hear that this is the case.

I hope this note may find you quite recovered from your
Indisposition. Betsy Tickell mentioned your intended trip
to some Sea Place—I forget where. May the Journey and
the Air be of Service to you, but it never was to me. Ozias
wrote rather *gravely* about you, so that I shall be really
anxious to have a good account from yourself. Betsy will
convey your letter.

Information about a proposed production at Drury Lane,
in regard to which William seems to have been serviceable
to the manager, Elliston, follows; Charles, I think, was
still holding the post of secretary.

I shall visit *Iver* certainly before I return to London.
How is Charles, and what has he been doing lately? Yrs
My Dear W. very truly   W. LINLEY.

The second letter, written from his own chambers in
Furnival's Inn on 29th of October, evidently with his own
pen, and in an agreeable and flowing Linley handwriting
has a note of cordial kindness that speaks well for both
brothers-in-law. It is addressed to Charles at St Helier,
Jersey, to be left at the Post Office till called for, and there,
is a note in red ink on the cover that two shillings and

twopence was paid for postage; this, as the letter consisted
of two sheets, would be the double postage, whence it may
be concluded that, as late as 1822 the charge for conveying
a letter to Jersey from London was a shilling and a penny.
That the post was as uncertain as it was dear appears from
the first sentence of this very letter; a communication from
Charles, dated on the 7th, had not reached William until
" this morning "—three weeks later.

I was not aware of my having expressed any Surprise at
your " drawing upon *Robins*," but let that pass; your bill
upon *me* has been duly honoured, and I was glad to hear
Robins say that there was no hurry for your return to the
desk, and that he hoped you would remain where you are,
till your health was quite reestablished. More of this, anon.
Now for the Dividend.

Charles's share, even after the deduction for repairs had
been made, amounted to £46 2s. 11d.; and owing to
the absence from Bath of some of the seat-holders, there
was something more to come. As William explains that,
because of the difference in the two seasons at Bath, the
Michaelmas receipts are always considerably below the
Lady Day ones, it appears that the Chapel was a profitable
property, bringing in well over a hundred pounds a year to
each of the three beneficiaries. The other Bath properties
are thus enumerated in this letter:

Spencer's rent £80—Miss Whitehead's 70—Benett's due
at Midsummer, 40, and Viner's Ground rent (3. 10). . . .
If you wish me to do anything with your balance, here, you
will send me your instructions accordingly. At your leisure
you will be so good as send me also your receipt. Your
explanation of the Lawyer's notice is quite clear; it was
very far from my intention, tho', to drive you into such an
irksome detail. Now as to your accounts of your health,

I am not *quite* satisfied with your account of yourself, the recovery of strength is a sine quâ non, with me. I trust therefore, my dear W., you will not think of moving from your Farm-House till *that* point is settled. I am not, as you well know, much of a Man of business but, so far as the execution of any straight forward commissions go, either Theatrical or otherwise pray command, and depend upon my best services. I don't know whether, as you have been so long accustomed to your Social glass, a total Abstinence from the good old Oporto would be most adviseable. As your strength returns, a glass or two will not, in my opinion, stop it's march. All Doctors are mortal enemies to wine in sickness and in health, and yet I know not a Class of Men, generally speaking who like it better, or are quicker putters about of the bottle. . . . I am not sorry that you have removed Charles from Mr Wyatt's. In my mind there is not much of the Milk of human kindness in him, and a Master who had a real regard for his Pupil, would not treat, as a mere *Drudge*, a young Man who had evinced so much steady application and ability as Charles has done. . . . I have availed myself of your permission to peruse the Correspondence upon this subject, and written to Iver to-day. . . . I arrived in London on the 23rd, after a sort of retrograding tour, in consequence of Poet Bowles insisting upon my seeing Fonthill Abbey. . . . I made my usual halt at Iver, staid a week at the Parsonage, and was as cosey and happy as I always am under Edward's hospitable roof.

Inside the cover is a postscript:

. . . I hope you will write to me again soon, and never think about *franks* to me. A letter not worth paying for, is not worth having, and I shall be really anxious to hear a *better*—yes I must, to be quite a satisfactory one, have a *better* acct. of yourself.

When and where Charles died I have not discovered, but as he is not buried at Iver, it seems not improbable that he

279

did not regain his health, but died at St Helier. His son, whose future seemed so promising, and who, young as he was, gained a gold medal for a plan of a cathedral—the drawing, which is carefully preserved and which I have seen, has great merit—fell a victim to consumption at the age of twenty-one, and his name is inscribed beneath his mother's on the stone in Iver churchyard.

Tom Sheridan, too, had died of the terrible disease so fatal to the Linleys, and had left behind him six children, all handsome and all gifted, more than one of whom was to die in the same way. Sam Tickell, away in India, had died in 1817, leaving three little children. Of Thomas Linley's grandchildren only Betty Tickell and Mary Ward were still living, and to them their two ageing uncles, Ozias and William, seem to have given all their affection.

A letter from Ozias to Mary (dated 7th of August, but without any indication of the year) is eminently characteristic. The writing too is characteristic, and not at all like that of his brother and sisters. It is upright, rather square, devoid of loops and flourishes, and the letters tend—as is often the case with the writing of people accustomed to write Greek—to stand separate from one another. Altogether it is a hand of modern aspect such as might almost belong to any professional man to-day.

MY DEAR MARY The Book which accompanies these few lines I must honestly own, I purchas'd for myself, allur'd by an elegantly written sentence which happen'd to strike my eye, and its treating of a branch of Philosophy with which I am totally unacquainted. Soon finding it however not calculated to afford me any pleasure or any instruction worth having, I determin'd to make *you* a Present of it not knowing but that may be rationally interesting to you which to myself is perfectly insipid. I was upon the point of adding

to my Present a good number of my favourite Hymns the
greatest part of them the Composition of the late Astronomer
Sir William Herschel, formerly one of my Musick Masters.
I treat my Congregation (or rather myself) with them very
often not only from respect to the memory of my good
Master, but because of their high *intrinsic* merit as devotional
Compositions. I say I meant to have sent you these Hymns
but learning from my Brother that you are prohibited singing
I thought I should only tantalize you by sending them. The
next time I go to Iver I will bring them over with me and
sing them to you myself. I must own I pay you a poor
compliment in presenting my leavings for your acceptance
but I beg my dear you would consider my present as an
earnest of those I will most gladly make you. Whatever
you may have a fancy for you have only to apply to me with
the same confidence as to your own Father & I shall exert
my best endeavours to procure it you. I am at present busy
in preparations for my Cheltenham excursion and have only
time to subscribe myself Your Affectionate Uncle O. T.
LINLEY. P.S. I thank you for the copy of your dear
Brother's Letter. When you have leisure Mr Ward may
have the goodness to permit me your Copy of his Journal.

Of Ozias as an elderly man our knowledge is far more
extensive than of William, thanks to the fact that in 1822
the Rev. John Sinclair became curate to the Rev. John
Lindsay. The latter was at the same time Vicar of Stanford
in Northamptonshire, and Fellow of Dulwich College; and
the duties of each charge were fulfilled sometimes by one
of them and sometimes by the other. Thus Mr Sinclair
became for weeks at a time a deputy Fellow, inhabiting his
Vicar's rooms and dining nearly every day in the College
Hall. There it was that, when he first visited Dulwich and
his Vicar-elect, he met Ozias Linley, "who made a deep
impression upon me by his talent and eccentricity."

I was fortunate enough to gain his good opinion for he said to me long afterwards: "You showed so much vivacity when we first met that I took you for an *Irishman*; which I assure you was not a little in your favour."

Indeed when Mr Sinclair was in residence at Dulwich it is evident that Ozias cultivated the society of his agreeable junior very assiduously. Unlike Ozias himself, Mr Sinclair must, I think, have been a good listener; and in later life, when he had advanced to the position of Archdeacon of Middlesex, he found, as good listeners are apt to do, that he had accumulated material for a volume of reminiscences. From that volume, "Sketches of Old Times and Distant Places," pp. 147 to 164, come all the details that render the figure of Ozias so living and so picturesque.

He was a good mathematician, a sound classical scholar, and an able metaphysician. He never read newspapers or reviews or indeed any modern performance of any kind.[1] The only works of fiction he cared for were *Tom Jones* and *Gil Blas*. With these he was familiar. His studies, properly so called, were limited to a small number of choice authors; and he had stated times for reading them. His arrangement, so far as I can remember, was as follows: on Mondays and Thursdays he studied Plato in the original; on Tuesdays and Fridays Newton's *Principia* and Hartley on Man; on Wednesdays, Dr Samuel Clarke's works, in particular his Controversy with Collins; and on Saturdays, Jonathan Edwards on the Bondage of the Will. He thoroughly adopted Edwards' theory as to the bondage of the will, but deduced conclusions from which Edwards would have shrunk. He conceived that, as there is no free will, there can be no demerit nor any punishment in the proper sense of the term. What we call punishments must in reality be

---

[1] His letter to Mary Ward, and indeed one of the Archdeacon's own anecdotes prove that there were exceptions to this rule.

chastisements intended in all cases for the recovery and reformation of the offender. Hence he inferred the ultimate repentance and salvation not only of all evil men, but of all evil beings whatsoever. He was, in short, an uncompromising universalist; and having made himself familiar with all the arguments from the original text of Scripture and from the Fathers, he delighted in doing battle for it at all times and against every adversary.

From my first acquaintance with him, I took pleasure in contradicting him, in order to draw him forth on his favourite topics. On one occasion, when I had been more successful in argument than usual, he took his revenge by an unexpected assault. " I wish," he said, " you were half as great a hero in the pulpit as you are in this dining-hall."

It was apparently the delivery rather than the matter of his young friend's sermons of which he complained, for he observed: " Give me a rival chapel in the same street and I pledge myself, in the course of a few Sundays to empty your church by preaching your own sermons." In answer to an inquiry what had become of the sermons he had been accustomed to preach,

he replied that having no occasion for them as Organist to the College, he gave them to Betty Slaughter, the chambermaid, who lighted his fires with them every morning until they were all consumed.

In conversation especially after dinner Mr Linley, who had a more than common share of sensibility, could not find phrases and comparisons strong enough to express his feelings. Yet some of his expressions it might be thought were tolerably strong. Of one man he would say: " He is an *unmitigated ass, brute and fool !* " Of another: " The fellow has no more feeling than a *butcher's block !* " Of a third: " He is like a cat, *eternally purring his own praise !* " Of a fourth: " The creature has contrived by dint of *cringe and crawl*

283

work to rise in the world." And of a fifth: " He begged for preferment with *wedge-like importunity*." To describe the haughtiness of Bishop Middleton, who, he imagined, had treated him disdainfully as nothing more than a minor canon of Norwich, he often said: " That man walks with such a strut, you would have thought he meant to kick the universe from beneath his feet."

His music Mr Sinclair thought " perhaps more remarkable for delicacy of taste and acquaintance with musical science than for powers of execution." Like his father, whose fineness of ear had been celebrated, Ozias was often doomed to hear music that afforded him no pleasure.

A performance which would satisfy many hearers was to him an intolerable nuisance. He would exclaim: " Mercy on my ears! A chorus of bull frogs; a chorus of warming pans; a chorus of bagpipes! "

On one occasion his friend sat near him when

a young lady was playing without book a grand concerto with surprising execution. Linley all the while indulged in the following half audible soliloquy: " Pshaw! How insipid all this is. Consummate ass![1] The same thing over again; I'd as soon listen to a chorus of cats. Well, I'm thankful she has finished at last."
. . . Linley's strong language was always enforced by suitable tones and gestures. He twisted his snuff box between his fingers more rapidly in proportion to his excitement and pulled his wig awry, till the back was foremost, and a large portion of his fine bald head became visible. He spoke so loud as to make the dining-hall resound, and struck the table so violently with his clenched fist as to put the glasses and decanters in serious jeopardy.

[1] This exclamation, it may be hoped, was for the composer rather than for the executant.

The heaviest blow of this kind I ever heard him give was when he conceived himself to have been superciliously treated by Mr Smith the Preacher of the College. This elderly clergyman, altho' more than 70 years of age, had not a little of the *petit-mâitre* in his dress, language and habits. Linley said of him that he was "all primroses and violets." As Fellows of the College the two old gentlemen lived of necessity in daily intercourse with each other, but having few points of resemblance they had continual altercations, which, happily, were always soon made up. The quarrel, however, which I now refer to, threatened to prove final. Mr Smith on being applied to had not at once consented to take Mr Linley in his one horse chaise to the ceremony of laying the first stone of St George's, Camberwell. Linley introduced the subject after dinner, and whispered to me: "He thinks I am not sufficiently a dandy to be seated by him on this grand occasion. The puppy! The eternal coxcomb!" Then turning to Mr Smith, he continued: "Now, Mr Smith, do condescend to tell me whether you do or do not intend to take me with you in your carriage to Camberwell." "Really, Mr Linley, I have a very great respect, but—nothing could have given me more pleasure, but—I should indeed have been highly gratified, but——" He was going on in this style when Mr Linley interposed: "Mr Sinclair, do you understand him? He is far too deep for my shallow intellect. Respect! pleasure! gratification! and after all there is an everlasting *but*. Do Mr Smith explain yourself. I am a plain spoken man; give me, I beseech you, either yea or nay" Mr Smith made another long speech, the tenor of which was a refusal. Mr Linley then in a paroxysm of rage turned to me. "Sir, you have heard him refuse to take me with him in his carriage. Now, remember, I do solemnly swear that I will never speak to that man again; no, not for ever and ever. *Amen*." He confirmed this *Amen* by a blow which made all the glasses and decanters on the table jump.

I was not a little alarmed at this outbreak, but the two friends met next day as if nothing had occurred.

But if such outbursts may have been sometimes a little disturbing to the collegiate tranquillity, Ozias could also break that tranquillity in a more agreeable manner. He had, it appears, a marked dramatic gift, and " would have been a first rate actor." Mr Sinclair had heard him " repeat scenes from *The Rivals* and *The School for Scandal* before a small party with such exquisite humour, giving additional touches off-hand that our sides were sore with laughter and we entreated him to desist."

The violence of Ozias's occasional language and demeanour being considered somewhat excessive, Mr Lindsay made a bold effort at reformation. He preached a sermon in the College chapel upon Anger,

and in describing the angry man gave a very pointed representation of Linley. We could not see distinctly the effect produced by this discourse, for Linley was seated in the organ loft behind a curtain; though I saw his eyes from time to time attentively fixed on the preacher. After dinner I introduced the subject by adverting to the excellent moral lecture we had heard in the morning. " For my part," said Linley who saw clearly that his own edification had been the object of the sermon, " I did not hear a word of it, for I was busy all the time reading *Robinson Crusoe*." This was of course an extempore invention.

The man who could on an instant produce this repartee was very much indeed the brother of Mary Tickell; just as his musical fastidiousness, his peals of laughter, his violent epithets and blows upon the table show him very much the son of his father. In his strong individuality, varied talents, eager likings and dislikings, and fundamental sweetness of nature, Ozias was typically a Linley.

In 1825, the Archdeacon tells us, "Linley was one among the vast number who considered themselves on the verge of ruin."

Speaking of that great monetary crisis, he would say "Nearly all that I possessed was in the hands of Sir John Lubbock. In an evil hour for him, some crazy old woman, staggering along the Poultry, fell down at the door of his bank. The passers-by stopped to pick her up; a crowd collected; a report was raised that Lubbock's bank was in jeopardy, and a run upon it began. The alarm reached Dulwich and I was urged on all sides to hurry off to town, and endeavour to secure my money. I dressed accordingly, put on my hat, took up my walking stick and then sat down in my arm chair for a few minutes to meditate. After some minutes, indolence or shame prevailed. I struck the floor with my stick and exclaimed; 'I'll sink or swim with Sir John.' You know what followed. The run ceased and my magnanimity was rewarded."

He entertained a high admiration for the Prayer Book and for the English Bible.

Speaking of the *te Deum* he would repeat with a solemnity which Kemble might have envied; "Heaven and earth are full of the majesty of Thy glory" and then add: "How can any man not destitute of moral sensibility read or hear without emotion these glorious words?"

"There are various passages" he would add "in the lessons for the day which I was never able to read in the congregation without betraying my emotion. Take as an example the chapter in which poor King Hezekiah, having read the threatening letter of the Assyrian despot, goes up into the house of the Lord and spreads it before the Lord. When I came to the pathetic appeal 'Lord bow down Thine ear and hear, open Thou Thine eye and see' it was too much for me I realised the whole scene, my voice began to falter and I could hardly read it because I could hardly see it."

Like William, he was on the best of terms with that excellent friend and uncle, Edward Ward, and was a frequent visitor at Iver, where he used to arrive, owing to the times of the public conveyances, after the hour of the Parsonage supper, and a special meal used to be prepared for him. The son of Edward Ward, who succeeded him as incumbent of Iver, well recollected Mr Linley and his oddities, and used to recall how he and the other children would stand around and receive from him dainty morsels from his supper—the delicacies that had lingered in remembrance being pork-pie and pickles. A letter remains that was written to announce such a visit.

COLLEGE 31st *March*. MY DEAR SIR Next Sunday being that next before Easter day the custom of my College imposes Silence upon the Organ; doubtless that the *penitential* feelings of the Congregation may not be disturbed by the impertinent flourishes of Mr Organist, or perhaps, this dismal silence may be intended to set off thro' the medium of contrast the loudness and hilarity of Easter-day's Hallelujahs. However, this treatment of the two Sundays is customary in all Cathedrals, and plainly shows that the Stage is not the only place where in order to heighten an intended Effect, the Imagination is played upon by dramatic trickery. Having then no organ duty to perform next Sunday I have it in contemplation to pay you a friendly visit and pass that day under your hospitable roof. I shall certainly put my Theory into practice and be with you next Saturday provided no Circumstances shall have intervened to render my Visit unseasonable in which case you will have time enough I hope to prevent it by the favour of a few lines. Your's most faithfully   O. T. LINLEY.

288

In March 1830, a year before his death, Ozias and his brother were both dining with Mr Edmund Byng. Several actors were of the party, and also Thomas Moore, who has recorded in his Journal how William Linley sang "Stay, traveller"—a charming song, it may be remarked, with a peculiarly haunting turn in its refrain. Ozias was "in agonies under it" and demanded, "'What dreadful stuff is that?' 'Ozias,' answers William, with a solemn and reproving voice, 'it is our father's.'"

Ozias, as he advanced in years, gradually dropped, his friend tells us, "those theological eccentricities" over which he had once been so hot; and his death was of exemplary piety. It occurred on the 6th of March 1831, and he was the last person to be buried in the vaults of the College chapel. He left all his property to William, but had made an arrangement with him that when he, in turn, died, the family pictures should be given to Dulwich College, where seven of them now appear in the Picture Gallery.

William's will, made soon after his brother's, divided his possessions between his two nieces, but before the time came for its being put into execution there was but one niece left. Mary Esther Ward died of consumption in 1833 at the age of twenty-seven, and was laid in the grave of her mother and brother. She was deeply, but by no means gloomily religious, and of a gentle but gay disposition. I have seen the journal which she kept of a foreign tour in company of her uncle and aunt, and which contains a little cabin scene showing the sufferings of the kind, polite Mrs Ward at the hands of a thoroughly uncongenial fellow-passenger. The tone and turn of this are curiously like those of the mother whom Mary did not remember.

William was now the only survivor. He lived the life of the amateur, wrote verses and published a volume containing his own and those of his dead schoolfellow, Charles Leftley—which volume is not to be found in the British Museum; wrote several novels, only one of which is there (and that one, I regret to say, I have not found readable), and wrote also a good deal of music, most of which is in the Museum, and much of which has considerable merit. His chief excellence—in spite of Ozias's "agonies," was his singing. By his singing he originally attracted the notice of that friend whom in his letter to his brother-in-law he designates "Poet Bowles," and he was the medium through whom Bowles became acquainted with Coleridge. To William singing as a boy, Coleridge wrote some verses; and of William after his death Bowles wrote the obituary notice that appears in *The Gentleman's Magazine*. It contains a description of his singing which is as obscure as it is interesting. He is said to have been

perhaps the only person living who had the peculiar talent of taking up in the several voices, with the most animated feeling, two tenors, treble and base, the leading parts representing some of the most splendid passages of Handel's choruses so that the auditor might almost consider himself present at a full performance.

The statement sounds as though William Linley possessed the miraculous power of singing four sets of notes at a time —that is, of singing chords. But since this is patently impossible, we must conclude that he could command both an unusual range of natural voice and an unusually successful falsetto, and that he was also a musician so extremely skilled that he could pass from the one register to the other and back again with perfect ease, and thus almost produce the illusion that four men were singing in rapid succession. He was a member of several musical societies, among them being that interesting body, the Madrigal Society, and seems fully to have deserved from his friends the praise which Bowles accords to him of possessing high and honourable principles and "the sweetest and kindest temper." But, though he was always courteous, and even perhaps genial, he seems to have had no gift of self-communication, and I doubt whether any living person ever knew him as well as even at the distance of a century we are able to know his sisters and Ozias. His is a pathetic, semi-effaced figure, and nothing of him emerges from the half tones of his portrait except the vivid impression made upon Bowles by his singing.

In St Paul's, Covent Garden, is a tablet to his memory bearing the following inscription:

In Memory of William Linley Esq. Who departed this life on 6th May 1835 Aged 64 years. The last of a family endowed with genius, He delighted in cultivating his own And in rewarding that of others. His religious feelings were humble and sincere. This tablet is erected by a grateful and affectionate niece whom in life he loved and in death remembered.

Betty Tickell, who was of course the niece in question, was, as her uncle had been, the last of her own generation. She lived for many years at 23 Charlotte Street, Bedford Square, and died there, unmarried, in 1860, when she must have been about seventy-nine. Thus out of the twelve children born to Thomas and Mary Linley, only the two eldest daughters have left descendants, and each of them only through one son. But the charm that belonged to so many of them has not wholly died with them;

it seizes those persons through whose hands their letters pass—as it seized Mr Sichel; or those who look upon their portraits—as it seized me, many years ago. To impart some feeling of that charm has been the purpose of this volume.

AUTHORITIES QUOTED

BURNEY, FANNY, *Early Diaries*, 94, 95.

Busby, "Concert Room Anecdotes," 118.

Creevy Papers, 108.

Crouch, Mrs, "Memoirs" (vol. i), 8, 121, 140.

Egerton MSS., British Museum, 17, 20, 107, 118, 174 note.

Eyton, "Antiquities of Shropshire," 2.

Fitzgerald, Percy, "Lives of the Sheridans," 85, 92.

Green, Emanuel, F.R.S.L., "Thomas Linley, Richard Brinsley Sheridan and Thomas Mathews, their Connection with Bath," 5, 24, 32, 42, 49, 82, 85, 120 note, 139, 185.

—— Proceedings of the Bath Natural History and Field Club, 9, 13, 17.

Kelly, Michael, "Reminiscences," 7, 8, 46, 106.

Moore, Thomas, Journals, 38, 47 (Rogers quoted), 79, 99, 289

Oliphant, Mrs, "Sheridan," 103.

Parke, "Musical Memories," 118 note.

Rae, W. Fraser, "Sheridan," 24, 38, 42, 69–81, 86, 87, 92, 93, 106–109, 114, 154.

Sichel, W., "Sheridan," 24, 38, 47, 93, 101, 106, 112, 121, 147, 158, 173, 273, 291

Sinclair, Rev. J. (afterwards Archdeacon of Middlesex), "Sketches of Old Times and Old Places," 181, 182, 275, 281–288.

Smith, J. T., "Nollekens and his Times," 15.

Walpole, Horace, 97.

INDEX